CENTRAL COAST ROSE MANUAL

Creating a Personal Rose Garden

JOSEPH TRUSKOT

MASTER CONSULTING ROSARIAN

MONTEREY BAY ROSE SOCIETY

*With more than 150 color photographs of roses
recommended for coastal climates.*

*One dollar from each purchase will go toward the maintenance of the
Monterey Bay Rose Society's Display Garden
at the Santa Cruz County Fairgrounds.*

MBRS board member Tomiko Edmiston's Rose Garden in Royal Oaks. Pictured are Oregold, hybrid tea (1970); Perfect Moment, hybrid tea (1990); and Scentimental, floribunda (1999)

Library of Congress Control Number: 2011900785

Table of Contents

Acknowledgments

The board of directors of the Monterey Bay Rose Society (MBRS) deserves my highest praise for its commitment and support of this project, and for sharing its expertise and infectious enthusiasm for growing roses in the communities surrounding the Monterey Bay. My gratitude also goes to the American Rose Society and its Northern California, Nevada, and Hawaii District for their dedication to America's National Flower.

My special appreciation is loudly proclaimed to the following individuals who assisted in the production of this book: Ruth De Bord, former President of the Monterey Bay Rose Society and a first-rate proofreader, Otto Lund and Janey Leonardich, fellow Master Consulting Rosarians with the MBRS for their assistance with content and dissemination of *The Bay Rose*, the MBRS newsletter from which much of the content was derived, Kris Sinclair of Sacramento for her willingness to share both editorial advice and horticultural information, Andy Easton, Salinas-residing orchid hybridizer for use of Thomas Mawe's *Everyman His Own* Gardener, Jean O'Brien and Elizabeth Schneider of Old Monterey Book Company for their support of the project from its earliest stage, and Mark Skeem for graphic design and layout.

One dollar of every sale of the *Central Coast Rose Manual* will go to support the maintenance of the Display Garden of the Monterey Bay Rose Society, located at the Santa Cruz County Fairgrounds, 2601 East Lake Avenue (CA State Highway 152), Watsonville, California 95076. Please visit its Web site at www.montereybayrosesociety.org. I hope that the Display Garden will long serve as a Visitor's Guide to roses which do well on California's Central Coast.

To the best of my knowledge, the photographs contained in this *Manual* were all taken by me in my garden in North Salinas, at the Monterey Bay Rose Society's Display Garden, or in other gardens on the Central Coast.

The photograph of *American Honor* which graces the cover was selected by a survey of more than one hundred people. Interestingly, it's the exact rose which won the Queen of Show Trophy at the Monterey Bay Rose Society's Annual Rose Show for me on two occasions! Even more interestingly, it was hybridized by Jerry Twomey in the early 1990s in Watsonville, California. Mr. Twomey generously allowed members of the MBRS to help themselves to nearly two acres of his roses when he closed his operations in 1995.

Rosa alba semiplena, alba (before 1867) growing up a bay laurel

Although it is no longer in commerce, individual bushes may be available through MBRS members.

A special word of thanks to HelpMeFind Roses. It is a wonderfully informative database that needs everyone's support. Check it out at: HelpMeFind.com.

MBRS Board of Directors
James Sauvé, president
Dennis O'Hara, first vice president
Otto Lund, second vice president
Judy Sauvé, treasurer
Janey Leonardich, secretary

Marge Callahan, member-at-large
Tomiko Edmiston, member-at-large
Paul McCollum, member-at-large
Brenda Wood, member-at-large

Activity Calendar

January

- Sharpen shears and loppers
- Prune roses growing in shade
- Rake and discard old leaves
- Plant bare root roses
- Move established roses
- Make cuttings from pruned canes
- Clean gutters and downspouts
- Pay Rose Society dues

February

- Prune roses growing in full sun
- Finger prune low down and multiple shoots
- Install drip irrigation
- Spread alfalfa pellets
- Keep bud unions moist
- Check garden drainage
- Bait snails
- Bend supple canes to increase bloom

March

- Feed roses organic fertilizer
- Remove wrongly growing canes
- Check for aphids
- Shape bushes to allow easy access
- Start pulling weeds

April

- Keep inside of bush open
- Disbud hybrid teas and clusters
- Feed chemical fertilizer
- Water roses generously
- Keep pulling weeds
- Watch for insect attack

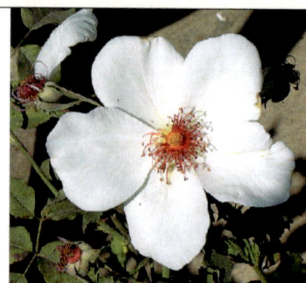

May

- Check stakes and ties
- Assess newly planted roses
- Water and feed roses
- Begin to dead head spent flowers
- Check garden for invading tree roots
- Let spring bulb leaves wither

June

- Water roses amply
- Remove all black spotted leaves
- Dead head spent blooms
- Fertilize roses
- Apply summer dormant oil
- Shape vigorous roses
- Disbud hybrid teas
- Tour gardens

Activity Calendar

July

- Reapply dormant oil
- Trim back one-time bloomers
- Dead head spent blooms
- Evaluate your garden
- Monitor roses in pots
- Fertilize only if you are around to water
- Remove dead leaves and weak growth

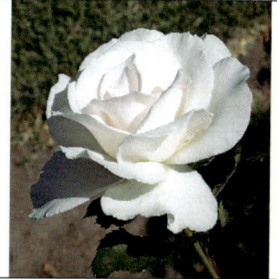

August

- Water and feed roses
- Keep your garden weeds under control
- Spread additional compost
- Remove all spent flowers
- Reshape bushes

September

- Allow roses to produce hips
- Apply pellets
- Remove spent petals only
- Check bushes for air circulation
- Remove any clogs from drip system
- Plant new roses
- Assess your garden

October

- Stop all chemical fertilizers
- Prepare for wet weather
- Clear gutters and downspouts
- Check Drainage of garden
- Tie down new growth on climbers
- Rake and discard all fallen leaves and petals
- Remove deadwood and spindly growth

November

- Condition soil with organic additives
- Plant new roses
- Monitor water use
- Plant spring bulbs
- Harvest rose hips
- Order garden catalogues

December

- Keep garden paths clear
- Check climbing rose supports
- Shovel prune bad roses
- Check drainage
- Move good roses

The Place to Begin

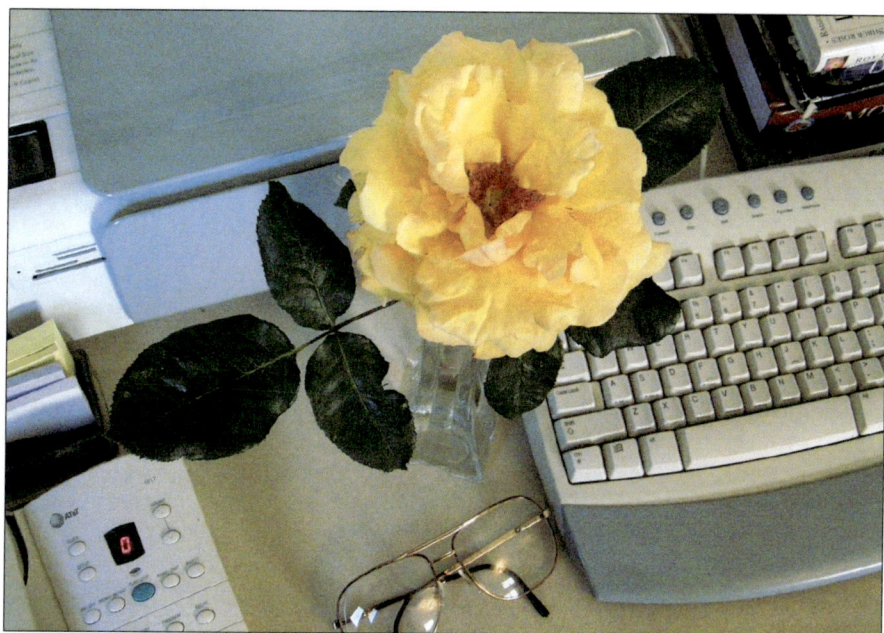

Tahitian Sunset, hybrid tea (2007)

A fully opened bloom of *Tahitian Sunset* is sitting next to my computer screen as I write this introduction to the *Central Coast Rose Manual*, a handbook dedicated to growing roses in the communities along California's Northern and Central Coast. *Tahitian Sunset* is next to me because it represents the culmination of 18 years of striving toward my own beautiful rose garden, of trying to invest a minimum amount of time for a bountiful result. The variety of microclimates which exist along the California Coast and immediate interior areas hasn't made this effort easy. Along the way to this goal, I have made plenty of mistakes and spent needless sums of cash which I want you to avoid.

Unfortunately, getting good advice usually happens *after* problems arise when gardeners have already invested substantial time and money in attempting to create their own paradise. They end up feeling inadequate to the task. Take my advice. You can grow great roses.

The summer in Salinas and other similar communities can be severe. Yes, severe—for most roses. Mornings begin cold, foggy and damp, the pavement often wet from the low clouds blowing in from the ocean. By mid-day, the sun burns through the marine layer and blazes down. An hour or two later, the wind picks up tossing the shrubs around like greens in a salad bowl. Then, clouds appear again moving slowly and steadily across the blue sky. The temperature drops into the chilly 50s and we head indoors shivering. The weather pattern is unique to this glorious part of the world and a real challenge to growing roses. Yet, here stands my bloom exhibiting all the colors of a Tahitian sun going down. Its yellow petals accented in red are ruffled on the edge. Darker colors are displayed on the reverse side. Its leaves are pristine—no blackspot, no powdery mildew, no rust. I even had to decide which flower among the many on the bush to cut and bring indoors—all single blooms on tall straight stems. The fragrance is not overpowering, yet present, some say licorice-like, others say a mix of tropical fruit and flowers. I'm smiling broadly. I did this. I grew this flower and it brings me pride. I want to share what I know about producing roses so that you, too, can experience this great feeling.

A garden doesn't exist without a gardener. Gardening takes dedication and constancy but you'll receive rewards along the way; magnificent, show quality flowers decorating your house and garden, raves from visitors who pass by, inhale, and gush with enthusiastic appreciation. You can get heartfelt kisses from those to whom you give flowers, not for a special occasion, but because the rose exists and the friend exists and you brought them together.

During the spring of 1994 when the garden was barely a year old, I invited a great lady and a terrific chum, Virginia Stanton, to visit. Virginia had firm opinions on just about everything—and everyone—and had seen quite a lot of everything *and* everyone in her all-too-brief 90+ years. We were off on an adventure and had stopped at my house to check the garden's progress. She, the garden, and the sunshine were behaving themselves on that particular sunny day and produced a great memory for me.

Virginia walked out into my yard, looked around slowly and methodically, paused for a moment, and said very softly to herself, and perhaps to me, "Everywhere you look there is joy." It's been my gardening motto and my principal goal ever since. In all our hard work, we too frequently forget that our purpose in growing roses, companion plants, and whatever else, must be to make the world better for us and for others—especially in that part of the world we can control—our gardens. Virginia, a former editor at House Beautiful magazine, passed away that November and is still greatly missed.

Buddy at the Garden Gate with Russelliana (1846) in full bloom

In the summer of 2002, a stray cat with a bobtail wandered into my yard and decided to stay and help. No more mice. No more roof rats. And the neighbors cheered, "No more gophers!" Buddy still hunts birds and mice, adores the water from a can of tuna fish, and chases petals from an Old Garden Rose tossed into the air above his head. His special prowess is assisting me as I pull out the long strands of invading Bermuda grass along the back fence. It's been great to have a cat in the rose garden. The watering goes much faster when Buddy sits next to me on a stool as I hold the hose and he protects me from startled moths.

In January 2000, Chris Rabe, then president of the Monterey Bay Rose Society, asked me to be the Society's newsletter editor. *The Bay Rose* was an eleven-year run which resulted in the content of the *Central Coast Rose Manual.* Participation in numerous lectures and workshops, visits to many gardens and nurseries, and general conversations with those who love growing roses added to the book's content.

Continuing in that tradition, here's my first piece of advice. Keep a good garden journal. It doesn't have to be anything more than a spiral bound notebook or a computer spreadsheet. Record the exact names of the plants you put in your garden, where and when you acquired them, and, if necessary, when they left the garden—regardless of circumstance. To get help, you will need to know the exact name of the rose you tried to grow. The dates which follow the variety names throughout this Manual are the dates the roses were introduced to commerce. These should help you gauge a rose's stamina and popularity.

Our climate causes us to search for the roses perfectly suited to its challenges—ones which will still display all the qualities we desire. Many varieties were created decades ago and might have been forgotten. Others will enter the market this very year and merely need to be given a chance to prove themselves.

This book is not intended as a cover-to-cover read. Similar information is repeated in different months. And, as in every other part of life, there is more than one way of doing things. I know what I did. I know what I didn't do and I know that my job as a home gardener will never end. The journey is the reward, not the destination.

JOSEPH TRUSKOT
SALINAS, CALIFORNIA
AUGUST 19, 2010

Read This
Before You Do Anything Else

Backyard Overview

Anyone interested in growing roses or helping others to grow roses, needs to understand a few basics regarding this remarkable plant.

Roses are members of the *Rosaceae* Family, closely related to apples, cherries, almonds, and quinces. Rose hips, the fruity section surrounding the seeds which develop at the base of the flowers, are one of the plant kingdom's richest sources of Vitamin C. No part of the rose is poisonous. Most varieties of the genus *Rosa* are deciduous. However, several rose species originating in subtropical regions of Asia are tender and essentially evergreen, although their leaves are fairly short lived. All roses are native to the northern hemisphere. The leaves of roses are usually composed of an odd-number of leaflets from three to as many as nineteen or so. The thorns on the canes and under the leaves are more accurately called "prickles."

The genus *Rosa* encompasses a vast array of species and cultivars with varying growth habits, flowering cycles, fragrances, color, disease resistance, and charm. Most rose species can be interbred resulting in a myriad of hybrids. More than 50,000 registered cultivars exist and thousands more are created each year by amateur and professional hybridizers. Flowers come in all colors except blue, as roses lack the gene that provides true blue color. The minimum number of petals is five, although there is a petal-less Chinese rose. The diameter of a flower can be a half-inch to eight inches.

General guidebooks on roses tend to describe growth inaccurately for California. We usually produce rose bushes twice the size of what they are on the East Coast or in England. Flowers are often half-again as large as the description in reference books. Many of the top-rated varieties in the nation perform miserably in Central Coast gardens.

Species and Cultivars

Classifying roses has become a great challenge in the past thirty years. Hybridizers, set free from pre-existing notions of what a rose should look like, have experimented with awesome combinations of parental stock. Their efforts have produced English roses, landscape roses, hand-painted roses, micro-miniature roses, patio roses, just to name a few.

The classification system of rose varieties is often confusing. Even species roses, those which reproduce themselves from seed, can demonstrate a wide difference based on geography and climate. The most common species growing in the wild on the Central Coast is *Rosa californica*. You can find it along road sides usually on a stream bank or drainage ditch. Many cultivars have also naturalized themselves in our area. Settlers from the padres on have brought roses to California. The names of many of these roses which have outlived the people who planted them are long since forgotten. Rose enthusiasts who "rediscover" them but can't identify their original names have given them new ones. These roses are called "found" roses. Many are eventually identified by diligent rose historians.

It's not certain who first discovered the ancient practice of grafting one plant onto the roots of a more vigorous related plant—once referred to as *inoculation*. But once a desirable rose (or apple, or cherry) was identified, a gardener could quickly multiply the number in his or her garden by taking a small portion of the good variety (for roses it's just one bud eye) and inserting it into an already established root system of something else. Grafting roses onto vigorous root stocks has been practiced since the creation of nurseries in California. It's not uncommon to discover *Rosa multiflora*, *Rosa odorata*, and *Gloire des rosamanes* (a.k.a. Ragged Robin) growing in old and abandoned places. They were commonly used as understock for fancier more appealing but considerably less healthy hybrid teas, teas, and other types of rose.

Old Garden Roses, a.k.a. Old European Roses, can be divided into Albas, Centifolias, Damasks, Gallicas, Scotch Briars, and Musks. They have been hybridized with themselves, with mutations of themselves, and with species roses. With a few exceptions, they are once-flowering, producing blossoms of white, cream, pink, red, purple, or maroon; striped, mottled, or picoteed.

Pierre-Joseph Redouté (1759-1840), the renowned French painter of roses documented more than 160 varieties of roses growing in several garden collections during the first decades of the 19th century. Some were regional variations of the same variety. Curiously, the collections included roses with bizarre leaf variances. These included the lettuce-leafed, celery-leafed, willow-leafed, peach-leafed, and hemp-leafed varieties of rose. (Many of these may now be extinct. The lettuce leaf or *bullata* variety is still commercially available from specialty nurseries. Certainly the novelty of the hemp-leafed variety would have a following if it was ever rediscovered!)

Also several of the roses Redouté and his botanical collaborator Claude-Antoine Thory depicted were roses which sported balsam scented, moss-like

Rosa eglanteria, species rose refered to by Shakespeare in Oberon's speech from A Midsummer Night's Dream

glands below each flower. Still other roses had highly vegetated and elongated sepals—that part of the flower which protects the petals while still in the bud stage.

Most importantly, a few recently introduced roses from China and India were identified by Redouté. This was prophetic. The focus of rose hybridization soon became the flower, its shape and its remontancy—its ability to rebloom.

China roses revolutionized rose hybridizing in the 19th century. What the European imperialists often brought back as "new Oriental species," we now understand to be the end results of talented Chinese and Japanese hybridizing gardeners. Nevertheless, European rose growers swiftly understood the significance of remontant specimens and the expansion of colors which included yellow, orange, geranium red, and russet that these plants made possible. Early hybridizing programs were tried between European and Chinese species roses and a few resulting examples continue to be in commerce. The beauty of the initial "Tea" rose specimens in their form and fragrance was not lost on hybridizers. Nor was the cluster flowered habits of polyantha roses.

The word "tea" became associated

Charles de Mills, gallica (1840)

with roses because of the similarity between the intoxicatingly beautiful smell of crushed green tea leaves and the fragrance of certain oriental roses. It has a lighter fragrance than the typical "rose" fragrance that the perfume industry acquires through the distillation of damask varieties. A group of roses called "Hybrid Perpetuals" were developed and hundreds of named varieties were created and introduced in the mid-1800s. Barely a handful has remained in general commerce. The popularity of Victorian-era rose shows and private gardens led to further improvements in a rose's ability to display its upright form and substance. The hybrid tea rose was the result and they have reigned supreme ever since. Hybrid teas were subsequently bred with polyanthas (cluster-flowered varieties) producing the floribundas.

The first official hybrid tea rose was *La France* introduced in 1867. This date is used by the American Rose Society to differentiate between Old Garden Roses introduced before and modern roses introduced after.

Miniature roses came into their own in the middle and end of the 20th century producing exact small replicas of their popular cousins, the hybrid teas and floribundas. Several creative hybridizers, such as the legendary Ralph Moore of Visalia, California, re-introduced qualities in his miniatures derived from the moss roses, striped roses, and climbing roses of the past. His objectives were distinctiveness, healthy leaves, and abundant flower production.

David Austin created the line of English roses also going back to the Old Garden Roses for their shape and habits. Sam McGredy IV developed a unique line of roses referred to as "hand painted" which in their flower contained blended petal colors making each blossom appear uniquely splashed with colors with great variations depending on the season.

Terminology

anvil pruners: a hand tool with one cutting blade which descends on a flat surface while making the cut, not recommended for pruning roses

basal break: a cane growing out of the bud union on a grafted rose bush

blackspot: a common, nonpathological airborne fungal disease associated with periods of wet then dry then wet weather made worse by insufficient air circulation and varietal susceptibility, displays characteristic black spots on otherwise healthy leaves and results in the death of the infected leaves

blind shoot: a cane growing on a rose bush which produces no flower buds at its end, a variety-specific character

bud eye: that area on a cane from which a stem will grow, found immediately above the junction of a leaf and cane on new wood

bud union: the site of the graft between the root stock and the named rose

bypass pruners: a hand tool with one cutting blade and a second non-sharpened blade which bypass one another during the cut

cane: the stem of a rose bush, can be flexible as in many ramblers or stiff as in many hybrid teas

chlorosis: a lack of chlorophyll in the leaves resulting in yellowish leaves with green veins, usually associated with the plant getting insufficient nutrients, causes can be multiple including nitrogen deficiency or water logged roots

deadhead: removing the spent flowers, usually best done down to the first full, outside facing leaf

disbud: removing side buds on hybrid teas leaving one bud per stem, also removing the short-stemmed central bud in a cluster of flowers

dormancy: a period when the metabolism of a plant slows down or stops due to excessively cold, hot, dry or reduced light conditions; usually associated with the onset of winter or drought. On the Central Coast, however, roses—especially those with subtropical genes in their ancestry—don't reach a true state of dormancy.

finger prune: pushing off with one's fingers undesirable sprouting canes

hips: the fruit of a rose bush often similar in appearance to its cousin, the apple

graft: placing a bud eye from the desired variety into the top cane of an established root stock, once referred to as "inoculation"

greenwood: the living portion of the rose usually referred to when scraping off the deadwood and bark on top of the bud union

peduncles: the lower portion of a flower bud which eventually develops into the rose hip

loppers: long-arm pruning shears needed to remove established canes with diameters larger than ¾ inch

powdery mildew: a common, nonpathological airborne fungal disease associated with cool wet nights and hot dry days made worse by varietal susceptibility, affected leaves display characteristic white spores on the leaf surface, stems and peduncles

prickle: sharp projections from the side of a rose cane which emanate from the surface bark of the cane and vary in size, shape, and abundance, commonly referred to as thorns

rust: a common nonpathological airborne disease usually prevalent in the spring and fall and dependent on varietal susceptibility

sepals: the outer covering of the flower buds which protect the petals as they develop, eventually folding back under the bloom, can be elongated or curled in some varieties, but are usually nondescript

shovel prune: a euphemism for digging up and throwing out sick or non-producing rose varieties

stem-on-stem: one stem growing from the side of another stem, disallowed when showing most modern roses at a show

systemic pesticides: combination fertilizer/pesticide products which cause the plants to incorporate the pesticide into its cell structure

thorn: sharp projections from the stems of numerous plants which are adaptations of a side stem

Rose Gardening Essentials

Secret, hybrid tea (1992) standing before the backyard garden

If I had it all to do again, my garden would be better. If I could have suppressed my desire for immediate gratification—abundant roses during the first season—and focused instead on a much longer view, hours of my time could have been devoted to reading great books, attending concerts, and shooting the breeze with the neighbors. But no, I was in a hurry to build a rose garden.

If I had it all to do again, I would have removed the pre-existing plants in my intended rose bed: jasmine, ivy, struggling dwarf fruit trees, passion vines, trumpet vines and the following list of invasive bulbs and rhizomes: arum italicum, calla lilies, montbrecia, gladiola, scillia, and flowering garlic. I would have designed the rose beds more carefully so that when weeds did show their healthy little faces, I could have wrenched them from the earth with little effort. I would have amended the soil and had the garden bed tilled to a three-foot depth, and repeated this process adding more compost and sand for at least six months. I would have let the beds rest for a season until I saw where the sun rose and set during the year. I would have made sure that the fences around my garden were strong enough to stand straight for another decade, fending off the intense gusts of wind during winter storms. But no, I was in a hurry to build a rose garden.

I bought my house in December 1991. In January 1992, I bought 250 bare root roses as cheaply as I could find and proceeded to plant them, all with about a foot or so between them. I had done some reading about this and felt that I was certainly no novice. I knew I had to have a plan. Here was my plan: the peach-colored ones would go at the back of the house and fade into the light pink ones in front of the jasmine vine and the dark pink ones would enhance their color if placed right next to them. The red ones would begin beneath the plum tree and on the north side of the shed. The orange ones were prominent under the apricot tree and the yellows in the back by the fence and the white ones under the apple tree. I read somewhere that it was a good idea to plant multiple rose bushes of the exact same variety so that you could pick a dozen or so identical flowers to put in a vase or give as a gift. So of each color, I bought about six and selected about four varieties of each color.

Six months later, I realized that roses are not petunias. I had problems, serious problems.

Basic success at growing roses means that you fully understand and provide the following six horticultural essentials: sun, air, soil, water, food, and great roses. I would also like to add a word I found on a floral postcard from ninety years ago, "Constancy." That's the quality of being unchanging or unwavering in your love or loyalty. Roses do need constancy, but thankfully not as much as people or animals.

SOIL

Much attention needs to be paid to soil amendments *before* a rose is planted. If you are planting a large rose garden, get your soil professionally tested. Sandy loam best suits rose cultivation. It's a mixture of sand, silt, clay, and organic material.

If your soil is heavy clay, you need to prepare it by adding sand and composted organic material before you plant your bush. If you just add sand to clay, you'll get concrete. If you just add compost to clay, you won't get the drainage roses require. To make certain that your roses prosper, grow them in beds which are raised. This allows for good drainage and subsequently adequate air beneath the soil. A healthy root system needs to be your primary focus. From it, all success grows. You won't need much height. A shallow trough in front of the rose bed is usually sufficient and it adds to the appearance of the garden by defining a visual line demarcating the bed.

If your soil is mostly sand, add compost and as much top soil as you can afford. Also, incorporate as much compost as you can find. Cow manure, mushroom compost, disintegrated yard waste, finely shredded palettes, anything that will give the sandy soil some ability to retain moisture.

Established roses also benefit from periodic organic amendments. Alfalfa pellets (rabbit food) supply plants with a growth enhancing enzyme, called "triacontonal." This particular additive allows the rose to absorb more of the nutrients in the soil. Make sure you get the plain variety, not the type containing molasses. It has the added benefit of composting quickly right in the soil giving the soil that much more organic content. Alfalfa meal is identical in content but more concentrated and expensive. I like to add it at the first sign of growth in the spring and let the rains wash it in.

The addition of blood meal to the soil beneath your rose will result in dark and healthy leaves. It's an organic source of nitrogen, the principal element lacking in most soils in Central California. Bone meal aids flower production. Epsom salt is actually magnesium sulfate, an important minor element required by all plants. It's a growth enhancer and should be added (1/2 cup per bush, only in the spring). Magnesium is used by the plants to transfer nutrients in the soil up to the leaves and stems.

Roses prefer a balanced to slightly acidic soil pH factor of 6.5. Because our ground water is alkaline, you need to make sure there is a healthy amount of compost and organic material in the soil. Adding additional chemical nutrients (Triple 16 fertilizers, really any fertilizer that has a double digit number in its composition) needs to be accompanied by an ample watering.

A heavy winter downpour will saturate your soil which is a good thing as long as any excess water runs off in a day or so. To ensure this, keep your drainage ditches deep. Roses can take two or three days—maybe a week in winter of total submersion, but after this, they suffocate and die.

Rain in California is generally a good thing so I'm not complaining. We just need to be super-prepared for flooding if our property is located on essentially level ground or at the edge of a stream.

Disco Dancer, floribunda (1984)

Species roses in their natural settings usually inhabit what is called "broken land," such as the areas at the edge of a forest, along stream banks or hedge rows, or other well lit, disturbed lots. The common characteristic of these areas is the soil type. It's usually a sandy loam with lots of mixed-up organic matter. That's ideal. It's loose enough for the rose's roots to get established. It's light enough to drain sufficiently and open up the underground air passages. And, it's organic enough to hold some moisture close to the plant.

Good rose growing starts with taking the time necessary to prepare the garden bed. It's really easier to bring in good top soil and discard what you have, rather than trying to amend what you have to bring it to a sandy loam state. Put some bone meal in the bottom of the hole where you intend to plant the rose. It's not necessary to mix it in. In fact, the rose's roots seem to benefit more if the bone meal is in clumps. Gertrude Jekyll, the legendary British horticultural-ist, advocated that whenever you were planting a perennial, shrub, bulb, or tree, you should place a dead rabbit in the bottom of the hole, cover it with composted leaves, and plant your rose on top. Just think about the history of roses in graveyards. I love to insert a steak bone beneath the rose bush. The roots will eventually find the nutrients in the bone. Former MBRS president Ruth De Bord always inserted a dead fish at the bottom of new planting. Not only did it serve as a source of nutrients, but it also deterred gophers.

Play sand can help the friability of your soil and make digging in the garden a little easier. To be effective, it needs to be well mixed in. Green Sand is a relatively new additive, new to me anyway. It's a mixture of iron oxide and potash, and is mined. It's crushed sandstone which has the ability to bind sandy soils together so nutrients and water don't flush right out. It also has the curious property of separating heavy clay soils by giving them a grainier texture.

WATER

Motivation and energy are such curious human qualities. I managed to clean out the gutters and down spouts on the front of my house, but never could get around to the ones on my back patio. I simply put this job off until Christmas vacation. Mistake!

With the multiple inches of rain we received beginning with the start of my Christmas vacation; I had no time left to clean out anything. The water kept coming down and over the top of the gutter draining, willy-nilly, onto the patio and eventually into the backyard.

One morning upon falling out of bed and heading for a cup of coffee, I looked out of my living room window onto the patio and noticed that my back yard had now flooded. The high-water mark was dangerously close to the sliding door of my living room. So with pajamas, flip-flops, and a

Blush Damask, damask (1000)

shovel, I mustered up a startling burst of energy for 6:30 a.m. and started to clear out the ditches which drain my back yard.

Roses love water. You can forget to provide every other thing and a rose will survive. But if you don't water, the rose will die. I prefer to hand water my roses to make sure each plant is getting a sufficient amount. Pay particular attention to roses in containers. I don't add strong fertilizers to roses in small containers. I keep them moist, never let them dry out, and look for a good home in the ground for them.

Overhead watering first thing in the morning allows the leaves to dry off in the morning sun. It will also reduce

Lyda Rose, shrub (1994)

powdery mildew on your leaves. Unfortunately, it uses more water than you might want to pay for and it encourages weeds. An occasional squirt with the hose in the morning will clean off the leaves and also enhance the look and the health of the plant.

Many plants prefer getting their water at the end of the day and having all night to drink it up. With roses, you will run the risk of fungal diseases if you allow water to remain on the leaves for more than a few hours.

Roses standing in water will start to rot after five days depending on the temperature. Their cell tissue ruptures and starts to break down. If you have heavy adobe clay and garden on flat land or at the bottom of a large hill or grade, you must make sure that your garden drains properly. As many of you who have visited my garden know, these are my conditions. In order to prevent my roses from drowning in the days of steady rainfall and rising water table, I've had to elevate the beds in which they grow and dig 12" drainage ditches in front of them.

I'm now quite used to them and rarely stumble over them. They do drain the garden and carry the excess water to the street. They also separate the lawn from the rose garden and keep the grass from invading the roses. This is a particular problem for those of us who have combined lawns with rose gardens.

These ditches also provide Buddy, my bobtail cat, with a great hiding place to hunt birds. He's been my garden companion ever since he strayed into the yard in June 2002. I thought he was a neighbor's pet but he'd pretty much been working the entire neighborhood and keeping it free of mice, rats, and slow birds. I found him knocking a snail across the patio one September and crushing it into a slimy

mess. That deserved a pat on the head and a crunchy, tartar-controlling treat. *Good kitty!*

Roses need water regularly. It's the one agent that makes everything else about growing roses successful. More water means more growth as long as there is sufficient drainage. If you flood the base of your bush and the water in midsummer drains into the soil in 10-15 minutes then, you've achieved a desirable consistency. Roses never want their roots to be totally dried out. Three to four inches of coarse mulch will accomplish this. Watering in the early morning is ideal. Watering in the middle of the day is not. There's too much evaporation. Watering in the evening, best for most other garden plants, is only okay for roses if the leaves don't get wet.

A good soaking in the summer really does seem to be a terrific tonic. It helps the rose build a root stem which goes down deep instead of light watering which might cause roots to fan out too near the surface.

AIR

A mistake made by many new rose gardeners is misjudging the amount of space it takes to grow and maintain a quality rose. Most hybrid teas need at least five feet of garden space for themselves, plus another foot or so for the gardener to get around them. If you follow this practice instead of planting them much closer together you will see the number of disease problems diminish and the quality of the leaves and flowers expand.

Improving the air circulation around your rose helps stimulate healthy growth. However, roses prefer to have some shelter from constant winds. They truly love growing on the south side of a house, wall, or fence. Winds in the summer tend to pull the moisture out of them. Be conscious of this and prevent leaf and flower desiccation by watering in the early morning.

I recently read (looked through is a more accurate description) a beautifully produced coffee table book extolling the beauty of Impressionism and promulgating the use of roses in Impressionistic garden designs. The exquisite photographs showed tangled garden beds with roses, foxgloves, and clematises. A quick look at the picture, of course, showed that the bottom third of the rose bush was void of any leaves, the middle third was dreadfully blackspotted, and the top part had roses and the few green leaves which fought through the tangled vegetation and managed to get some air. The best roses at Monet's garden, Giverny, and several others featured in the book, were all growing against a wall, over an arbor, freestanding near a pond or grafted onto standards. In each of these instances, the redeeming factor was air!

Buddy and Rose Hips from Honorine de Brabant, bourbon (1850)
which are bright red at Christmastime

Before you plant your rose bushes, make sure you understand how tall and wide they are likely to get. When you select the spot make certain you can walk around at least a half of the fully-grown bush. It's much more fun to tend roses when you don't have to struggle to get at them. I can't imagine what our own little Givernys would look like, if we allowed them to get tangled up like those in the picture. Taste, of course, is a personal matter. You will probably enjoy your garden more, however, if you plant your large bushes five to seven feet apart so that air (and you, the gardener) can circulate around them.

Roses like air, but they aren't wild about the wind. Avoid planting tree roses on which hybrid teas have been grafted in areas which get constant, full force wind. The longer canes are likely to snap or bend over. If you want to create a natural look in an area with trees, plant the rambling, scrambling, climber roses on the windiest side of the tree. You want Mother Nature to blow the long rose canes into the tree's foliage, not continually blow the rose out of the tree.

A tall fence growing in the northwest corner of a rose garden is likely to protect your hybrid teas and allow them to develop beautifully straight long canes.

Livin' Easy, floribunda (1992)

LIGHT

If your garden is not exposed to at least six hours of bright (not filtered) sunlight, don't try to grow roses. A lack of light will produce longer canes, smaller leaves, and fewer flowers; plus it will foster many of the common disease problems roses have.

Roses love sun and the growing fields in Wasco, California in the San Joaquin Valley are a testament to it. Roses don't mind being out in the open and getting as much sunlight as possible.

The need for hours of continuous direct sunlight increases to eight if your summers put you under the marine layer. Morning and afternoon sun is better than afternoon and evening sun. Some variation to this exists. For instance, I grow six roses on the side of my house which doesn't get six hours of direct sunlight. It does get a lot of reflected light from the side of my neighbor's white house twelve feet away and the roses seem to thrive. In certain areas, afternoon sun is far too hot and the roses get toasted. Some light shade in the mid-day hours will help your blossoms look better.

In the inland areas which get intense heat in midsummer with frequent day time temperatures in the hundreds, roses will shut down. If these are your growing conditions, don't avoid roses. Just know that you'll have to water early in the morning, use lots of heavy mulch, and expect many fewer blooms during the hottest part of summer. You should also look around your neighborhood at the height of a heat wave to see which varieties of rose hold their colors. I suspect if you choose whites and light pinks, you'll be more satisfied. Many of the roses, especially the "hand-painted" and "blended" colors might become monochromatic in the intense heat.

FOOD

Once there is six inches of new growth on roses, it's time to begin feeding them. I prefer the hose-end convenience of balanced fertilizers such as MiracleGro®. They contain not only the nitrogen, phosphorous, and potassium needed by all plants in major proportions, but they also contain minor elements such as magnesium, sulfur, zinc, copper and trace elements like boron. Triple 16 or other balanced fertilizers are fine for roses as long as you water deeply first, add the handful of Triple 16, and water again. Smaller amounts of chemical fertilizers provided regularly are better than a whole lot given occasionally.

Perhaps the most dramatic change during the 18 years I spent gardening has been the move from chemical fertilizers to organic sources of nutrients. I still use chemicals at the height of the growing season, but many of my fellow rosarians now only give their roses organic food.

Fish emulsion is fine as an alternative source of nutrients. Cow manure is an excellent soil amendment, better than a food source. Chicken manure can be too "hot" a fertilizer and should be added with care. Better to mix it in with the soil and let it break down before you add it

Iceberg, floribunda (1958)

directly to the soil. Fresh animal droppings will increase the bacteria level of the soil and raise its temperature. Warmer soil increases a plant's metabolism and allows it to grow faster and produce more flowers. Be careful, however, not to add stall sweepings as they may contain a high salt content. Better to let this material compost somewhat.

Organic fertilizers such as chicken manure or fish emulsion take longer to break down into a usable form. After October, stop giving the roses any chemical fertilizers and apply some steer manure or fish emulsion to give the roots some nutrients during the winter.

Some gardeners recommend a 0-10-10 application which is meant to stimulate the production of fruit and flowers for next season. I might add this to once blooming varieties because they will store the nutrients in the canes for next year. It doesn't make sense to add it to roses which will get a good trimming in January. An occasional banana peel buried under the mulch at the base of the plant will

add some potassium to the soil. Banana peels disintegrate quickly and blacken even faster than that. The added potassium helps to make the petal color more intense.

The chemical nutrients roses need in their food supply can be divided into three categories: major elements, minor elements, and trace elements.

The major elements are the three numbers on fertilizer labels (10-10-10, 5-1-1, etc.) and are essential to growing healthy roses. All rose growers need to become familiar with reading fertilizer labels. There can be a vast difference from one package to the next.

The first element and first number listed in this major group is **Nitrogen**. Fertilizers contain this element in three different forms. Nitrate nitrogen is the most readily available source. Ammoniacal nitrogen is less readily available but in the correct soil will convert to a nitrate form and become more available. Urea nitrogen is the least readily available and also needs to be chemically changed by fungus and bacteria in the soil to become available to the rose. *Nitrogen stimulates growth and produces dark, healthy foliage.*

Phosphorus, the second major element and middle number, is also available in three forms, but is highly sensitive to the pH level of the soil. The more alkaline the soil, the harder it is for the plant to absorb it. *Phosphorus stimulates a healthy root system and promotes flowering.*

Potassium, the third major element, is readily available to the rose and remains in the soil for some time. *Potassium is essential for photosynthesis and helps roses store nutrients. It intensifies bloom color and promotes vigorous growth, especially hip production.*

Roses need other elements but in smaller doses. These are known as the minor elements and are listed in no order of importance.

High Spirits, miniature (1983)

Sulfur is an essential element in adjusting the pH factor of the soil from alkaline to acidic. It also aids the creation of organic compounds necessary for overall healthy plant growth. It leaches quickly from the soil and needs to be replenished. It's available in organic material.

Calcium helps to build strong bones in us and has a similar effect on roses. It promotes the strength of a plant's cell walls giving the bush a truly vigorous and healthy appearance.

Magnesium aids the transportation of nutrients, especially nitrogen and phosphorus, throughout the plant. It's richly contained in Epsom salt.

Roses also need trace amounts of several elements. These are **manganese, boron, zinc, copper, molybdenum,** and **chlorine**. They are all sufficiently available in a healthy soil mixture and are contained in most city and well waters. **Iron** is the most problematic trace element. Not that it isn't present, but in alkaline soils like we have in most of California, the pH factor is too high for plants to extract it. *Iron is essential for chlorophyll formation and fixing nitrogen in the soil.* We do not recommend the products sold to improve iron in your soil as they can also contain proportionately high levels of arsenic and selenium which are poisonous to living creatures. In a well-composted humus soil, sufficient iron should already be readily available.

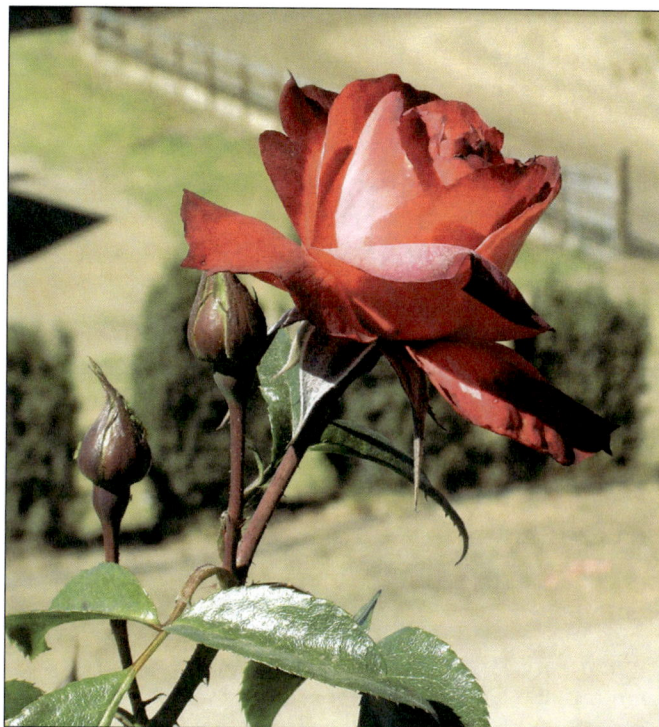

Hot Cocoa, floribunda (2002)
at the Display Garden, Watsonville, California

SOURCES OF NUTRIENTS

Hundreds of different products are available on store shelves. They will vary in price—often for the same chemical product—so shop wisely. They also vary in the practicality of application methods so think about how much time you want to spend feeding the roses. The concentrations differ, so be careful of your measurements. And they vary in what I call "boutique" appeal which makes some of them ideal for the "white-pants-wearing" gardening crowd. There are two groups: chemical and organic. Plants can't tell the difference. Nutrients are nutrients. However, organic sources have the benefit of providing safer, slower degrading, insoluble, more evenly supplied nutrients.

CHEMICAL FERTILIZERS
The products of huge processing facilities, chemical fertilizers are soil nutrients reduced to the bare elements and nothing else. They are available in dry forms, time release versions (Osmocote and plant spikes), and water soluble powders. The higher the numbers, the greater the concentration and the greater danger you will burn your roses. The dry forms commonly come in the following numbers 10-10-10, 16-16-16, and 20-20-20. Shop around. Fertilizer is often on sale. For instance, MiracleGro® is available at Kmart, so is their house brand K-Gro which is identical.

I do not recommend systemic fertilizers and pesticide products. The fertilizer part of the mixture is probably fine. However, the pesticide part is extremely lethal to the environment. If you have the money these "all-in-one" products cost, just buy bat guano.

ORGANIC FERTILIZERS
Some common organic fertilizers are listed below. Their approximate percentages of nitrogen, phosphorus, and potassium are listed in parentheses. These percentages can vary somewhat from product to product.

Blood Meal. (12-0-0) This dried blood from cattle slaughter houses is a rich source of nitrogen. Do not apply more than recommended rates because it's concentrated enough to harm plants. It's also likely to contain trace elements including iron. Hoof and Horn is a similar source material and its odor may not confuse your pets as much. After each application of blood meal, water well. This may keep your pet dog (or your neighbor's) from digging up the plants out of confusion.

Bone Meal. (6-12-0) This is a slow-acting fertilizer that releases phosphorus gradually. Bone meal is good for bulbs that don't sprout for several months after they are planted and for alkaline-loving plants such as clematis and lilac. Don't mix it into the soil. The rose roots will find the clump of bone meal and use it up slowly.

Cottonseed Meal. (7-3-2) In warm soils this fertilizer is a readily available source of all nutrients with little danger of over fertilizing. Use it for acid lovers such as rhododendron, blueberry, and azalea, too.

Fish Emulsion. (5-1-1) This is a well-rounded fertilizer consisting of partly decomposed ground fish. The smell is strong but will dissipate in a day or two. It confuses pets that can't get past the fish smell. It has a high concentration of nitrogen and can burn plants if overused or not watered in sufficiently.

Seaweed Extracts. (9-2-7) Seaweed is an especially good source of trace elements that your plants may need. Its odor is not as strong as that of fish emulsion, but it's more expensive. It's also referred to as kelp.

Manures. Nutrient concentrations vary widely depending on the kind of animal the manure is from. Cow manure is the weakest and serves best as a soil amendment rather than a nutritious additive. Poultry manures (Chicken, Turkey, Pigeon) are stronger and need to be added in smaller amounts. Bat Guano is stronger still and way more expensive and needs to be added in only small amounts.

Although concentrations in manures are lower than in manufactured fertilizers, manures improve soil structure and increase its water holding capacity. Fresh manures can cause food-borne illnesses. They also can burn tender roots. Use composted manures or apply fresh manures at least 60 days before harvesting any garden vegetables that will be eaten raw.

Matangi, shrub (1978)

Avoid barn sweepings, unless you have allowed them to decompose and leach out somewhat. They usually contain too much salt which is not good for the roses.

HOME BREWS AND RECIPES

Concoctions such as alfalfa teas, soil soups, slurry slops, sludge pots, and night soil all have intrinsic nutritional value. Various recipes exist and are promoted by some local vendors. Always take care when handling fecal material as various bacteria are harmful to humans.

Grandma's kitchen fertilizers can't be beaten for their accessibility. Egg shells are a source of calcium, but they need to be ground up and composted. Banana peels, coffee grounds, tea leaves, stale cat food, steak bones can all be applied directly to the base of a plant. Steak bones should be saved and dried in the sun, if you can keep predators away. Then add them to the bottom of a new planting hole. They take years to break down and are a steady source of food.

APPLICATION METHODS

WATERING SCHEDULES

Always deep water the day before you apply any fertilizer. Always lightly water immediately after applying any fertilizer. If your leaves show a drying out at the very tip in both old and new leaves, this is fertilizer damage. You can't reverse the effect of the burned leaves, but reduce the amount you are giving in the future. It's better to add just a little fertilizer with every other watering in the growing season than to add a whole lot of fertilizer once or twice a year.

Drip irrigation systems might not reach the place where you applied fertilizer. Drip irrigation systems need to water and feed all of a rose's roots. Make sure each nozzle is in its proper position Always check and hand water places where fertilizers aren't getting watered in. Watering by hand has the added benefit of allowing you to observe what is going on with your rose bushes. Are there diseases present? Are pests evident? Are the canes growing in the right direction?

DRY FERTILIZERS

Apply at the base of the rose bush and as far out as the shrubs branches reach. Chemical fertilizers should be added regularly (every other week at the height of the growing season) but in smaller amounts. Hose-end applicators have some advantages: no need to bend over, leaves absorb some nutrients, leaves get a good washing which allows them to function better as leaves, water sprays cut down fungal spores as long as the leaves can dry off by sunset

Old fashioned watering cans are still useful. You really can direct where the water and fertilizer are going. You have to use a bucket for fish emulsion as its particles will clog the watering can nozzle.

Peace, hybrid tea (1942)

Fixing mistakes is part of gardening. Water is the all purpose correcting agent in feeding roses. If you screw up on concentrations and over fertilize, just give more water. I once confused the time-release lawn fertilizer with the time-release general plant food. I just watered more and got some of the largest, greenest bushes ever. The flowers were average and not particularly abundant but I did no damage.

APPROPRIATE CULTIVARS

We choose roses for lots of odd reasons, too many of which are non-horticultural. At one time, I grew *Just Joey, Joseph's Coat, Uncle Joe,* and *By Joe.* I wonder why? I also have had in my garden *Maria Callas, Kathleen Ferrier,* and *Helen Traubel.* I wonder why? The first roses I really wanted to rush out and get eighteen years ago when I started my garden were: *Mister Lincoln, Tiffany, Frau Karl Drushki, Peace, Sterling Silver,* and *Talisman.* It was a perfect collection. It contained one of each color. Others which have been highly praised or associated with famous gardens and gardeners I once knew were also among my first choices. The result: too many, too closely planted, virused, mildewed, rusted, and nonperforming.

Life's too short to experiment in your yard. Select varieties which are already known to do well in your neighborhood. When you see people growing healthy roses you admire, ask them if they know the names. If they don't, find out how many years the rose has been growing there.

Learn to care for roses which respond to care easily! Healthy roses which are constantly producing flowers are not difficult to come by.

Try to make a few other general observations. What's its petal count? Does it produce single buds with some side buds or does it produce a candelabra-like stem? Is it fragrant or not? Is it constantly in flower or does it tend to have flushes of bloom? Is it a color you like? What color?

Roses have specific needs, but when those needs are addressed you will continue to reap a harvest of gorgeous blooms. The Monterey Bay Rose Society helped me to see how my own shortcomings were affecting my gardening and wasting my money. Skip this part of the learning curve.

Select your roses from garden centers with climates exactly the same as your garden. If you select the roses in the fall, you will have seen how they responded to a summer on the Central Coast. Buying roses in the springtime will give you the widest selection to choose from. However, the vigor the roses display was not acquired locally. They stored up their energy from the previous summer while they were down in the bright and hot growing fields.

HYBRID TEAS, FLORIBUNDAS, GRANDIFLORAS, SHRUBS

Pink or Pink Blend
Duet, Fame, Gemini, Great Century, Kathleen Ferrier, Miss All American Beauty: a.k.a. Maria Callas, Secret, Tiffany, Tournament of Roses

Red or Red Blend
Crimson Bouquet, Ingrid Bergman, National Trust, Nicole, Olympiad, Reba McEntire, Perfect Moment, Picasso, Veteran's Honor

Yellow or Gold
Apollo, Chinatown, Easy Going, Gold Medal, Golden Holstein, Helmut Schmidt, Julia Child, Sun Flare

Apricot, Coral or Orange
Apricot Nectar, Artistry, Bill Warriner, Chris Evert, Disco Dancer, Gingersnap, Impressionist, Just Joey, Matangi, Oldtimer, Sunset Celebration, Sheila's Perfume, Tahitian Sunset, Vavoom, Westerland

Mauve or Mauve Blend
Barbra Streisand, Blueberry Hill, Heirloom, Lavender Pinocchio, Midnight Blue, Purple Heart, Singin' the Blues, Stainless Steel

White
First Kiss, French Lace, Iceberg, Margaret Merril, Pascali, Sally Holmes

Modern Climbers
Altissimo, America, Berries 'n' Cream, Dublin Bay, Fourth of July, Lavender Lassie, Pearly Gates, Purple Splash, Soaring Spirit

Maria Callas, hybrid tea (1968)

Disease Resistant Repeat Blooming Older Roses
Cécile Brünner, (bush polyantha), *Crépuscule* (noisette), *Duchesse de Brabant* (tea), *Honorine de Brabant* (bourbon), *Jeanne d'Arc* (noisette), *Madame Alfred Carrière* (noisette), *Old Blush* (china), *Phyllis Bide* (polyantha), *Sombreuil* (large flowered climber), *Ragged Robin* (china), *Rose de Resht* (portland), *Perle d'Or* (polyantha), *Marie Pavié* (polyantha), *Portland from Glendora* (portland)

Disease Resistant Once Blooming Older Roses
Alba semi-plena (alba), *Cécile Brünner,* (climbing polyantha), *Henri Martin* (moss), *Isfahan* (damask), *Madame Legras de St. Germaine* (alba), *Maiden's Blush* (alba), *Newport Fairy* (rambler), *Russell's Cottage Rose* (Russelliana).

Disease Resistant Miniature Roses
Apricot Twist (light apricot), *Crazy Dottie* (pink/orange), *Cuddles* (pink), *Cupcake* (pink), *Gourmet Popcorn* (cluster flowered, white), *Hot Tamale* (dark pink, orange), *Incognito* (mauve, yellow), *Irresistible* (white), *Jean Kenneally* (apricot), *Jeanne LaJoie* (pink), *My Sunshine* (single, yellow), *Natchez* (single, pink), *Old Glory* (dark coral), *Palmetto Sunrise,* (pink/yellow blend), *Pink Petticoat* (tall, pink), *Peggy T* (single, red/white blend), *Pierrine* (salmon), *Popcorn* (white), *Pride 'n' Joy* (orange), *Puppy Love* (red/yellow blend), *Rainbow's End* (red, yellow double), and *This Is The Day* (dark coral).

Roses By The Month

Liverpool Remembers, hybrid tea (1992)

In the late 1700s, English gardener Thomas Mawe published his gardening manual entitled *Everyman His Own Gardener* which documented much practical knowledge regarding growing vegetables, trees, and flowering plants. I've quoted his references to growing roses throughout the *Central Coast Rose Manual*. His advice, as you will soon read, was given at a time when all farming was organic! Roses need to be treated a certain way to get the best results. Those methods still apply. What's more, the kindly Mr. Mawe organized his presentation of horticultural advice on a month-by-month basis. I echoed this monthly advice over the years in *The Bay Rose*'s regular feature, Roses By The Month. The following section is meant to be read at the beginning of each month as much information is repeated.

January

In a horticultural sense, December and early January are perhaps the easiest months of the gardening year. There isn't much you can do when the wind and the rain dominate daily routines. Winter storms can cause serious damage to homes, fences, and property. The earth gets drenched with abundant rainfall and becomes supersaturated. The dangers of mud slides and uprooted trees are ongoing concerns. Rose gardens move down on our priority lists.

Now, it's time to return to the garden. Weeks of long cold nights have put our roses as close to dormancy as they will get. Generally, the more that roses rest in the winter in our region, the more nutrients they are able to store and the greater their first burst of flowers will be. A cold wet winter in California is great for the roses. Yet, what can we possibly do when the ground is so full of water?

CHORES IN THE WINTER GARDEN

One January, I got up at 6:00 a.m. to let Buddy outside. A quick survey of the frosty rooftops and grass sent me right back to the bedroom for another couple of hours of sleep. "What's the point of gardening now?" I remembered thinking just before returning to dreamland.

Tending roses, however, was still on my mind when I woke up again. I made coffee and toast and leafed through R. H. Shumway's latest *Illustrated Garden Guide* (advertised as "Good Seed, Cheap" and a great source for heirloom and unusual plants, call (800) 342-9461, they've been around for 134 years), then I reorganized my computer files and hours passed. After I turned a pan of scalloped potatoes from a holiday party into a wonderfully hearty potato soup and fortified myself, I finally braved the chilly wind and absolutely soggy yard. It was now past noon. An inch of rain fell at Christmas and in Salinas we were up to the average for that time of year. The garden was truly saturated, but dry enough to walk on.

A few of my hybrid teas (and any other roses with Chinese ancestors) growing in the warmest part of the yard, were still producing flowers, but the winter storms had whipped them about and I would have had to have done some extraordinary "fluffing up" to get them on the table.

Walking in the bright sunshine, you could almost feel the plants snoozing. In fact, the *Rosa eglanteria, Rosa setigera,*

Abracadabra, hybrid tea (1991)

and all the rugosas were virtually leafless. The damask, gallica, and alba roses had donned yellowed or tough leaves and need me to pull off the younger ones to force dormancy. The roses with more tender parents like the *Rosa banksia* varieties, hybrid musks, teas, noisettes and, of course, hybrid teas, floribundas, and miniatures were still leafy but many of their lower leaves had dropped, probably from a combination of blackspot and old age. They looked leggy and prime for pruning.

GETTING READY TO GET OUT IN THE GARDEN

As I walked about the garden, I was taking mental notes of which canes were going to go and the approximate height to prune to. I learned several seasons ago not to follow the instructions in the general rose books and manuals, but instead observe what long time rosarians do in this unique climate and follow their lead.

Isfahan, damask (1832)

I began working in my potting shed and realized it had been a long time since I had last been out there organizing things. There was a considerable amount of water on the table top which didn't alarm me as the storm was a powerful one, the winds could have blown the torrents through the lattice work and thus flooded everything. I discovered four packages of daffodil bulbs in a bucket containing about eight inches of water. I forgot to plant them in October, I guess. I drained the water and sure enough they were well on their way—an unconventional way to force them. I looked over at the garden bed just outside the shed and my eyes fell on a rather poorly producing, unnamed miniature that had been a gift. I decided that was the spot for the daffodils.

A soaking wet cardboard box of succulents was removed (also a gift) and the plants lay in a heap under my *Isfahan* until I could deal with that mess. As the work table got less and less cluttered I felt a bit odd, like I was being watched. Then I looked up and saw two green eyes, a white face and black nose staring down at me through the cracked corrugated, green fiberglass ceiling. Buddy was watching me through the new hole in the roof, thus the abundant water on the work table. It's always something.

In order to replace the roofing, I'll have to remove the eight-foot mound of roses growing up there (from North to South: *Phyllis Bide*, *Climbing Cécile Brünner*, *Isfahan*, and *Newport Fairy*) and cut the canes right down to the roof line. There goes my open garden in the spring that I've promised everyone in the world they would be invited to. What to do, what to do. Duct tape! I'll replace the roof in the summer after the party and hope the duct tape will stop the current leak.

Another success, I found my diamond blade sharpening tool. It was expensive but never wears down and keeps the blades sharp. I'd been looking for it since August. Half-heartedly looking, mind you, but still it was great to find it again and especially at this time in the gardening cycle.

I finally identified the leafless mystery bulb which I upturned in the summer and had set on the table to investigate further then totally forgot—it was clearly a cyclamen from an abandoned pot someone had given me. I gave it a new home near the entrance, gathered up the freesia bulbs which got knocked over and re-potted them in a hanging basket this time.

One of the most useful gardening aids for this time of year is an old shower curtain liner. I spread it out before the bed where I wanted the daffodils to go, sat down with my legs spread, pushed aside the cat who had joined me on the liner *a lá* summer picnic, and surveyed where to begin. With the soil so saturated, it took no effort to grab the doomed miniature rose by its base and lift it out of the soil, shake off the mud, and cast it aside. The soil is in beautiful condition, which further infuriated me because this rose had everything it needed to look wonderful AND IT DIDN'T! The daffodils will do very well in this spot and maybe I'll plant some annuals here instead, just to send a warning to the rest of the roses!

In rearranging the potting shed, I found all the tools I will need for pruning: my blade sharpener, a pair of kitchen scissors, my Felco one-inch pruners, my Corona loppers, my pruning saw, and my hatchet. I still haven't found my small sized leaf rake as I will need it to sweep up after the pruning begins.

WATCH YOUR WATER

If there's been an exceptionally dry December, it's necessary to keep the roses well-watered, especially those in containers or in south-facing, raised beds. A good drink in the winter does last longer than at other times; but care must be given to see that the roses aren't totally ignored and allowed to wither. The climate can be cold and dry and, ultimately, destructive.

Once the rains have begun, we will witness a series of changes in our gardens. Rain is a great cleansing agent. It dissolves salt and carries it away. It also helps nutrients work their way from the top layer of soil down into lower layers where most of the important roots are. Its leaching properties, however, also remove water soluble nutrients. Not to worry though, roses don't really need many nutrients at this time of year.

Blue Girl, hybrid tea, (1964)

It's most beneficial to roses when rain drains off within a few hours of falling, but don't be alarmed if it falls quickly in great quantities and you watch your roses soak for a day or two. It's important though that after two days the water finds a way to dissipate; otherwise, you risk the danger of the plant smothering. Your soil should be a sandy loam which retains some moisture but allows excess water to drain.

Brave the storms. Pretend you are King Lear, "Blow, winds and crack your cheeks! rage! blow!" and check your roses periodically to see that they aren't drowning.

START RIGHT NOW TO PRUNE

The correct time to prune your rose garden is mid-January until mid-February. Several reasons exist which support this. If you prune too early, your roses may respond to a minor heat wave, come out of dormancy before they have rested sufficiently, and freeze when a cold blast returns. It will also cause them to produce weak canes because sunlight is at its lowest level. It's also easier to prune if you give the rose a chance to swell its bud eyes. In other words, pruning in mid-January is a bit easier because nutrients have begun to flow again. The new growth has swollen bud eyes making it easier for you to place your shears in the correct location.

But, don't let me get ahead of myself. I need to discuss the essentials of rose pruning before I begin sharing my observations.

Although the optimum moment to prune roses in our area is mid-January, you can begin earlier with some of them. Start with those which are in partial shade at that moment. If you begin to prune the roses which are in the warmest, sunniest part of the yard which is definitely a temptation at this time of year because it's warmer there for you, too, they will come to life too soon and be at risk for a late February frost. The length of daylight has much to do with producing substantial growth and you want everything to be growing at its best. In addition, if you prune the warmest part of the garden first, the blooming cycle will be ahead of the colder, darker parts of the garden. My aim is to invite people to tour the backyard when everything is in bloom at the same time.

I couldn't resist and went to work on *Golden Wings* (1956). It's a large shrub which has only been in the ground for two seasons. This is likely to be THE season it grows into maturity. For a shrub, I like to envision what the ultimate shape of the plant will be. I quickly disposed of the wimpy lower canes and topped off the one or two canes which grew much higher than the rest of the bush. Now when it fills out in the spring it should have an attractive overall shape.

The next on my list were any canes which prevented my easy movement about the garden. If a rose has snagged me more than once, it got pruned regardless of any other factor. My garden, my paths, my clothes. Rose—grow where I say grow!

While I was sitting on the liner in front of a rose bed, I seized the moment to snip away the inconsequential growth coming from the lower canes of *Jeanne LaJoie* (1975) and *Sombreuil* (1880) in front of me.

Pruning will also go much faster if you remove any potted plants or other obstacles which are near the roses. With only a few days available to me for pruning, I have to make sure that I can get as much done as possible. **Remember.** All roses will respond better if they receive some pruning. The hedge clipper method, though crude, is better than doing nothing at all.

A sunny day in mid-January, however, is the epitome of perfection, especially so for rose growers. A respite, however brief, from the necessary rains of winter is quite welcome indeed.

BUT BEFORE
YOU START PRUNING

Now is the time to trim back the hybrid teas, floribundas, grandifloras, English roses, polyanthas, and miniatures. It's essential to get some advice from an experienced grower on this important rose topic. Attend a pruning clinic or call the consulting rosarians listed at www.MontereyBayRoseSociety.org. Ask some questions regarding the specific varieties you grow. For instance, *Peace* (1945) doesn't respond as well to a good pruning as *All*

That Jazz (1991). A little experience with the roses in your own yard will teach you this.

I divide up my garden into several sections. Then I set out only trying to prune one of these sections and no more! That way I can feel like I've accomplished something and if two or three weeks go by before I get back out there, at least the roses within the finished sections will be on the same growth/bloom cycle.

If you have decided to get rid of certain roses, do that before you start pruning. It will give you more space to work. If that's not possible then cut the departing bush down to one or two canes to act as handles for extracting the plant later.

Digging up a rose bush can take time, especially if you are taking away an intact root ball. I won't start this project until I'm certain I have a new home for the rose. Pruned and dug out roses will keep during the winter for a couple of weeks, however, if stored in a heavy black plastic bag and kept moist.

USE SHARP SHEARS AND LOPPERS

We all operate with the understanding that we want the most from our gardens with the least amount of time and effort. One of the best ways to save time and lighten the burden of pruning your rose garden is to use very sharp shears and loppers. Invest in a really good, diamond tool sharpener and keep it handy and occupied. They're expensive but truly worth the money in your garden and kitchen. (You will be amazed at how easy it is to cook when your kitchen knives are sharp.) Keep your tools well honed as you prune. Don't forget to sharpen your loppers as well. And, keep all moveable parts of your shears and loppers well oiled. WD-40 usually does the trick.

Buy good pruning equipment. Don't spend money on anything that doesn't have replaceable blades. Felco bypass pruning shears are available at the best garden centers. They cost a lot but are again worth every cent. Don't ever use anvil shears as they crush the cane ends and make the plant susceptible to a number of common diseases and pests. By making quick, clean diagonal cuts you will avoid dieback and insect invasion.

Invest in a good pair of short loppers, a pruning saw which cuts on the pull action and glides on the push, and a hatchet. A good wire brush with a long handle like those sold for your BBQ grill will help to clean up a woody bud union. This action helps produce future canes.

Pushing yourself to get the pruning job done quickly is not a good idea. With the sharpness of the tools, you can easily snip right through your glove and do damage to your hands. Pace yourself and know your own limits.

One of the handiest tools I own for pruning miniature roses is a vegetable scissors available in the gadget aisle of most grocery stores. They snip cleanly in small spaces. Bypass pruners, of course, are versatile, but are too thick and clumsy to get into the little spaces you have to work when trimming a miniature.

More advice: Don't use vegetable scissors when the job calls for pruning shears. Don't use pruning shears when cane removal requires a lopper. Don't use loppers when the limb calls for a saw. Don't use a saw when the root really needs a hatchet.

USE COMMON SENSE AND BE CAREFUL

Start your pruning chore by protecting yourself. If you wear glasses, that's adequate eye protection. If you don't or wear contacts, use sunglasses or safety goggles when pruning rose bushes. Not only to prevent sawdust or dirt from landing in your eyes, but to offer interference from toppling canes. Eye protection is of particular value when pruning climbing roses. The angle is awkward. It should be obvious that reaching up and cutting canes will make them fall down, usually onto you. I also find that lots of debris comes down with the canes including dust and leaf litter. I can cite plenty of near misses from which I departed with a scratched cheek or punctured nose. Be careful.

Invest in a good pair of gloves. Leading hardware stores carry ones made from goat skin. I find them to be the most protective from rose thorns and quite versatile,

Mermaid, hybrid bracteata (1918)

but they are by no means impenetrable. Mail order supply houses sell versions which have goat skin palms and long suede covered sleeves to protect forearms. Don't waste your money on plastic or rubber versions of these. I was given a pair once and had to toss them after one morning of use on a *Mermaid*. More accurately, roses don't have true thorns but have "prickles." Regardless of the botanical nomenclature, they can make a lot of blood run down your arm. I recently bought a really fine pair of top grade cowhide gloves. What they lack in flexibility, they make up for in thickness. They weren't cheap but were once again well worth the price.

At this time of year, most rose thorns have dried to a lethal stiffness. The wood may be soft, as wood goes, but it's still wood and inflexible. Wear a tough pair of jeans and a shirt you don't mind tearing.

Make decisive and clean cuts on your roses. I like to make all cuts at a 45° angle to make sure that water doesn't sit on the cane ends, direction of the angle not too important. After every fifth rose bush, you should probably stop and sharpen your clippers. It won't take too long and the results are so much better. Dip the blade in Lysol between every bush to kill the malefactors which cause cane dieback.

BASIC ROSE PRUNING

Follow this simple exercise: Place your right hand on a table with the palm facing up, the wrist at the edge, and the fingers and thumb stretched out wide. Slowly bring the tips of your fingers and thumb up while keeping them spread out and equidistant with the back of your hand remaining against the table. When your fingers are at an angle of 75° to the tabletop, you have before you a model of the perfectly pruned hybrid tea rose bush. Onto this model visualize a swollen bud eye right where the middle of your finger nails are.

Keep this model in mind. Five canes may be more than what your garden specimen produced, but three is quite adequate. If you only have one or two good large canes, do the best you can and water and feed well throughout the year to see if you can get the plant to produce a basal break or two.

To save time, study each rose bush before your start cutting it back. You will learn to see where you can make just one or two cuts and remove what could take five or six before you get there. I have never read, heard, or witnessed any advantage to pruning in slow meticulous stages. I like to work at a steady rather fast pace disposing of the canes as I go.

ROSE PRUNING RULES TO REVIEW AND KEEP IN MIND

- Clear out any canes regardless of how healthy they appear to be if they dissect the center of the plant.

- Remove any canes on a hybrid tea or floribunda which are smaller in diameter than a pencil. Adjust and apply this same ratio to miniatures and climbers.

- Make good clean cuts on the ends of the canes which are at about a 45° angle to the ground. This allows water to roll off the cut. If it just sits on the cut, you'll get cane dieback. Position your cut at about a half-inch above an outward facing bud eye sloping into the plant.

- If possible, make your cut below any stem-on-stem growth. The remaining canes on a hybrid tea should be uninterrupted from bud union to cut. You may allow some stem-on-stem growth in shrubs such as hybrid musks or repeat blooming Old Garden Roses.

- Remove any and all deadwood especially from the bud union.

- Get on your knees and use a wire brush to scrape off the hardest bits. Then, put some mulch or light soil on top of the bud union to keep it moist.

- Finger prune (push off with your finger) any bud eyes which have started to grow in the lower half of the pruned cane. These will not produce substantial growth and will inhibit good air circulation. If two shoots arise from one bud eye, pull off the weaker of the two.

- Hybrid teas and floribundas only need to be pruned down to 18 to 24-inch long canes. This is longer than what you will read in most rose care literature.

- Clean up the pruned refuse and litter in the garden. An ounce of prevention is worth a pound of cure.

- Keep some regular old Lysol household cleaner mixed up with some water in a bucket and swirl your shears in this pail after trimming each rose bush. This should help cut down on "die back."

To me, there are essentially five types of roses to prune: miniatures, climbers, shrubs, hybrid teas/floribundas, and tree roses. These types aren't scientifically divided, but rather a grouping of different pruning challenges.

Tootie, miniature (2003)

MINIATURE CHALLENGES

Miniatures aren't too difficult to prune if they are in pots. At their easiest when all you have to do is set the potted miniature on a table, and sit and prune. One esteemed member of the Monterey Bay Rose Society who has been growing roses since before God has all of his miniatures in pots. When pruning time arrives, he unpots them, shakes off the old soil, divides the root mass with a hatchet, replants the strongest section in fresh soil, and places the pruned-off portions on the raffle table at January's MBRS meeting. The method makes a great deal of sense and, since I have won many of his excellent discards with the pick of a ticket, I hope he continues it. This is considered asexual reproduction which is illegal if the rose is still patented.

If the miniatures are in the ground, it means more work. Get out an old blanket or shower curtain liner and just lie yourself down beside them to snip off the inconsequential growth, deadwood, and hips. I have also pruned the miniatures right down to soil line. Miniature roses are all on their own roots. There is no graft involved so that the roots will produce the rose once again. This right-to-the-ground method will work but it sets back the size of your plants. It's best to leave more of the old canes intact.

CLIMBING FRUSTRATIONS

Climbers are my favorite type to prune because I can do it without stooping, squatting or lying down. It isn't a particularly fast job because the plants are large and need much attention. I also like to replace some of the bindings. I use jute string which rots away after a season or so. I use it because it gives a little as the rose grows. Wire won't and will restrict the flow of nutrients up the cane. Plastic clamps may take more hands than you have. Stretch plastic garden ribbon works, but it is ugly. When it's pruning time, it's also time to replace (or at least inspect) the bindings. A freshly pruned climber is tranquility itself.

My garden is considerably smaller than my enthusiasm and my appetite for growing roses. One solution which has presented itself over years of growing a variety of roses is to seek out show stopping climbers, position them carefully in the corners, and elevate the garden. Growing climbers on all sides of my back yard fence has created an effect for the eyes not dissimilar to surround sound stereo. Everywhere your eyes fall, there are roses and no straight lines. At least that was my intention. Plants growing in a straight line works during the pruning cycle.

I have taken great care to select the best climbing roses I can and brace them against the fence which surrounds the yard or the posts holding up the patio roof or the lattice work which hides the potting shed.

In the past, I lost three of the wilder types of climbers when I tore down a rusted old shed and cut down the plum tree on which they grew. The *Rosa moschata plena* (before 1530)

Sombreuil, large flowered climber, (1888)

Chrysler Imperial, climbing hybrid tea (1957)

turned out to be *Rosa brunonii* (1820) which grew and grew and grew and flowered for all of about five minutes each year. I lost my *Mermaid* (1918) which made me sad, but my yard was too small to contain her. I lost my *Rosa woodsii fendleri* (1820) which still hurts. What a wonderful native rose! I saved a cutting and grew it in a pot outside my office window. I also gave a piece to a friend in Mendocino County and it has brought his wife and him much joy. It attracts bees which is a good habit if you plant it near a vegetable garden, orchard or vineyard. These big roses darkened my yard too much and drained energy from the more refined plants, such as *Climbing Étoile de Hollande* (1931) and *Climbing Chrysler Imperial* (1957) and *Climbing Talisman* (1930).

I actually got a jump start because of some free time in my garden. I was cleaning out a couple of beds hit hard by some Thanksgiving frost and taking advantage of the relatively dry garden bed. I chopped my hydrangeas and bush fuchsias down to ground level, removed the dead leaves from a clump of yellow callas, and pulled out some invasive trumpet vine which unnoticed by me had grown right into two climbing rose bushes. In the process of removing the vine, I broke a few spindly canes and in cleaning them up said "What the hell, it's nearly time" and pruned them back.

These two bushes hadn't gotten much trimming during the past two seasons and had really taken off. They both needed work. One is a hybrid musk named *Nur Mahal* (1923) and the other a noisette *Crépuscule* (1904) [French: twilight] and both grow in partial sun. A few warm days won't bring them out of dormancy.

One season, I never got to prune my C*limbing Chrysler Imperial* (1957) and it never once had what I would call a superior looking flush of flowers. It was always congested and scrappy looking. This past week, I went to it and really brought it down to a beautiful shape. I reduced it by one third in general length and made certain that the oldest and weakest canes were removed. All the insignificant growth along the canes was removed. The long canes which arch over the fence were retied and trimmed down to the lowest bud eye. It looks great and I'm certain will have a wonderful blooming cycle.

Climbers need a little more attention. Most need a length that will grow vertically from the bud union and then another bit that will go horizontal to the ground and produce the flowering stalks.

Some, like *Climbing Cécile Brünner* (1894), are really weeds in our climate. They grow and grow. The April bloom is fantastically beautiful and then that's about it. It's a vigorous climber and will overwhelm most other roses planted near it. So I suggest that if you grow this rose, keep it away from all others. I have such a big chore ahead of me chopping it way back to a manageable size and allowing the *Phyllis Bide* (1923) (in many ways a much better climber) a chance to breathe.

If you're really good and clever, you would grow your climbers on a trellis with removable fasteners. (Not weave them in and out of the trellis itself, but keep the canes all on the outside of the trellis.) As the bush produces longer and more canes, you add more fasteners. Then, when it's time to prune, you simply remove the fasteners, lay the bush on the ground, prune it and then refasten it to the trellis. Like I said, you'd have to be very good and very consistent. This is the best way to grow good climbers.

SERIOUS SHRUBBERY

By shrubs, I mean most of the old European roses I grow. They average about eight feet in height. Shrubs can also mean more modern ones such as the free standing *Sally Holmes* (1976) located in my front yard. It takes about two hours to get it in shape. The time is spent mostly chopping up the pruned canes and leaves to fit in the yard waste container. Some floribundas actually grow more like shrubs than hybrid teas.

Many of my older varieties such as the hybrid musks *Danaë* (1913) and *Nur Mahal* (1923), the polyanthas *Perle d'Or* (1884) and *Chatillon Rose* (1923), and the repeat blooming OGRs *Salet* (1854) and *Honorine de Brabant* (1850) won't shrink away from a thorough pruning. It's like a haircut. Sometimes I let them get big, sometimes I whack them back. The plants are really well established. They are healthy and will take whatever shape or form I want.

HYBRID TEA TOTALING

Pruning the hybrid teas is the easiest job to me. One, I don't really grow that many of them. Two, I seem to eliminate and replace more of them than any other type. Three, I want them to produce the big blousy flowers I love. And four, I've planted them in the most accessible parts of the garden so it's easy for me to get around them.

I was finished pruning the thirty or so I intend to leave where they are in less than an hour. Several have produced no canes last season which were larger than the canes from two seasons back. Although I may give them one more year, this trait makes them a candidate for a trip to Elsewhere.

The good performing hybrid teas were pruned back to just four to six really strong canes increasing the likelihood that they will produce magnificent blooms in April and May. I've left canes a bit longer this year. It's an experiment to see if a little more atmosphere might do them well.

Pruning a floribunda usually requires leaving more canes on the pruned bush than for a hybrid tea. Many floribundas produce clusters of flowers and experience will tell you how much they tolerate. Shape the bush, open the center, and leave a few smaller canes on the top.

Gold Medal, grandiflora (1982)

STANDARD AND PATIO ROSE TRIMMING

Generally speaking, the pruning advice for bush roses applies to tree roses. Roses grown on a standard (commonly known as tree roses) are actually three different varieties. The root stock is one rose, the standard or trunk portion is a different rose from which all the bud eyes have been excised, and finally the attractive species which you purchased is grafted onto the top of the standard. So pruning depends on which rose is on top.

For upright, hybrid tea roses, prune them as a shrub except the canes need to be considerably shorter in length, perhaps eight to ten inches. Keep the center section unobstructed and remove all spindly growth. This reduces the weight on the bud union and decreases the number of flowers on the tree later. This will provide for new canes and much larger flowers on the bush.

For cascading roses which might be climbers or landscape (recumbent) varieties, shape them but do not shorten them too much. You want to create an umbrella-like form. With weeping standards you want to make sure that you have an ample number of new canes from which the flowers will cascade. A weeping standard needs to be symmetrically balanced not only for aesthetic reasons but for practical ones as well. The weight on the upper bud union—if lopsided—can cause the top to snap off during a wet and windy storm. When this happens, the plant is not repairable and must be discarded. Additionally, pruning time affords a great opportunity to replace any weak upright supports. The larger the tree rose gets, the more stakes it needs.

Winter Magic, miniature, (1986) blessed with a delicious scent and vigor

Newport Fairy, rambler (1908)

ROSES THAT SHOULD NOT BE PRUNED

Now is NOT the time to prune once-blooming roses such as albas, damasks, gallicas, species roses, and ramblers which bloom on year-old wood. You should remove any dead canes (or nearly dead ones) from these varieties and any hips and withered flowers from last season. The time to cut back these plants is AFTER they finish blooming in the summer, leaving enough time for them to grow new canes. Most one-time bloomers do better with just a good cleaning out and not a reduction in size. The bigger they get, the greater the number of blooms they produce.

Other roses you should not prune are new cuttings or seedlings. Yes, remove deadwood and damaged canes, but not much else. I may snip off the very end of a newly sprouted cutting, but only an inch or so.

Do very little cutting on any bare root plants you have recently bought and want to plant. They were already downsized in the growing field. Look for broken canes and remove the part which has cracked by making a nice, clean cut just below where the break occurred.

OTHER PRUNING CONSIDERATIONS

A well-pruned garden is a thing of beauty, not because of its blooms but because of its simplicity and promise. Hybrid tea roses do not need to be heavily pruned unless you have some other intention. As noted above, a healthy, large hybrid tea could be pruned to 18 to 24-inch long canes and be quite the better for it. There is a great deal of energy stored in

those canes. With longer days and warmer weather, the canes will produce magnificently. There's no need to cut them to 10-inch stubs unless you are trying to promote the production of basal breaks. A basal break is a brand-new cane emerging from the bud union. These are the goal of every rose garden because they mean two or three seasons of new flowering stalks.

It may be time for you to prune away canes on your roses which have been gradually producing fewer and fewer flowering stalks and leave thinner, weaker looking but younger canes to pick up the slack.

Generally speaking, prune heavily and you will get larger-size hybrid tea flowers but fewer of them. Prune lightly and you will get many more blossoms but they won't be exceptionally large. You can't kill a rose by pruning it. Many have observed that the more you contemplate pruning a single rose bush, the smaller it gets.

Your ultimate goal is to have:

- Three to five strong canes growing out of the bud union.

- The area immediately above the bud union being open with no canes growing straight up.

- All growth thinner than a pencil eliminated.

- The bud union resting at the soil level with its upper part visible and its out edge buried.

All leaf litter, botrytis-ruined buds, and old canes raked up, burned or discarded. Never use rose debris as part of your compost—at least, compost intended for use on the roses. Common disease spores are likely to survive the composting process and re-infect the plants.

ADVANCED ROSE PRUNING

In general, prune your yellow hybrid teas, floribundas, and grandifloras less than you do other colors. Something in their yellow ancestry, probably *Rosa foetida* (1597), makes them less vigorous after a pruning. If you grow or once grew *Peace* (1945), you may have noticed that it doesn't like to get a severe pruning. Many wild roses also do much better and look much prettier if left alone, such as *Mutabilis* (before 1894) and *Rosa woodsii fendleri* (1820). Make sure that you plant them in a location where they can grow unimpeded.

Pruning gives you the best opportunity to evaluate each of your roses. If they don't do well after being in the same spot for two growing seasons, dig them up and put them in a different spot: more sun, less sun, less wind, better drainage, less crowding. Analyze the condition and test another spot.

If a rose bush is growing in a direction you don't want, you can alter this by hard pruning one side of the bush while encouraging the other side by pruning a little less. When the

Pink Petticoat in bud, miniature (1979)

new canes appear going in the wrong direction, push them off with your thumb while they are still soft (finger pruning).

The rose you planted may have done too well and needs more space. Now is a great time to thin out the garden and diminish overcrowding. I have two roses I will dig out this winter and not replace. I'm certain that after April, I won't even know that another rose had been there.

If you are pruning your rose bushes for exhibition at the Annual Rose Show in late April or May, you should probably prune at the end of January. Leave only three canes on the rose. You want to encourage large size blooms supported by a strong straight cane with perfect leaves. During the re-growth period, you may want to limit the new canes on the rose to no more than two per pruned cane. Each of these canes will sport only one rose per stem. That's how to grow a show specimen. Great exhibitors will also build wind shelters and other devices which will protect these canes from snapping off in the wind. They are also very severe with their spraying for insects. Perfection and size is their main objective, not a great looking garden.

GET RID OF THE ROSE TRASH

Make sure that you travel with your trash can while you prune. Fill it immediately as you make your way from rose to rose. You never know when the rain will start again. I also spend the time necessary to snip the pruned canes into smaller pieces which pack nicely in the refuse container.

The canes you will be removing have been on the bushes for several months, if not years, and the thorns have dried to a particularly dangerous stiffness. Be careful. Be very careful and wear really old clothes.

Rake up all the old leaves and canes which have fallen onto the ground and remove them from the rose bed. If you have the time and money, you may even wish to remove all the mulch and place a fresh batch on the ground immediately after you've finished pruning. It's much easier to spread mulch when the roses aren't in the way.

Certain other rose classes, such as chinas, noisettes, and hybrid musks benefit from a little shaping at this time of year. Reduce the overall plant size by about a quarter. Cut out any awkward growth which distorts the plants' appearance and remove, of course, any deadwood, hips, faded flowers, or inconsequential growth. You may have to pull off and discard leaves as some varieties in our climate are nearly evergreen.

Once you have pruned your entire garden, rake up all the old leaves and stems to cut down on transferring diseases from one growing year to the next. Then, spray the remaining canes and the top dressing around the roses with a winter dormant oil spray. Follow the manufacturer's instructions carefully. Coat the canes and bud union well as they can harbor scale insects as well as air borne spores. It's not difficult to do and is excellent garden hygiene. Disease is easier to prevent than to cure.

Pink Petticoat in full bloom, miniature (1979)

Zigeunerknabe [Gipsy Boy], bourbon (1909)

PLANTING NEW ROSES

The distinguished British rosarian Graham Stuart Thomas gave good advice for this all important topic: "Make sure you dig the hole big enough."

Check out the location first by determining:

- Does it receive at least six hours of sunlight during most of the growing season?

- Will the rose have sufficient space around it when it's fully grown for you to care for it properly?

- Is it at least twenty feet from any tree, thereby not competing with the tree roots for nutrients?

Prepare the soil in your garden before you plant your bushes. Roses prefer a sandy loam which is about 45% sand, 25% silt, 25% clay, and 5% organic material. For a large planting, get a soil test done. Firms that do this are advertised in the yellow pages. For a smaller garden planting, try to incorporate into your soil what it needs to achieve the above consistency preference. I regularly amend the Salinas adobe soil I have with sand and cow manure and make sure there is adequate drainage. Roses respond well to a good soaking but if the roots don't get enough oxygen, the plant will suffocate.

Dig the hole about a foot in diameter larger than the bare roots or root ball require. It should be deep enough and wide enough for you to spread out the rose roots without them curling around or turning back in on themselves. If you have gophers, plant the rose inside the gopher cage and let the topmost portion of the wire appear above ground. Dig about a foot deeper than necessary and incorporate some good soil into the lower portion of the hole.

Into the very bottom of the hole, place either a dead gopher, some left over soup bones, or some commercially polite bone meal. Don't mix it into the soil. Apparently, the rose roots enjoy it more when they enter a large mass of bone meal instead of a saturated area. (I don't know how experts know what they do, but I've grown roses and this practice does work better.) It takes years for the rose to use up this vital source of phosphorus—the middle number in fertilizer charts.

Place the rose in the center of the hole, adjusting where necessary so that the bud union rests right at surface level. Spread its roots around. If you are transplanting from pot to ground, it's important to know how long the rose has been in the pot. If it's been two years or more I would shake off the soil from the pot and free up the roots to absorb new soil. You may find that many of the roots have curled around at the bottom of the pot and truly need separating.

ADDING BARE ROOT ROSES TO THE GARDEN

Bare root roses hit the market in January and selections are at their widest. Ask the merchants in December when they expect their bare root rose shipments and then be among the first shoppers to arrive. Choose the best varieties for your area and buy the healthiest specimen available. If the bare root rose has already sprouted, you can be sure that it's been out of refrigeration for several weeks.

Don't try to save money by rescuing badly treated plants. Start with the healthiest specimens possible. Running a rose hospice won't score you any points in Heaven. Life's too short. Shovel prune (dig out) lesser performing varieties and replace them with something new. Start small and learn to care for the roses you grow. It will be much more rewarding.

Make sure that the rose you purchase in those packages hasn't been on the store shelf too long and that it is still sealed tightly. If the price of the bare-root rose is too good to be true, it probably is. Don't buy anything less than Grade A Number 1 roses from a name brand supplier (Hortico, Weeks, J&P). Cheap roses are often not quality roses. They are frequently infected with a mosaic virus which disfigures the leaves with unsightly splotches of yellow and reduces flower production. You will hate it.

The bare root rose you purchased should be unpacked immediately. I like to spread the sawdust in the garden somewhere. Trim off any broken canes or roots and immerse the rose in a tub of water with about a 1/4 cup of bleach added to it. Let the rose soak for twenty-four hours if you have time to spare, but at least four hours, and not more than three days.

Pull the bare-root roses from the tub one at a time and again examine each carefully. Be on the look out for damaged roots and canes you might have missed at first inspection. Snip off a broken root with a clean cut about a half-inch from the break. If a cane has cracked at the bud union—even if it is still partly attached, remove it. The injured portion might invite a smothering crown gall or just break off completely from the weight of the flowers six weeks later.

Trim up any broken or lopsided canes. Place a short cane from the pruned off scraps between two canes you feel are just too close to one another. Sometimes you can hook this separator on opposing thorns and it will stay. Later in the season, after the canes have hardened in their new position the separator will just fall off having achieved its intended result.

Make a conical mound in the bottom of the hole, place the bud union on the peak of the cone, fan the longer roots out, and slowly add the soil, compacting as you go. You don't need to hard pack the roots. Merely make sure that you haven't left any large air pockets which may cause the rose to sink. The roots should be pointed down at a 45° angle and fanned out as much as possible. Slowly, shovel in more soil to cover the roots. In our region, the bud union (of grafted roses) should rest on or slightly below the soil line. Too far down and the rose isn't reaping the benefits of the graft, too far above and you hamper your chance of producing basal breaks and encourage root stock suckering.

Pack the soil in and around the base of the plant. If the garden is well drained, plant the rose in a slight basin to facilitate and maximize your watering. Give the area good

Ingrid Bergman, hybrid tea, (1984)

soaking. If you notice the rose has sunk somewhat, add more soil or maybe some extra mulch, but keep the bud union at the proper height.

I've observed that the two worst practices about planting roses, or most other shrubs, are the poor research associated with individual varieties and the location chosen for the shrub. Choosing the correct plant and placing it in a location which allows it to thrive is an indication of good horticulture.

Novice gardeners will think they are getting good results from the first blooms coming from their newly planted bare root rose. Actually, the rose's energy is stored in the plant's canes from the past summer's growing fields. The key to success, given these circumstances, is growing even better roses the second season after planting. Provide good soil, at least six hours of sunlight, ample nutrients and water to allow the rose to continue to use and store energy.

MOVING ESTABLISHED ROSES

In the middle of my first day at pruning a few years ago, I arrived at that part of my garden where my three *Maria Callas* (1965) had been growing for eight years. She's sold around the world by that name but in the United States she's referred to with the unexplainably silly name of *Miss All-American Beauty*. (Not only was Maria Callas an extraordinary soprano and one of the best-selling classical artists of all time, she was born in New York City.) *Maria Callas* is a dark satiny pink, generous with blooms and canes, and a

Secret, hybrid tea (1992)

highly recommended rose for the Central Coast. Two of these terrific plants have done well, but the one planted behind them has never done anything special compared to the others. She's too much in their shade to be their equal.

I got my shovel and dug out *Lynne Anderson* (1995). It's a good rose but had the name of *Oh My God* in the pre-introduction growing fields. It got far too big for my small garden. As I had the shovel in my hands, I dug out the hidden *Maria Callas* and moved her to a much roomier and brighter spot. When I find a great rose for my garden I try to buy two or three bushes. I enjoy cutting flowers and giving them to others. Having a triple supply of the same flower assures you of a really nice presentation bouquet. I learned years ago that it isn't possible, practical, or desirable to grow every single rose that is. The "one-of-each-type" approach might be fine for collecting coins or stamps but it doesn't work in rose gardening.

When I got the hole large enough and mixed up the soil and some of the top mulch, I tossed in some air-dried bones, covered them with dirt and carried the *Maria Callas* over to its new home, pruning while holding the diva in my arms. I positioned her with consideration given to how big it will get not how big it is now.

The shredded palettes which I applied two years ago as top mulch have mostly broken down and I've been gradually incorporating them into the soil. This means that before the roses get going again, I need to set aside a day or two to apply new mulch. I also like to toss some construction sand out onto the top of my Salinas adobe clay as I replace roses. It's easy to till these top items into the newly dug hole so that the soil is always improving its malleability. It's easier for your nutrients to get to your roses if the soil is plenty porous. The decaying palettes now part of the soil invite insects and bacteria to take up residency. This activity heats the soil along

Golden Holstein, floribunda (1989)

with the summer sun and allows a better absorption of the nutrients you'll start applying as the roses return to life.

Alas, the third *Maria* lasted only one full season in the garden. Once in a better location, it nearly doubled in size. It also displayed severe rose mosaic which I somehow had missed in its darker location and may have resulted in its original poor performance. So it got yanked out and a rooted cutting put in, directly from the pot to the ground. This "Mystery Rose" was taken from my mother's garden. It had a light, loosely shaped yellow bloom. I imagined it to be very old and rare. Once under my care, its color deepened, its size increased, and its name became evident—*Golden Showers* (1956). It's very common here. I had one already growing on the back fence, and really not a bad rose.

TAKING CUTTINGS, MAKING THEM GROW

Helping others with pruning chores is a great way to acquire cuttings. Otherwise, they will just go in the recycle bins. There are those who say it's best done in the fall, others say spring, still others say summer. Many argue that the winter pruning is the best time of all.

I have had some success at every season of the year, but I'm certain that was due more to dumb luck, a good rooting hormone, and a cooperative variety. I have also had abysmal failures every season, too.

The best cuttings to take are those from the base of a rose bush growing on its own roots. It's easy to find a relatively young cane and remove it from the parent with some roots already attached. Replant it in some loose soil and allow it to build a good set of roots. These plants will be ready to pass along or put in the soil in only a few months. The more roots you have attached or the more scarring (the brown skin of the cane which forms beneath the soil line) the better your chances of success.

I saved several of the specimen flowers from a rose demonstration a few years ago held in early May. I mixed up a batch of potting soil with equal parts of Perlite. It's purposely very loose. I half filled some 3-inch square starter pots and inserted pencil-written labels. The canes were all ones which had already born a bloom.

I then cut the stem so that two bud eyes would be buried in the soil and two exposed above. I left only one leaf attached and removed the spent flowers, remaining buds and all other leaves. At the very bottom of the cane, I scraped the skin slightly exposing the inner layers. I jiggled the scraped end of the cane in a jar of Rootone, stuck my index finger into the soil at a 60° angle, and carefully inserted the cutting in the hole made by my finger. I then placed the potted up cuttings in a shady place beneath one of my Old Garden Roses and watered it and its neighbor liberally. I never let the soil dry out or get too soggy.

Soaring Spirits, large flowered climber, (2004)

After about two weeks, I discarded any of the cuttings which were shriveled and clearly not going to make it. I watered the remaining ones with Sure-Start and monitored closely. Some good prospects didn't make it in the end and I discarded them. Still, others showed signs of growth. Five of my showiest specimen roses came from these cuttings, including my specimen of *Newport Fairy* (1908) which I refer to often in the *Manual.*

You just never know whether you will be looking for a home for all the rooted cuttings you now own or cursing the time you wasted trying to get at least one to take. If your efforts to produce a rose creates an abundance of roses, bring them to the rose raffle at the MBRS's monthly meetings. There is always a rose society member pleased as can be to own something new.

TRY PROPAGATING YOUR FAVORITE ROSES

The best roses I have passed on to others have been ones that had a really strong root system. These were a result of bending a long pliable cane down to the ground, making a tiny slit on the underside and burying it in loose soil and mulch, and then allowing the end of the cane with the leaves still on it to grow in full sun.

The process is age old and simple. It's easier to achieve with varieties that produce supple canes and harder (but not impossible) with the stiffer hybrid teas. Basically, the new plant receives nutrients from its attached parent while the buried portion is producing a root system.

This method works very well with many of the Old Garden Roses and climbers. I have started the process in the summer and allowed the plant to get accustomed to the position before it lost its leaves in the fall. The winter is a good time for root production. By spring, the plant should be ready to be separated from the parent and may even be sending out new shoots based on its own roots.

I have left these new plants attached for an entire season and then given the offspring away when it was convenient for me to do so. The recipient got a good sized bush that was ready to go back in the ground. One specimen was left attached to the parent plant for nearly three years when I finally convinced someone that it would be a perfect addition to her garden. It did well for her immediately.

This method is well worth trying and one that will certainly please the recipient of the rose you propagated yourself. Again, it's easiest to do with roses that have long pliable canes.

GROWING ROSES FROM SEED

If you would like to experiment with growing roses from seed, now is the perfect time to gather your air pollinated rose hips. You will only know for certain the seed parent, so select hips from one that you like. The genetic make-up of all roses (except true species) is a complex matter. You will not get a duplicate of the parent, but you *will* get something. It's fun, not hard to do, and rather exciting to know that each sprouted rose is unique.

Extract the seeds from the healthiest hips you can find. Simply slice through the outer fruit layer and pry out the seeds. It's startling to discover that the size of a seed from a miniature rose is about the same size as a seed from a thirty-

Newport Fairy, rambler (1908)

foot climber. A large hip means more seeds not larger seeds. Place the seeds inside an envelope fashioned from damp paper towels, place them in a zip lock sandwich bag, and put them in the vegetable compartment of your refrigerator for a month.

Pull them out in late-February; place them in a seed tray that has individual compartments and a clear cover. Place the trays in full sun where they will be protected from the rain and any jostling around. Make sure the soil remains damp. Germination takes a couple of weeks. By mid-March your babies should be sporting a few leaves. As the weeks go by, discard any plant that gets mildew or blackspot. Move them into a larger container when their roots appear below the seed tray. Surprisingly, the seedlings will produce flowers in their first season. You will discover how many of the off-spring are slow growing, lack any distinction or redeemable character, and revert to pink. The effort will make you that much more appreciative of the roses in commerce and the considerable effort it takes a professional hybridizer to get something marketable.

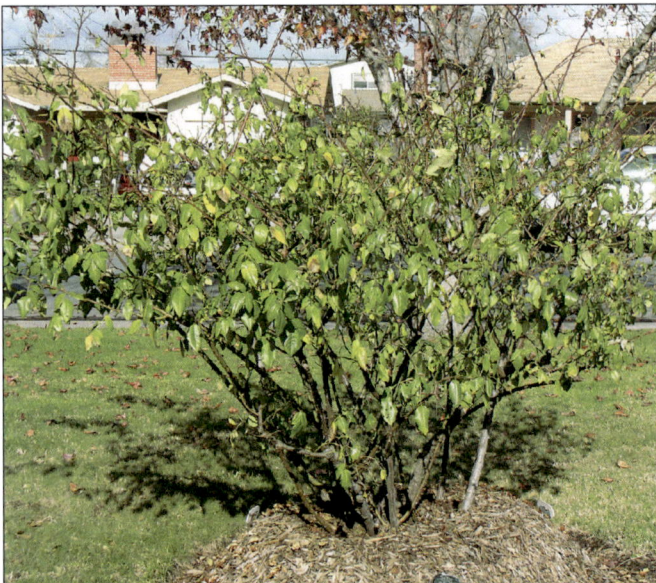

Sally Holmes, hybrid musk (1976) ready to prune

OTHER GARDEN MATTERS

I noticed a good deal of oxalis growing around the perimeters of my yard. Spray cheap white vinegar on the oxalis leaves. The vinegar at bottle strength won't hurt the tougher roses, but will kill the oxalis leaves. You may have to spray on several occasions but it does work. Because oxalis emanates from tiny bulbettes along its main root, pulling it up might spread it like crazy. Whether you decide on vinegar or just a quick tug straight up, don't let it get big enough to bloom. Its seeds disperse and you'll get more.

If there is also an abundance of sprouted fescue and general weeds in the garden bed, you definitely need to re-mulch the bed. I use the cheapest material available, shredded palettes, applied to four inches or so. It looks great and stays around for a good two seasons.

I also removed from the garden the perennials which renew themselves from the roots. This, too, will give me more room to maneuver.

SIT BACK AND WATCH THE ROSES GROW

I love the look of a freshly pruned rose bed. It's so clean and so full of anticipated results. After the pruning is done and the rain has made yard work too messy, all you can do is watch as the roses come out of dormancy. Enjoy the spring flowering bulbs you planted a few weeks back. I better get this mulch out before those bulbs start coming on too well.

Oh, it's always something when you have a garden . . . .

Sally Holmes, hybrid musk (1976) half-way pruned

ADVICE FROM THE PAST

All deadwood should be cut away; also where the branches of different shrubs crowd one upon another, let some be pruned out, and shorten long rambling shoots and rude luxuriant growths; for the shrubs in general should be kept clear of each other, so that each kind may be seen distinctly; and clear away all suckers that arise from the roots.

After pruning, as above, the ground between the flowering shrubs and ever-greens should be digged; observing, as you go on, to shorten long straggling roots, taking care not to disturb the plants. This will do good to the shrub, destroy weeds, and the places will appear neat.

Thomas Mawe, London, 1797

Sally Holmes, hybrid musk (1976) pruned

February

Perhaps the quietest month for roses on the Central Coast, February can still have ample chores and many unexpected events in store. Take pleasure in walking about the garden and looking at your pruning efforts from a few weeks back. With nearly three months of cold nights—several with hard frosts, and in spite of a few days of near record heat, the bushes are the most dormant they will ever be. The buds are swollen but the plants are only just barely leafing out.

Make sure you notice certain clean up jobs that await you. It's easier to rake a dormant rose garden than one in full bloom. Clear out all the old leaves and dead canes you possibly can. You may not have much time between the downpours in February and early March to get stuff out of the way. So pay attention to what needs doing and in a free moment, do it. I personally would rather rake moist garden trash than the dry stuff. I'm less likely to inhale the dust and mold spores and that means freer breathing.

Lastly, look about the garden and notice where you might plant some spring bulbs next year. Daffodils are great. Mine look terrific along a border. Why hadn't I put more in last October? Daffodil leaves are mostly ready to dry up when the roses are in full bloom. Crocuses are even better in that regard.

Now that the rains have saturated the soil, the days are lengthening, and the mid-day sun is heating up, we will see new growth on our roses.

FINISH YOUR PRUNING

We all have a forgotten rose bush or two in our yards. One of mine is a *Gourmet Popcorn* (1986) which is on the *wrong* side of the front walk and got overlooked. I must get to it soon or its growth cycle won't match its twin on the *right* side of the walk. Check around your yard. Have you overlooked a bush?

Hybrid tea climbers also like a good reshaping. Look for some long new canes and make sure they are bent somewhat horizontally so that all of the leaf buds will produce flowering stems. A good technique for a pillared rose is to wind the canes around the pillar, barbershop pole fashion. This, too, will cause the buds to pop.

Look closely at your climbers and identify your oldest canes. Does it look like these will continue to produce ample flowering stems for you this year? If you have several newer

Sombreuil, large flowered climber, (1888)

canes, eliminate the oldest growth right at the bud union. Get down there and scrape the dead bark until you reach greenwood. Keep the bud union moist with light soil or mulch. This will help the bush produce basal breaks—our best source of new flowers.

If your canes are still growing, pull off all of last year's leaves and snip the tip a couple of inches back to a swollen leaf bud. **Remember.** Any growth too small to support a good sized flower for that particular bush, should be pruned away. Be extra gentle with the new long canes produced by our climbing hybrid teas. It doesn't take much force to snap off the entire cane.

FINGER PRUNING—THE EASIEST MAINTENANCE JOB

If you pruned your roses in late-December or January, you should see growth on the recently trimmed canes. Save time. Go through each rose bush you pruned and break off with your fingers any new side growth appearing on your hybrid tea and floribunda canes which is low on the plant or looks like it will send a cane diagonally through the center of the bush. Just push it off with your finger. The growth is very soft.

Bee's Knees, miniature (1998)

It may hurt at first to push off a new sprout. After all, isn't that what you have been feeding, watering and pruning to get? However, your goal must be quality. And to achieve it, you need to direct the plant's growth.

The priority candidates for removal are strong sprouts growing from outside canes directly into the center of the bush. Keep that area clear. You want basal breaks emanating from the bud union. To get them, keep that area free of overhead growth. This will provide sunlight and air which seem to stimulate the new cane producing function of the union. You also need to keep the area moist throughout the growing season. Never let it turn to bark.

Frequently, two or three bud eyes will emerge from the same general location on a cane. Choose the strongest one, usually the center one, and pinch off the others. If the strongest one is heading toward the center of the plant, remove it. The bush will redirect its energy to an outward facing sprout. Your objective is strong growth and significant blooms, rather than abundant, weaker growth and less impressive flowers.

For a hybrid tea, anything appearing on the lower eight inches of a cane is worth pushing off now. Don't let it grow. The best flowers will come from the top. Keep the center of the plant, immediately above the bud union nice and airy. It will ward off the two worst afflictions of roses in February: blackspot and rust. Good ventilation allows the plant to provide some natural resistance.

Please don't finger prune your basal breaks. (It's like trumping your partner's ace!) Your new and best canes will come from the bud union, usually from its circumference. Basal breaks are much larger, often a vivid reddish color in many hybrid teas, and more vigorous than simple side growth so they should be easy to distinguish.

The end result of finger pruning will be healthier plants, more attractively shaped bushes, and larger flowers growing on straighter canes. As a general rule, on a healthy hybrid tea with three or more canes coming out of its bud union, remove any and all side shoots eight to ten inches up from the ground. Unless, of course, one of those shoots appears to be a dominant cane heading toward an empty area of the plant. It's a judgment call, but shouldn't be too difficult to make.

FINAL CHANCE FOR PRUNING

Remember. Snipping back something is better than just letting the rose be. Your one time blooming roses excluded, all your hybrid teas, floribundas, grandifloras, miniatures, climbers, and tree roses benefit from a good pruning. At the barest minimum, get rid of your deadwood and spindly growth. Cleaning up as many of the leaves, fallen hips, and snipped canes is good, healthy gardening and will reduce the number of blackspot, rust, and mildew spores near your plants.

One advantage of waiting until the bud eyes have begun to grow before you prune is seeing which sprouted eye the rose prefers. For some reason, a rose bush does not send an equal amount of nutrients to every bud eye. Most, in fact, stay dormant. A pecking order exists and you can take advantage of it, especially if you notice that the strongest new growth is coming from a location midway down the cane. Simply remove all growth, a half-inch above the new growth. The nutrients from the plant are already heading to this

Veteran's Honor, hybrid tea (1997)

cane. The shut-off valve for the old cane will eventually close and the upper portion of the cane will die back. Prune it away now and be done with it.

I love to go back two weeks or so after pruning a section of my garden and inspect. Missed canes need to be shortened to conform with the overall shape of the bush. What looked like substantial growth during the pruning process, appears skeletal and deformed when viewed from your kitchen with your coffee cup in hand. You need to fix them, then forget them.

TOUCH UP YOUR OLD GARDEN ROSES

By now the canes on your once-blooming, Old Garden Roses should be lined, up and down, with swollen buds. I find this the best time to give them a quick once over. It's easy to determine the dead and exhausted canes from the vibrant and alive ones. If you wait until the canes leaf out, you run the risk of tearing them off or breaking them as you yank out the deadwood. I was surprised at how much of it there was tucked away underneath and inside the numerous prickly canes of *Isfahan* (1832), *Charles de Mills* (1840), and *Henri Martin* (1863); all of which are probably eight feet tall and six wide. I also tried to tighten up as many of their supports as possible. The plastic coated clothes line that I use stretches a bit during the year, but I find it's the best material to tie a large heavy rose to a fence. Its unsightliness, so apparent now, gets hidden once the leaves appear. Jute string is more attractive but won't hold the really big canes of large climbers.

It's important that any long canes on your OGRs not be allowed to grow more than three feet straight up. Bend these canes down to the left or right if supported by a fence, or around if supported by a pillar. If you have a climber or OGR growing over an arbor, take the time necessary to attach the long canes on top of the trellis or lattice work. Most of the one-time bloomers, send out their flowers from bud eyes on last year's canes. The more horizontal the canes are, the more bud eyes will pop and produce flowers. Do whatever it takes to prepare your one-time bloomers for the most floriferous and extensive blooming cycle possible.

WILL YOU BE SAFE IN YOUR GARDEN?

I spent some exciting moments one afternoon during a brief interval of warm sunshine. I was sitting on an inverted bucket underneath *Isfahan* (1832), my old damask rose, planted against my potting shed and was snipping off withered flower stems while trying to miss the healthy canes. (The American Rose Society spells the name of this rose in-

correctly as "Ispahan." It's named after the great Persian city which I once frequently visited.) I use the word "exciting" for this particularly tedious task because at the very moment I was reaching into it to clip off a mixed-up tangled bunch of last year's leaves and stalks, the bucket beneath me which I was tilting to put me closer to my reach, suddenly jolted me into the bush.

Fortunately, I was wearing gloves and regained my balance before I hit the rain soaked soil and flooded ditch next to the bed. The neighbor's barking dog and his own yell, plus the fact that I, *Isfahan*, the bucket, the potting shed, and the entire neighborhood continued to shake, told me there wasn't anything funky going on in my middle ear. We had had an earthquake. Oh well, it wasn't the big one. I surveyed the damage. A four foot, healthy cane got snipped off in the confusion. The paper later reported that the temblor was "a 4.0 felt by many without incident." I lamented the accuracy of newspapers.

Henri Martin, moss (1863)

START FEEDING YOUR ROSES ORGANIC FERTILIZERS NOW

Begin feeding your roses once the new growth is three or four inches long. Start feeding with organic fertilizers. February is an ideal time to put a double handful of alfalfa pellets at the base of each plant, rose or otherwise. It's available at most pet food stores. Figure one pound per every three feet a rose has in height. Ask for the non-molasses type. You don't need to attract ants. Alfalfa facilitates your plants' ability to extract nutrients from the soil.

If your roses are further along with two or three fully formed leaves showing, add a half-cup of Epsom salt to the base of your rose. Epsom salt is not a salt at all, but is magnesium sulfate. Magnesium is one of the essential minerals for healthy roses. It, too, is a growth enhancer. It's best to add it to the soil around your roses, at the end of a rainy spell for two reasons. One, it dissolves rather quickly and the rain will distribute it more broadly than your hose. Two, the sunlight on the leaves will also spark growth. You'll get the best response from it when you have never added it before. It does stay in the soil so you only need to add it every couple of years or so. It will increase the size of your plants' leaves almost before your eyes. I apply Epsom salt only at the start of the year, and then only every three years or so.

Do check out the following website: www.epsomsalt-council.org It claims that studies show applications of Epsom salt in the garden will: help seeds germinate (including weeds?), make plants grow bushier, produce more flowers, increase chlorophyll production, and improve phosphorus and nitrogen uptake.

Here's what they say about application amounts: Roses: one tablespoon per foot of plant height per plant; apply every two weeks. Also scratch a half-cup into soil at base to encourage flowering canes and healthy new basal cane growth. Soak unplanted bushes in a half-cup of Epsom salt per gallon of water to help roots recover. Add a tablespoon of Epsom salt to each hole at planting time. Spray with Epsom salt solution weekly to discourage pests.

The Epsom salt applications also encourage basal breaks. Magnesium is a true growth stimulator. When used in combination with good drainage, ample air circulation, and six or more hours of sunlight, your roses should be off to a great start.

There is one downside of using Epsom salt. If your grafted roses have been infected with one of the rose mosaic viruses, Epsom salt will make this readily apparent. These mottled or streaked looking patches on your leaves are not your fault. The bush was infected back in the growing field either by the bud source or the root stock. Unlike viruses which affect humans, rose mosaic virus won't spread to your other roses.

There is no practical garden cure for rose mosaic virus except, when possible, ripping up the plant, taking it back to the garden center where you bought it, and telling the proprietor to give your uninfected money back! Unless customers demand better products, growers will just provide what is most economical for themselves.

Once the roses are truly leafing out and you see more leaves than canes, give them a few more additives. In North Salinas, our soils are particularly deficient in nitrogen at least in the form that the roses can use. A cup or more, depending on the size of the bush, of blood meal worked into the soil just above where its roots are will produce spectacular results. You will get the most professionally grown looking

Singin' the Blues, floribunda (2008)

leaves possible by giving your bushes blood meal. They use it up quickly. This year, I will make the effort to get it into the soil about three times. It's expensive, but it works.

Fish emulsion is also a common additive which will give your plants a full range of nutrients. Your yard might smell like the ocean for a day or two after the application but the roses enjoy the nourishment for several weeks. The garden is likely too wet for you to be entertaining visitors. Steer manure has nutrients in it, but they are in relatively lower amounts. It's used best as a soil amendment—more organic material in your soil benefits your roses. Chicken manure, also available from local nurseries, is stronger and must be added with caution. It could burn your tender young leaves.

As an added, readily available treat throughout the year, I eat bananas and bury the peels beneath a rose bush. They decompose quickly and are also high in potassium which improves flower abundance and color.

One last organic item I have experimented with includes old cow and sheep bones cleaned of any remaining meat and gristle: steak, shank, neck. I purposely bleach them in the sun and rain not for any horticultural purpose, but just so I will remember to get them in the ground. I will eventually bury them down where the edge of the roses' roots are. And I mean bury, a good 15-20 inches down. They will provide a steady source of phosphorus and some potash for years to come.

We used to advise people to add chelated iron to darken rose leaves. Unfortunately, the common products offering it are cut with several elements harmful to the environment in general and earth worms in particular. We now don't recommend its use at all. It's better to stick with organic sources of nutrients, compost, manures, and fish emulsions. Also if you have mosaic virus in your roses, a good dose of chelated iron has been known to disguise the mottled leaves.

Long-time rosarian Joe Ghio recommends adding a teaspoon of Boraxo in February to each bush. It provides the trace element boron which gives the roses a little extra to maintain their health. If you use, MiracleGro® or any similar hose-end product, you won't need to do this. These products contain all the major, minor, and trace elements roses need.

Gloire des Rosomanes, hybrid china (1825)

KEEP BUD UNIONS COVERED AND MOIST

In this region of California, your grafted roses should be planted with the bud union right at the surface of the soil. Keep a handful of loose compost or mulch on the base at all times, but especially now. We want to make sure that the warming sun and lengthening days don't dry this area out, but instead help the rose to produce a new cane. Basal breaks, new canes coming from the bud union, ensure there will be ample roses this season and several seasons to come.

If there is one thing I spot while visiting gardens planted by novices, it's this. The bud union is up too high. It needs to be just at or a little below the soil line. An inch is too deep. When making your adjustments, add some fresh soil and loosen the soil at the base of the plant. Don't dig too deep. You don't want to damage roots, just loosen up the top so that the soil will absorb water better.

Excepting May with its high rose tide, February for me is the most exciting month in the rose garden. Major pruning coincides with our coldest weather and the roses have been as dormant as they will ever be. Dormancy means rest—for the rose—not the gardener.

RELOCATING YOUR ROSES

Several of my roses were planted in the winter of 1993 and have stayed in these original places adorning their areas of the garden supremely well. Others, for numerous reasons, have been planted, dug up, planted, moved over, dug up, put somewhere completely different and then satisfied, remained there. My general rule is a three-strikes policy. I've caught myself asking certain varieties out loud, "What else do you want?" When, after relocating them to the sunniest spot, amending the soil to the point of planting them in dirt entirely different from the rest of the garden, giving them sufficient water and adequate drainage, and gentle but regular feeding, they still JUST SIT THERE AND DON'T GROW. The climate here on the Central Coast of California isn't the right one for them. Dig them up and give them to someone who lives where nights are warmer than ours, and days drier.

There are also other reasons to move your roses. Some just get bigger than expected and need to find a spot where they can have much more room. Many of my roses have been healthy plants acquired on the raffle table from cuttings nurtured by members of the Monterey Bay Rose

Portland from Glendora, portland (1882)

Luis Desamero, miniature (1989)

Society (the best source of roses which do well here). This means that they are growing on their own roots and are not budded onto another variety (root stock). After a number of years, roses grown on their own roots will produce side shoots. These can be removed along with some of their associated roots and planted elsewhere in your garden or somewhere else.

We are at the end of the prime relocation period—dormancy. So one day, I donned my garden clothes and went right down to rose level. A few weeks prior, I had removed a large rambler from my back fence which left a hole in the ground and the garden. Before I finished my job, I stirred up the soil and mixed in some sand. The top-dressing mulch also got incorporated into the soil. Intentionally, I let it sit for a few weeks and returned to it later. I added composted cow manure and mixed this in well.

A *Rosa eglanteria* offshoot from an original plant I dug up and gave away had finally gotten too big for its location so I dug it up and put it back against the fence where it will have plenty of room to grow. The eglantine roses are perfect hedge and barrier roses which mean they have numerous prickles running up and down each cane which create a thicket. They also produce ample side shoots which will fill in a row with new plants. Eglantines aren't as invasive as other roses and will submit to some attractive shaping.

Even though they are one time bloomers, when digging them up and moving them, you have a perfect moment to prune them up. Remove all inconsequential growth. Prune away any busted up roots. Even though I advocate keeping as much of the root ball intact as possible, I never seem to be able to do it. The soil just falls away and I end up with a harvested bare root rose. Shake all the old soil off. It's mostly spent anyway. Dig your hole large enough. Dig down a foot

or so below where you will place your bush and mix in the good soil, cow manure, and sand. Put a dead rodent at the bottom of hole, cover it with compost and soil, and plant your rose on top.

Pink Robusta (1987), another rose growing in the wrong place, got dug up and discarded. I decided even though I've grown it since 1995 in a back corner, I never really was satisfied with it. Too much blackspot. Too long an interval between blossoms. And way too leggy. Its canes were a naked five feet long before any leaves. There are just too many good roses to grow so I shovel pruned it! Two more short growing roses were moved to empty spots closer to the front of the bed. A miniature growing in a pot for three years was put in the ground. A brand-new shrub rose won at the January auction replaced the eglantine.

Although the optimum time to dig up and move plants is ebbing, you can still plant roses throughout the season. If you don't know where to put them, put them in a pot. The reason nursery pots are black: the color absorbs heat and elevates the temperature, thus enhancing the plant's ability to absorb nutrients, which results in increased growth. I have actually dug up roses to put them into pots—just to achieve this.

PREPARE YOUR GARDEN FOR THE SUMMER

One of the best things you can do for your garden now when all the bushes are at their shortest is take care of its future watering needs. Set up your watering system now. If you own a drip irrigation system, now is the easiest time to get out there and make repairs or sink new tubes and unclog spouts. Or, if you are like me and derive an odd pleasure from standing and watering with a hose, now is the best time to create or clear a nice little basin area around the base of your plant. Scoop out the soil so that the bud union is just at the surface of the bed. This way, you can fill the basin with water, let it soak in, and then refill it. These basins also keep any solid fertilizer you add from running off.

Occasionally, I have added a lot of organic matter to the soil while I planted my roses. Now is a great time to adjust the levels. Organic matter dissolves relatively quickly and shrinks in size, thus lowering the soil level in respect to the bud union.

DEALING WITH HEAVY RAIN

The exceptionally heavy rains which can fall from the end of December to the end of March are most welcome. Rain is always a good thing in California. It permeates the soil with essentially pH balanced water—not the alkaline stuff which we provide during the rest of the year from our garden hoses. And roses respond to it by giving us nice clean, new growth.

The heavy rains carry away mineral deposits and flush the garden beds of spores and old leaves. Decomposition is speeded up when water is prevalent and, to a degree, rains wash away insect eggs and drown adults. All of these are positive results of the heavy rains.

Now, for the other side of the story. Much of the nitrogen accessible to the roses is water soluble. The more it rains, the more the nitrogen and other soluble nutrients are leached out of the soil. If your soil lacks a sufficient degree of organic material, you are likely to lose a good portion of your soil as well. There is nothing left there to bind it and hold it firm. Organic material also has the ability to retain moisture longer. Therefore, when the rains stop, soil void of organic material will dry out, crack, and be otherwise difficult to work. Soil containing organic material keeps the soil friable and contributes nutrients to the plants as it decomposes.

OTHER GARDEN CHORES

As the rose garden gets pruned and cleaned out of last year's refuse, you will have plenty of room to maneuver. Now is an ideal time to shore up the stakes and posts, put a coat of paint on the fence, and redistribute mulch around your garden. I always tread with care this time of year, as I can't quite remember where I planted bulbs last fall.

I've noticed that my daffodils come on stronger than ever. The variety that I've had the most luck with is called *Ice Follies*. It's quite common and has white petals with ivory trumpets. *King Alfred*, probably the most common large yellow daffodil, needs a little more cold weather. I've not been successful with them in North Salinas. I have, however, had great luck with all forms of miniature daffodils. They are delightful edging plants which truly bring color when roses have little to offer and get out of the way when your roses are going full force. I like the following varieties: *Jack Snipe*,

Crépuscule, noisette (1904)

Tête-a-Tête, and *Rapture*. The common "pheasant eye" narcissus blooms much later in spring but has become a show stopping front lawn specimen. You must show patience with the expired leaves. I cut off the seed pods and let the leaves just dry out. You can push them aside but the nutrients must return to the bulb if you expect a great show the following year. I had some gardeners help with weeding one April and they cut back all of my *Ice Follies* while the tops were still green. The following year, I had not one bloom, not one. In years past, I had had a hundred or so!

I also noticed that my Society Garlic has stayed wonderful all winter long. I will definitely make sure to grow more of this throughout the yard. It doesn't spread like other forms of flowering garlic.

Several of the succulents in my collection have continued to grow and flourish. Springtime for succulents is exciting, too. While usually not very showy, the flowers are a welcomed change from the ordinary.

ADVICE FROM THE PAST

The borders where wall and espalier trees grow, should be kept remarkably clear from weeds: for these not only appear disagreeable and exhaust the nourishment, but they would promote snails, slugs, and such like creeping insects to the detriment of the fruit.

Therefore, when weeds at any time appear in these parts and where there is room to admit of hoeing between any crops that may be growing on the borders, let a sharp hoe be applied to them in a dry sunny day, by which you may soon stop their progress, and as soon as hoed, rake off all the weeds and rubbish, leaving a clean smooth surface.

Thomas Mawe, London, 1789

Midnight Blue, floribunda (2004)

March

As I am sitting here at my computer, a mocking bird is singing its little heart out in my backyard. This means four things:

- The heavy rains, which fell all night long bringing us the water we need, have finished.

- The sun is up and shining.

- Buddy is holed up somewhere outside in a dry place and doesn't want to venture out in the wet grass to terrorize avian visitors.

- Spring is here!

Much of the success of our roses depends on what happens in March. As our bushes come out of dormancy, they are particularly vulnerable to rain, wind, hail, frost, and several insects. We usually have a few frosts in November and December but are spared a truly cold winter along the Central Coast. I'm disappointed if I don't see a week of temperatures just below freezing. It puts the roses into a deep sleep. Brave the intervals of dry weather, put on sturdy, water repellant shoes, and walk through your garden.

With the heavy frosts many of our gardens received in December and January, our rose bushes were forced into natural dormancy. For two months, they barely stirred. Many of my roses actually dropped their leaves naturally with the frigid evenings, occasional rains and wind.

When exceptional rain steadily falls with cold winter storms, the snow lines can drop to 500 feet and Salinas looks like Switzerland. Reports from these "Salinas Alps" are that dormancy hasn't quite finished up there. I do remember one late frost that wreaked havoc on many of the roses up in Corral de Tierra. It killed the entire crop of new shoots and set the bushes back six weeks.

Cold weather is generally a good thing for the roses as it helps them rest and form their new growth more slowly. The pressure is on to get our bushes producing flowers for the Annual Rose Show in early May. My plants are just now beginning to leaf out. Once this begins, there's little to stop them from growing. Days become noticeably longer. Would that these beautiful leaves and vigorous new canes be a continual feature of rose cultivation! Let's enjoy them as long as possible before the various diseases and pests start their attack. When asked what constitutes a good rose year, I like to think that it is getting your first full bloom in before the onset of the conditions which cause fungal diseases and other pests.

American Honor, hybrid tea (1993)

FEEDING YOUR ROSES CHEMICAL FOOD

Roses are hungry creatures, as I've mentioned previously. They just can't get enough accessible nitrogen, phosphorus, and potash. Those are the three numbers you see on fertilizer labels. Start applying fertilizer now. I usually give my roses something to eat every other weekend throughout the growing season. Products such as Schulz' Rose Fertilizer, MiracleGro® for Roses, Peters, and others contain every major, minor, and trace element a plant needs. Most are applied through a hose-end feeder which means you will be giving your plants water and food at the same time; two jobs done at once. A balanced fertilizer, 10-10-10 or 16-16-16, is limited only to the major elements. These can be very useful—and economical—because they provide nutrition in an easily absorbable form, are readily available, and are relatively inexpensive.

All of the trace elements are already present in our tap water. Each time we water we are also providing necessary food.

Bubble Bath, hybrid musk (1980)

FEEDING YOUR ROSES ORGANIC FOOD

Throughout the growing season, you should give your roses (and every other important flowering plant in your garden) a hearty application of blood meal, bone meal, fish emulsion, and alfalfa pellets. Apply these nutrients immediately prior to a rain storm and let mother nature do the work.

Adding most organic material also helps acidify your soils. The tap water in California is often alkaline. So it becomes very important to use compost to regulate the pH factor. Animal manures, especially when raw, contain much bacterial content. When placed in the soil, the bacterial action involved in decomposing the manure elevates the soil temperature which helps the plant absorb nutrients.

Be careful of under-composed barn waste. It's quite likely to contain urea which is full of salt. This makes the pH factor tilt back to the alkaline range which roses hate.

Placing coffee grinds and tea leaves directly onto the plant won't hurt anything. But as they decompose they use up some nitrogen which the plant could also benefit from. As long as you are providing a steady source of nitrogen, this is harmless and may have some benefit.

My grandmother was a fan of adding crushed egg shells to her plants. It's a source of calcium—a minor element which again won't hurt and may help your roses.

I've discovered that that last banana I couldn't quite get to doesn't have to go in the garbage. Cut it up peel and all and bury it just under the soil in your garden. Recent taste tests have proven that raccoons love banana flavor above all else. Bury the banana deep if you have these masked marauders in your neighborhood. Otherwise, just like for us, bananas are a great source of potassium. They also disintegrate quickly and will be undetectable in about a week or so.

ORGANIC FERTILIZERS AND CONDITIONERS

As soon as the new growth has emerged to display a fully opened rose leaf, it's time to start feeding your roses. I recommend that you start easy. Give your roses some fish emulsion first. Then, toss a handful of alfalfa pellets around the base of each rose bush. You can't give them too much, so don't be stingy. The pellets are a bit unsightly when swollen. If you get the pellets distributed before a wet period begins, you won't notice how ugly the stuff is unless you are outside in a raincoat or under an umbrella. If a dry period follows a wet period, the now cow pie-like alfalfa will harden into a clump. It's easily broken up with one of those three-pronged cultivators and will do even more good for the rose when some soil has been mixed in with it.

Now is a great time to check out the state of your top dressing or mulch. If it's beginning to break down, spend a moment doing some physical activity and turn it into the soil wherever you can. The spring rains will help you if you can complete this major effort before a rainy period.

By turning the mulch into the topsoil, you will be aiding your roses tremendously. More organic material in the soil increases the bacterial action necessary to break down bark, twigs, straw, and dead leaves. It also improves drainage,

Chinatown, shrub (1963)

worm activity, and soil air circulation. Increased bacterial action also means higher soil temperatures. Higher soil temperatures result in a more favorable pH level in your soil. A more favorable pH factor results in improved root growth and better absorption of nutrients which, of course, gives you incredibly fantastic roses! It's worth the effort of turning your old mulch into the soil.

Bacterial breakdown does consume nutrients as well. So once you have significant growth (six-inch-long canes) which won't burn from the application of chemical fertilizers, it will be time to apply some stronger fertilizers in a regular pattern. A large amount at any time is not ever recommended. In fact, it's better to hold back on any chemical fertilizer if you are tempted to give the roses a large dose before you go away on a trip. Weaker, but repeated, applications are best.

Many rosarians have gone completely organic in their fertilizer programs. There are many different organic additives which are quite potent, but costly. Bat guano is one.

Gizmo, miniature (1998)

FINGER PRUNE YOUR NEW GROWTH

Your pruning efforts should now be evaluated. Go to each rose in your garden and flick off any side growth on your main canes which is growing within eight inches of the bud union. I like some sun to reach this important area so that the plant will produce a new basal break which might mean three or four years of more roses. Wads of new growth will straighten themselves out in a search for individual space. You can facilitate this process by removing the competing bud eyes. Helping your rose bushes send their nutrients to the most significant growth on the top of the bushes is a most important task and is easy to do if done now, today.

By clearing out this growth, you will accomplish two things. You will provide better air circulation through the center of your plant and thus help it to resist fungal diseases which flourish in unmoving, stale air. You will also save time later on when this lower-down growth needs to be pruned away with shears. **Remember.** The healthier the rose's leaves are, the better the entire plant will do.

Also, examine your uppermost growth. Occasionally a rose will decide it wants a lower bud eye to get more nutrients than the one you pruned down to. This is particularly true if there was a little bit of die-back on the cane end. The rose knows what it can support properly. Help it by getting rid of the upper, weaker growth.

Staring out my bathroom window with a toothbrush in my mouth, my eyes fell on a hybrid tea outside. "That shoot has got to go," I mumbled and, when I finished, went outside and snipped it off the cane. Do this now before the bush wastes too much energy on non productive growth.

Most importantly, direct the energy of your roses to the specific direction you want, not what the rose wants. You will notice that at the ends of some canes the rose will send out multiple shoots. It's very easy at this point to remove all but the strongest one—or the one growing away from the center of the bush. The growth may all look just fine now, but your major concern must be the long term health of the rose. You can achieve much better air circulation (and less powdery mildew and blackspot) if there is more air around each growing cane.

GET YOUR FINAL PRUNING DONE NOW!

Walking through my garden, I noticed I'd overlooked several roses. I intentionally put them off when pruning. I passed them by because they are climbing roses attached to a fence and are easy to prune standing up in a drizzle—which has happened more years than I care to remember. This is, however, your last chance to prune. They will still have a chance to muster sufficient growth to join their neighbors' blooming cycle. Even a little pruning is better than none at all. Take a hedge trimmer, if you have to, and at least chop the ends of the rose off.

ROSES GROWN IN POTS

I grow only a few roses in pots; two gallon cans and a redwood octagonal container. These pots have been sitting on the edge of the lawn for a few years. Last summer, I realized that my *Gizmo* (an orange single miniature, developed by

Tom Carruth of Weeks Roses and introduced in 1998), which has given me several years of pleasure, had some weeds and grass growing in it. I tried to pull the weeds out only to realize they were not surface plants. They were issue from deep down below. These gregarious botanical nuisances had found their way up from the lawn to entwine with the roots of the plant, steal all its food, and obliterate the sun from its leaves.

Two weeks ago, I decided I needed to clean up this unsightly mess. Yes, my work schedule had collided with my personal life once again and I ended up having to ignore a problem diagnosed months ago. When I lifted up the redwood container, its bottom stayed stuck to the ground, mostly disintegrated. The entire container was a tangle of Bermuda grass roots and yellow wood sorrel; plus, of course, my exhausted and overrun *Gizmo*.

Should you have plants in pots and face a similar situation, find a dry spot, dump the entire contents onto that spot, and start pulling apart the mess. The redwood container was, of course, shot without a bottom though its sides still looked so nice. I kicked it to pieces and discarded the wood and the metal bands.

I then began a two part operation. I pruned *Gizmo*'s top while separating its bottom from invaders. After the six years it had been growing in that same pot, I felt no remorse in tossing out the soil. It was by this time nearly void of nutrient value. I shook *Gizmo* as much as possible and pulled out the nasty grass roots which grew any and everywhere. Where it was just too tangled, I took a shears and cut the rose apart, eventually freeing the entire mess and creating three rose bushes instead of just one. This process is also known as asexual reproduction and is illegal to do with all patented roses, including *Gizmo*. But, as I said to the police officer, "I was swerving to avoid an accident."

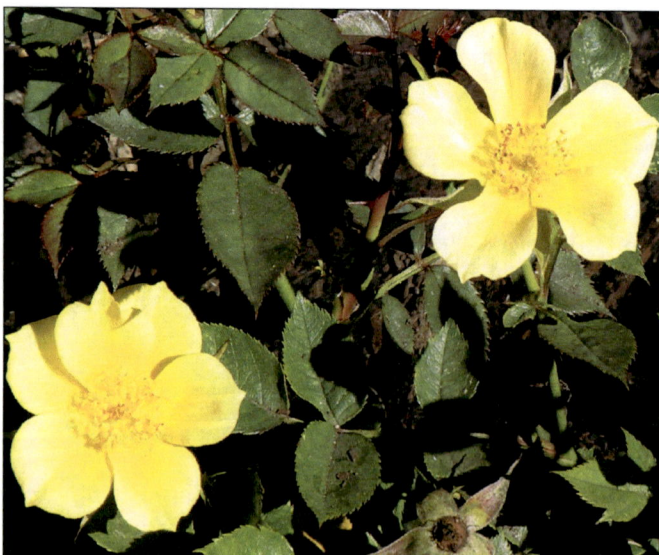

My Sunshine, miniature (1976)

So what had been one *Gizmo*, was now three. I got some fresh potting soil and filled a 15 gallon container with it. Took my Gizmi and arranged them nicely in their new home. I added a little water for security reasons and know that come spring, this will once again be an eye-catching rose bush.

Roses do better in the ground and become much more drought tolerant. However, in most circumstances they are very easy to grow in containers.

Remember. Terra cotta pots expire excess water which is counter to the needs of rose bushes. Don't try to grow roses in clay pots. A good black plastic pot also captures the heat from the sun, elevates the temperature of the soil which increases the bacterial breakdown of nutrients being supplied to the rose bush. Good things, all the way around.

CARING FOR YOUR CLIMBERS

The wild winter winds have returned: whipping through my neighborhood causing the fences to creak, tossing around the unreachable top canes of my *Climbing Cécile Brünner* and *Madame Alfred Carrière*, blowing away the remaining leaves of last season, and snapping many agèd and badly fastened climbing rose ties.

Avoid weaving a climber's canes through a trellis. Instead, fasten them securely to the outside of the support using sturdy plastic clothesline or jute string ties. This way, you won't have any problem pruning them. Simply open up (or cut off) the old ties and lay the climber down, prune it and tie it back with fresh, secure ties. Another reason not to push your cane in and out of a trellis has to do with dead canes. You can easily break the trellis by extracting the dead or dying canes. Be careful if you have to remove some canes. Don't attempt to yank them through. Instead, make several cuts and remove the roses in pieces.

Allow your climbing roses to send out new growth from the bud union of grafted roses or from the root mass of own root roses. One way of doing this is to remove the oldest and least productive growth on your bush and encouraging the newest and healthiest canes.

You will get most of your flowers on climbing roses from lateral buds. So make sure that once the rose cane reaches the top of the fence, you gently arch it over and secure it in several places. The more parallel the cane is to the ground the fuller the resulting bloom will be and the greater the visual impact. Downward facing bud eyes will right themselves over time. So don't be too particular about them.

If a cane produces two or three shoots from the same general area, knock off the weakest ones with your thumb. All the nutrients going to one cane will produce a sturdier base for a larger spray of flowers.

Climbing roses, by their very nature, are more vigorous than shrub varieties. They can be contained if regularly

Scarlet Knight, hybrid tea (1966)

Take a good look at your entire garden. If a rose bush is sending out lots of growth right into your garden path, now is a good time to encourage it to grow in a new direction. The canes are pliable and can benefit from being staked up, pulled over, or otherwise bound. Be very careful with new long canes. Their weakest spot tends to be right at the point where they emerged from the old cane. Too much pushing and bending will cause them to break off entirely. This is too defeating, so be extra careful.

WATCH YOUR SOIL WETNESS

With abundant rain, it's very important that you make sure your bushes are not sitting in badly drained areas of your garden. Our heavy clay soil in North Salinas turns to goo and it's impossible to do anything until the water drains away. It used to just sit there for days before I dug small ditches between my garden beds and the lawn.

My miniature canal system actually serves several purposes. My roses grow in beds which are six to ten inches higher than the grass. This adds dimension to the garden design. Elevation will help bring your eye directly to the blooming roses. A twelve inch ditch between garden and yard also helps to keep the invasive grasses out of the garden bed. I have real problems with Bermuda grass. Once it gets going underneath the rose bushes you'll have a serious problem.

Both yard and garden drain more quickly now. My back yard is lower than my front yard so I needed to make sure that the water has some place to flow to. I have interconnected these ditches. So rain that runs off the rose bed in the back yard drains into these ditches, flows under a fence along the side rose bed and out into the front yard

thinned throughout the growing cycle. They also tend to respond favorably to a good pruning.

I specifically held off pruning ten climbers because they are located on relatively drier ground. Wisely so, as the rains have saturated the gardens, front and back. Puddles of water are -here and there, indicating low points in the yard. It would be messy to prune the regular roses now. But I can stand up and prune these climbers. The raised beds on which my roses grow help to drain off the excess water.

The winter can be a bit longer some years with frost still appearing on the backyard grass and rooftops in late February. The roses have had a nice long rest and bud eyes are popping out everywhere.

SHAPING YOUR ROSE BUSHES

By now, all of your rose bushes should show abundant new growth. Please take the time to get down into each rose bush and pinch off insignificant looking side growth on your canes. Many pruned canes will produce two or three new growth stems from the spot where you snipped. Pinch off all but the strongest of these. It's very easy to do now and avoids the closely packed foliage which is likely to provide ample space for fungal spores to hatch. Good air circulation is vital in controlling these diseases which are rampant in our area.

With the frequent spring rainfall, thinning the new growth will allow it to dry out somewhat between showers and thus prevent blackspot.

Secret, hybrid tea (1992)

Russelliana, bourbon (1826)

Grass loves to grow at this time of year especially little seedlings among your roses. Don't let it get too well-established. It always seems to find those spots that aren't covered by protective mulch. It pulls out very easily because the soil is moist. But, it's a chore.

With the exception of bindweed (wild relative of morning glory) and a few other invasive tuberous plants, early extraction is the best method. At any rate, don't let your weeds go to seed. I like to let bindweed form a healthy clump of leaves and then paint it with RoundUp®. Yes, paint with a brush not spray. If you try to pull out bindweed, it breaks off far below the surface and becomes two or more plants a few weeks later.

Weeding is easy now because the roses aren't fully grown. Always plant new roses with sufficient space around them for you to tend them easily.

ADVICE FROM THE PAST

Rose-trees of most sorts . . . that are planted any time this month, will produce flowers the same year; but the sooner they are planted, the better they will take root, and the stronger they will flower.

But by transplanting these shrubs late in the season, you may obtain a late bloom. I have planted them in April and beginning of May, and they have flowered in July, August, and September.
Thomas Mawe, London, 1791

where it follows along the row of miniatures on my front walk and eventually drains down the driveway and out into the street. This system has transformed a flat yard into one of varying height. Because of the 18 years of top dressings, amendments, and mulches that I've generously applied, my back yard is now higher than the adjoining yards of my three neighbors.

Leaves that are smaller than normal with a yellowish tinge and dark green veins are an indication that the nutrients are not getting from the roots to the leaves. The culprit at this time of year could be water logged roots. Roses need air to grow. Although they will tolerate wet feet for a couple of days, they will eventually die if the roots don't get sufficient air.

START WEEDING NOW

My preferred weeding technique is extraction. Grab hold firmly to the base of the weed and pull it up slowly. This time of year, with the soil so saturated, it's quite easy. You won't die from the fumes, you'll benefit from the exercise, especially on high stress days, and you can't beat the price. I do spray oxalis, Bermuda grass, and bindweed with white vinegar especially before it puts out flowers or gets too established. I know this won't necessarily eradicate the plant, but it will slow it down, stop it from spreading, and make me feel that the effort was effective—at least for a short time.

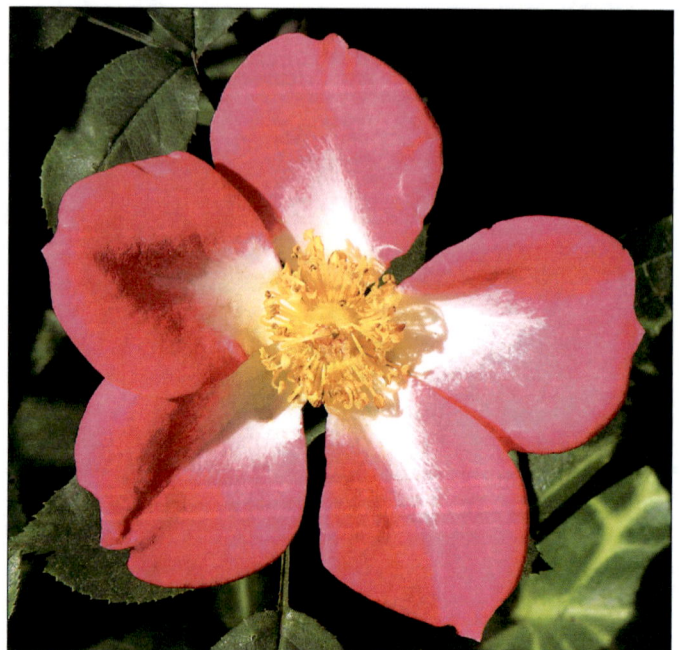
Peggy T, miniature (1988)

April

Even though my work schedule is relentless in April, I finally put my gardening foot down and am determined to have the prettiest garden ever. In my case, that means thinning out the poorly performing roses. It also means making plans to attend to a rotting roof on the potting shed, a couple of storm-injured posts on my fence, invasive tree roots from the sweet gum the City planted in my front yard, and rose beds invaded by Bermuda grass.

How is this year different from the past? The healthy roses are really healthy. They've developed incredible root systems which pump nourishment up into their numerous canes. I'm less caring about preserving roses, and other plants, which do not perform well in my backyard.

The past few weeks of sunshine and intermittent rain have put the roses on the express train back from the State of Dormancy. The strong, gusty winds of winter have done some damage to the new canes, but all in all, the garden is looking very nice.

The sunshine dried up all trace of the heavy rains except one—blackspot! I removed the leaves as soon as the disease appeared and discovered that this nasty fungal disease has ravaged most of the bushes which I pruned in late December and early January. The first set of leaves on these plants yellowed and needed to be removed and destroyed. Those forgotten bushes which never made it into my early pruning schedule and were only reduced in size in early March are absolutely pristine. Here's another reason not to prune too soon.

I had a dark day a few weeks back. A storm raced in and blew down my 13-foot tall *Madame Alfred Carrière* (1879) which was just going into full bloom. It was a mess and I was discouraged. It's happened twice before. This is a heavy rose. She weighed about sixty pounds and I had to carry her up a ladder on my shoulder to re-fasten her to the corner of my house which she adorns. So, I trimmed her back and tied her up a few canes at a time using newly screwed-in fasteners. I bound her up with fresh plastic covered clothesline with nylon and metal fill. This should hold for a few seasons, but I learned my lesson and will thin out the old gal this fall. This was a lot of work and I trampled on top of what had been growing beneath her.

This was my last opportunity to clear out a shallow basin in the earth below each of my roses. Once the canes get large, its harder to get underneath them. I always run the risk that my ample presence moving about the garden will eventually break off tender buds and canes. So, from the largest shrub *Sally Holmes* (1976), free standing in my front yard) to my tallest climber *Climbing Cécile Brünner* (1894), fastened anew against my potting shed) to my smallest miniatures (too many to list), I watered well giving each large rose bush at least ten gallons of water. I have so conditioned the garden soil that this amount is readily absorbed.

Sally Holmes, hybrid musk (1976) in full bloom

DO NOT USE SYSTEMIC, ALL-IN-ONE PRODUCTS

Several fertilizer-insect killer combination products are on the market and being heavily marketed. They are clearly labeled "systemic." That means you apply these concoctions to your plants and all your worries are over. Wrong! They provide nutrients and ward off pests by incorporating poison into the cell tissue of your roses. First of all, they are not necessary if you follow the general feeding principles outlined in this Manual. Secondly, inhaling the fumes and dust from these products while you are applying them means the poison is entering your lungs. Thirdly, the insects beneficial to

Sally Holmes, hybrid musk (1976) close up

and well watered. Give them good drainage so there will be lots of air in the soil. Air circulation around the roses is vital.

I have witnessed an infestation of thrips that damaged a crop of flowers. Tiny little holes appeared in every petal. I did nothing but continue to water and feed and clean up around each bush. Eventually, the minute pirate bug, a tiny little guy with a voracious appetite, found and ate up all the thrips. I had no further problems that season and no real recurrence in subsequent years!

People have noted that spraying pesticides for spider mite infestations ruthlessly kills off the predatory mites as well. Yes, there are mites which eat the ones causing the damage in the first place. It's a vicious circle, better not entered.

A few caterpillars have built comfy little houses by sticking together a couple of my rose leaflets. I pull apart their happy homes, locate the vermin, and squash the leaf eaters immediately. I then remove all leaves damaged by chewing and sucking insects hoping to send the plants energy toward new growth.

STILL MORE WEEDING

The weeds have returned in full force. It wasn't difficult for me to fill a 55 gallon cans with Bermuda grass roots ripped out of border perennials in my back yard. It's nasty stuff and had so invaded this area that I had to dig up some of my favorite companion plants, shake the dirt off their roots, and sift through the soil and plant roots to pull out the invading grass.

Don't let oxalis get established. The more it grows unchecked each season, the more you will find it the next. My best advice is to dig it up now. Insert your trowel around the growing oxalis and loosen the soil. Lift up carefully and then discard the soil and the weed. Try not to disturb the base of the plant and uncover the bulb and its bulbettes. Pick them out if they dislodge themselves and destroy them. In all cases, do not let the flowers of oxalis go to seed. If you don't have time to do this, spray the green leaves with white vinegar.

Plantain, dandelion, scarlet pimpernel, spurge, and several other weeds pull out easily. Don't let them flower and go to seed because the seeds are very fertile.

Bermuda, Kikuyu, and crab grasses are abysmal nuisances. Dig them out as much as you can. Then, return to the weeded bed in a week or so and remove all the new sprouts. Repeat as long as necessary. If the weeds are growing away from your flower beds and you don't care about the soil they are growing on, a good shot of RoundUp® will also do the trick. Nutgrass, however, is a huge challenge. Poisons only kill the top of the plant. Remove as much as you can of the grass, its roots, and its hundreds of bulbettes. Again, discard the entire mass. Its kernels are almost impossible to find and eliminate. Make sure you

your garden and the environment, such as honey bees are killed by them. (Systemic means the poison is incorporated into the plant, even its pollen.) Roses are edible plants and you've just rendered them poisonous. And lastly, systemic insecticides disrupt the ecological balance of the environment, not just in your own backyard, but globally. The insects that prey on aphids, thrips, spider mites, and the rest are higher up on the food chain. They don't recover as quickly as these pests lower down. Therefore you are just inviting more problems into what should be a harmonious scene.

CHECK FOR INSECT PESTS NOW

Aphids are hatching now and may start appearing in your yard. I don't use insecticides at all, but I do monitor insect damage. Mild infestations of aphids are easy to control with a mild soap solution and/or a forceful spray of water, or a gentle crushing between your fingers. Bottom line—get them gone. **Remember.** Aphids are BORN PREGNANT. If you kill one, you've killed hundreds!

For some reason, I only have aphids on one side of my garden and only on my climbing *Joseph's Coat*. It's a hard area to keep watered and the soil is substandard. So there's probably some strain involved. If this weekend is summery, I'll spray them with some dish soap and wash them off with the hose. I'd rather let nature control itself. Their natural resistance is considerable. When the plants get stressed, they become susceptible to disease and insect damage. Well cared for plants will soon replace whatever leaves and flowers have been destroyed by insects. Make sure the roses are well fed

Penelope, hybrid musk (1924)

For many roses which have the habit of sending up a large candelabra of buds, there is usually one bud which is larger than the rest. In many cases, it's on the stumpiest stem in the center of the spray. Snap this bud off with your fingers and trim the stub. The remaining buds will fill in the hole left in the spray as they develop and hide the spot where the biggest flower had been. These smaller buds will actually then grow somewhat larger. Again, the overall result will be a quality spray of fully developed roses.

As the petals drop from your first flowers, make sure you deadhead your bushes. Cut the stems back two leaves down on the cane. This is very necessary to encourage repeat blooms. You should easily be able to produce three or four bloom cycles on most modern roses during the season.

In addition, several diseases and pests can linger in your garden on the spent blossoms. It's very good hygiene to eliminate and destroy them.

don't spill the RoundUp® on the soil. It stays there for a long time and will retard the growth of anything it comes into contact with.

Another garden problem evident at this time of year is *Arum italicum.* I have successfully spread this relative of the calla lily nearly everywhere in my garden by moving around roses and soil. The longer you leave them in the garden, the more numerous the bulbs from which they stem will be. At first sign of the leaf, dig it out and throw it and attached bulbs away. It will form a two-foot-high clump of leaves supported underground by an increasing number of bulbs.

DISBUD YOUR SIDE BUDS AND DEADHEAD

Most varieties of hybrid teas produce one excellent bud and one to four other buds on the same long cane. Remove these side buds as soon as it's practical. It will help you guide your rose bush into producing an excellent show bloom. If you remove these side buds now, you will get a straight, unblemished bloom on a long stem. A side bud takes nourishment away from other parts of the plant, isn't as vigorous as the main bud, and usually distorts the shape of the hybrid tea. If you like a more naturally grown rose, leave them alone. For whatever reason, it's particularly hard for people new to growing roses to pick unbloomed buds and discard them. When you follow this simple practice, the quality of the rose will be enhanced and the garden will look so much better when your eye can fall on a single, gloriously grown flower. Floribundas and polyanthas are by their nature cluster-flowering roses and don't need disbudding.

DISCOVERIES IN THE GARDEN

I am greatly fond of discovering things in my garden. The *Geranium phaem* "Majlis" which I bought five seasons ago with a group of other species geraniums, has finally bloomed. It was down to one leaf a couple of seasons ago and some how, some way, this year it decided to grow. The bloom is a simple glorious blue-violet color held on a petite spire. I got such a thrill when something which was near death and a great disappointment finally produced results. It joins its sister plants "Mourning Widow" (black flowers!) and "Sillingfleet Ghost" (grey lavender) as controllable companion plants to roses.

Several of my roses have produced offsets which I potted up and will add to the raffle table. These great plants are things terrific! I have the old damask called *Blush Damask* (1759) which was one of the roses that the great Victorian gardener Gertrude Jekyll loved to plant. I'm hoping for lots

Picasso, floribunda (1971)

of basal breaks on several established roses. I noticed during my pruning that quite a lot of the bushes need to be producing some new canes. A new cane is a thrill indeed. Just be careful not to crack off these new wonders as their attachment to the bud union is rather tender when they are new.

Every year in California is different. One year at this time, it just wouldn't stop raining lightly. It never accumulated, wrecked the first flush of flowers, and set everything way off schedule. We had to cancel the Rose Show. The next year, after an absolutely perfect winter—enough rain and lots of very cold weather—usually good for roses—the moisture stopped in early April and never returned. We had weeks of hot, dry weather pushed us right from spring into summer.

WATER COMES FIRST

If rainfall is seriously behind where it needs to be and the steady wind from inland is desiccating the garden, get the hose out and water. You must learn to gauge how much water your roses need and this isn't easy. The dark, drizzling cloud cover is notoriously deceptive and can mask thirsty roses. I never installed a drip system. Many people swear by them and I understand the convenience they provide. They work extraordinarily well if your days have predictable weather and you can get a good average setting. But if the weather changes and a hot wind blows in from the Central Valley, the timer won't adjust for it.

I find sitting and watering the most relaxing outdoor activity there is, especially with a hat on, a hose in one hand, a Scotch and Soda in the other, and my kitty sitting next to me on the bench. Hours pass. I fill up the earthen basin below each bush with water and move on to the next rose in line and so on with all the roses around me. I return to the first one again and repeat the process. On the third trip around some of the second water is still in the area beneath the rose. This tells me the rose has had enough.

THEN COMES FOOD

As said on previous occasions, roses need a steady and ample supply of nitrogen, potassium, and phosphorus, and, in lesser amounts, magnesium, iron, calcium, boron, zinc, molybdenum and others.

One week use Triple 16, two weeks later Miracle-Gro®—or its Kmart equivalent which is about half the price, two weeks later fish emulsion, then back to Triple 16, then on to something else. Watch newspaper adds sometimes you can find a really good deal at a drug store rather than a garden center.

The shredded palettes I used seasons ago have deteriorated and the soil is again exposed. I'll need to get some new

Victor Borge, hybrid tea (1991)

mulch and spread it around. There is still a sufficient amount on the surface of the soil to prevent weeds and hold in moisture. The compost action, however, uses up nitrogen so I intend to use a little more nitrogen to replace what this process might be extracting from the soil.

I can't leave the subject of fertilizer without mentioning my adoration for blood meal. It's a miracle powder. It makes the plants look professionally grown because its readily-accessible nitrogen darkens the leaves and canes. This greener greenery can only help the plant's ability to acquire the other essentials which increase the number and color of the blossoms. Blood meal lasts a while in the soil and contains some trace elements. It's also very easy to apply, but needs to be placed in close proximity to the root system, i.e., take the time to dig it into the soil.

Fish emulsion is a great organic tonic. Buddy loves the smell but gets a bit frustrated when he can't find the source. I've been tossing his uneaten and all dried up cat food onto the roses. I'm sure this will give the roses some gumption. If you have access to fish scraps, get them in the ground. Ideally, if you know where you'd like to expand your garden in the future, start now burying raw nutrients such as this in the ground. Give them a year to decompose.

You can never give your roses enough organic material. The addition of good fertilizer right now is so important in the development of new canes which are the source of new flowers. Keep some compost or mulch on top of your bud unions and don't let them dry out. The roses are full of energy now and you want to help them make the best of it. Basic nutrition also helps your leaf color look its best and your blossoms all be show quality.

GIVE YOUR BUSHES A ONCE OVER

With fantastically sunny days, all your roses should be sending up shoots from every location. You may remember that I said I was going to take advantage of the winter frosts and the long dormancy by doing some heavy pruning on roses which need some new canes.

The response has been terrific. I'm getting very strong growth on some younger canes and a good response on the older wood. I'll continue to feed and keep the bud union moist to make sure some strong basal breaks happen. I think some sunlight on the bud union helps a lot so I'm examining each bush in the garden and pulling off any new growth that is heading inwards to the center of the bush.

I'm also removing all but one multiple shoots from the same location. The result I'm trying to achieve has to do with the quality of the blooms not the quantity. I want this rose season to be spectacular.

FIRST BLOOMING ROSES

Every year I try to gauge which rose bush is most likely to flower first. One year, it was *Madame Alfred Carrière* (1879). The next year it was *Climbing Cécile Brünner* (1894). The following year it was a miniature out by the driveway, all ones which have hard to reach or overlooked canes.

Maverick blossoms appear some years. *Black Prince* (1866), a hybrid perpetual got only a modest trim and produced an early flower. Three weeks went by before its next bloom opened. *Perle d'Or* (1875), a polyantha with some

Black Prince, hybrid perpetual (1866)

Madame Alfred Carrière, noisette (1879)

Chinese tenderness also sent out some early sprays of flowers. I didn't quite finish pruning it and it was happy. I don't mind not doing anything to the big roses on the potting shed when I know that after they bloom they'll get whacked back.

Usually, I get a good first bloom on my miniatures as they are out in the full sun. On a couple of occasions, I truly gave them a clipping to remember. As a consequence, I have some fantastic new canes coming on strong, but don't have a large number of flowers.

DARK CORNERS UNSUITABLE FOR ROSES

Companion plants to grow with roses can be particularly useful in those corners of gardens which are too dark for even the most shade tolerant bush. I give high marks to *Fuchsia thymifolia*, a small shrub (30-36 inches tall) which bears fleshy little thyme-like leaves and a quarter-inch fuchsia-colored blossoms with white stamens. There's also a white variety but it wasn't as vigorous as the fuchsia-colored one. It's adored by hummingbirds and perfect for that corner of your garden that gets little or no light. I have a hedge of the stuff under the eave on the north side of my house. It does not suffer from the mites which disfigure the fancier ornamental fuch-

Madame Legras de St. Germaine, alba (1846)

sias. During the summer, I will separate some of the lower branches which have rooted and plant them elsewhere in the garden. It will burn if given anything more than dappled sunlight. I've also had great luck with *Fuchsia x.* "Red Rain" (which is about 3 foot tall) and *Fuchsia magellanica var. molinae* (which can grow to ten feet). Leather-leaf ferns are useful and are great to include in a rose bouquet. Many of the other ferns spread rapidly and are really difficult to remove—should you eventually wish to. I've had really good luck with the four hydrangeas on the north side of walls and fences and often thought I should grow more of them. The liriope at my front door receive no direct sunlight. They produce lovely purple spikes of flowers every fall and give visitors, especially the mail carrier, a visual treat for three months. It's commonly known as creeping lilyturf.

HOUSE REPAIRS AND ROSES

In order to get some parts of the house painted, I had to trim back the roses which use it as support. My house painter, Mike Lopez, untied the stays and used a rope to pull the not-quite-leafed-out roses away form the house. He staked the ends of these ropes in the ground and gave himself ample space to hand paint the house.

Among the many words of advice Mike insisted on imparting to me every morning as he showed me what he'd done the day before, while I was at work, were these words about roses:

• My *Madame Alfred Carrière* (1879) which was fifteen feet tall and is now thinned out and reduced to about eight or nine had been tied to the house through eye bolts in the eaves. The weight of the rose and the force of it moving in the wind has over time worn the edge of my composite shingles back to the house line. This is a serious issue. I'll have to devise a way so that the rose is secure and upright, but it doesn't rub against the shingles anymore. The blossoms which have come out of this newly trimmed noisette are about a half-again as large and fragrant as they ever were.

• The heavy mulch on two sides of the house had risen above the foundation slab and was burying the house sidings. This only invited earwigs, pill bugs, and worms to wiggle up under the combed cedar shake siding. Mike removed all the mulch which was against the house. He sealed any spaces which invite insect vermin to lodge and put a couple of heavy coats of paint.

• Mike trimmed a few of the one time bloomers in order to paint behind them. This reduced their size enormously. The biggest one near the garage was *Russell's Cottage Rose* (1846) (a.k.a. *Rosa russelliana, Souvenir de la Bataille de Marengo,* Old Spanish Rose,

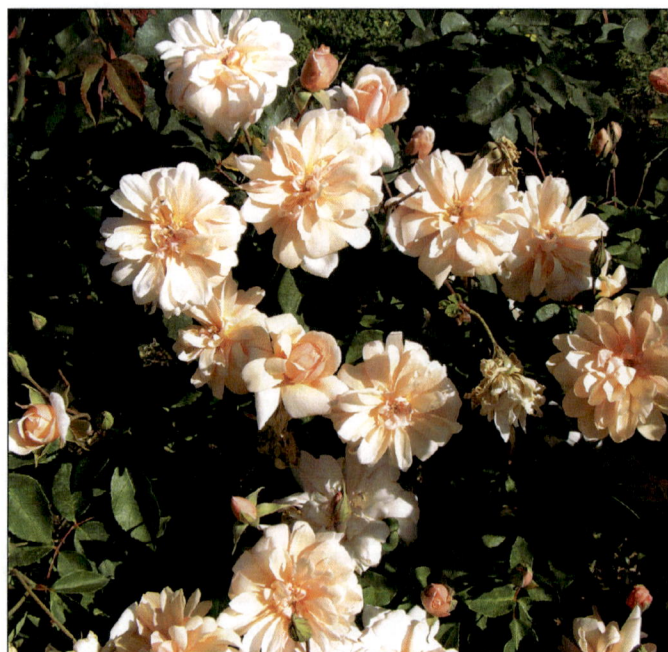

Perle d'Or, polyantha (1875)

and several others). It's a much less rangy looking shrub and much more attractive now. There's plenty of old wood left. So we shall see what effect it might have.

- By the time everyone visits my yard in July, there shouldn't be any trace of the painting left and the house will be sparkling. Several of my older hybrid perpetuals loved being left horizontal for a month. They are blooming like they never have before.

Remember. There's always much to do in April. Don't have more bushes than you can care for appropriately.

ADVICE FROM THE PAST

In planting shrubs and trees of every kind, let all convenient expedition be made in doing it, so that they may be planted as soon as possible after they are taken up, or brought from the nursery, or elsewhere, that their roots may not be dried by the sun and wind; but when the shrubs are brought from any distance, and cannot be immediately planted, untie the bundles, and lay the roots in a trench, and cover them with earth, to lie till the places allotted for them are ready to receive them.

Thomas Mawe, London, 1797

Sombreuil, large flowered climber (1880)

May

On California's Central Coast, we experience "high rose tide" in May. Most evident of this seasonal phenomenon in my yard are the four big roses on my potting shed. Random blooms begin to appear on *Climbing Cécile Brünner* (1894) and *Phyllis Bide* (1924), both polyanthas in late March or early April, then in mid-April my old damask rose, *Isfahan* (1832) shows pink and the large rambler, *Newport Fairy* (1908), starts to open its huge clusters of satiny, light pink buds with white eyes at the end of April. By mid-May, the potting shed is a mass of flowers.

What a month of flowers! Ample sunshine and heat make certain our roses are abundant and high in quality. We often get a rotten little bit of rain in April. Rain isn't the problem. When the leaves get wet, then dry out, then get wet again, blackspot develops and spreads. It's an airborne fungal disease which leaves a telltale blackspot on the rose leaflets. The fungus will kill the leaf eventually and cause it to drop from the plant. The disease will not kill the rose, but the plant's lack of green chlorophyll producing leaves will cause its growth to slow down.

Certain roses are more resistant to blackspot than others. When you see blackspot in a climate which gets no rain from May to November, it's due to the atmospheric condition described above. Some roses aren't resistant at all and, when growing in too close proximity to other roses, will dispense the spores and the disease will spread. I spent one past weekend, my first free weekend in a month, removing any and all blackspotted leaves from four or five bushes.

Since I do not spray my roses with pesticides (that term includes insecticides, fungicides, and herbicides), I am forced to pull off and discard all infected leaves. I prefer to

keep my bushes well watered and well fed. I do intend to spray my mildew prone bushes with some white vinegar or dust them with sulfur powder. I hesitate spraying too much with vinegar as I want my garden to exude the natural smells that roses have: damask and tea, melon and clove, myrrh and licorice but NOT PICKLES!

TENDING ROSES IN FULL BLOOM

Utmost in importance in prolonging your blooming cycles and shortening the period between blooms is water and food. The plants are exerting the greatest amount of energy at this time and need plenty of water to support the abundant blooms and to make new foliage, canes and buds. The base of your rose bush needs to be constantly moist in order for your rose to produce the basal breaks it needs for future flowers.

I find roses growing in my heavy clay soil prefer a good soaking and then a good rest to allow air to enter the soil. The length between waterings depends on how hot the days are and how intense the sun is. A good drink can work miracles.

This great growth effort needs to be fueled as well. You shouldn't have any problem at this time of year giving your plants a dose of fertilizer at least every other week all summer long. Triple Twenty (20-20-20) or Triple Sixteen (16-16-16) are often on sale, as is MiracleGro®. Look for them, buy them cheaply, and get them onto your plants.

Unlike watering, regular feeding of smaller amounts of these strong fertilizers is safer and better for the roses than a large amount at any one time. Water your roses well the

Phyllis Bide, climbing polyantha (1924)

day before applying your fertilizer. Add fertilizer around the base of each bush—spread it around. Don't throw a big clump of it right on the bud union. **Remember.** Most of the roots are further out. Then, water the fertilizer in. Let the top of the soil dry out somewhat; always moist but never constantly soggy.

Phyllis Bide, climbing polyantha (1924) close up

ASSESS YOUR NEWLY PLANTED ROSES

Roses vary from garden to garden because of differences in soil, water, air, nutrients, sunlight, and specific varietal characteristics. We too frequently plant roses based on how they did growing in another climate. Inevitably I end up disappointed by the results.

Disease prone varieties aside, I often have other difficulties. The roses I planted in the back of the bed turn out to be shorter than those planted in the front. I'm irritated that I hadn't better judged the size; admittedly, one of life's smaller peeves, but one nevertheless.

Now is the worst possible time to move any of your roses. They most likely will go into shock from which they may or may not recover. Wait until the summer bloom cycle is finished before you think about relocation. Better yet, hold off moving anything until late October. The plants grow much

better roots when they don't also have to grow stems, leaves, and flowers. It's also much easier to handle a pruned, leafless bush than a fully developed growing one.

However, if you do need to switch things around, make sure the rose's roots and the soil where they've grown remains intact. Do this reshuffling at the end of the day, not first thing in the morning or in the middle of the hottest, brightest part of the day! Then, water thoroughly with ample amounts of Vitamin B1 to help re-establish a functioning root system. You probably have noticed that the first part of the plant to react to its relocation are the new canes and buds. If they don't lift their heads up in a day or two after the move, prune them back to prevent any additional strain.

FEED AND FEED AGAIN

I like to vary the fertilizers I use making certain that I always water before I feed and again after I feed. Roses like water. Roses like some air in the soil, too. Roses like the soil to be warm. It's not always easy to control their water intake because the heat, humidity and wind direction affect our roses on the coast. A little fertilizer frequently applied is much, much better than a lot of fertilizer occasionally dumped on the bush.

Don't forget to put organic material in the soil around your roses. It helps sustain the nutrition if you go for a period without fertilizing. Fish emulsion is the easiest organic material to apply. Composted cow manure is also cheap and readily available.

If your bushes start to decline in flower production and the leaves look a bit tired and yellow, put some more alfalfa pellets around the bush and let the water soak its beneficial qualities into the soil. If you haven't added any bone or blood meal, try some now and water it in well. It's a very healthy way to keep your roses looking their very best. Plant your over ripe bananas beneath one of your rose bushes. (Forget this if you live in an area frequented by raccoons as these furry critters are particularly fond of banana flavor.) Bananas contain high levels of potassium and they degrade very quickly.

WATER AND WATER AGAIN

If your work and personal schedules get as complicated as mine, you may have to forego just about everything in caring for your roses. But, the one thing you can't abandon is the watering schedule. Play close attention to your roses' most critical need—the need for ample water. I am often fooled by the cool coastal weather and the drizzly low clouds. I am easily lulled into that proverbial false sense of security. Then I happen to inspect the yard and the good Salinas soil has hardened into adobe and the plants are nearly desiccated.

Valencia, hybrid tea (1967)

those which are in pots. You can't be too generous with water in well drained pots. If you have placed roses in terra cotta pots, you must be especially vigilant in keeping the soil moist. Terra cotta breathes freely and loses much water in the process. Evaporation also dispels heat which can be good, except that roses need some heat in the soil to absorb their nutrients sufficiently. My suggestion is to grow your roses in plastic pots which fit into the terra cotta pots.

If you use hoses, be careful not to damage the roses by pulling the heavy hose through them. You can easily knock off a new cane or snap a rose bud. If you overhead water, be sure to do so in the morning so that the water on the leaves will evaporate in the sunlight. Common knowledge once dictated that roses should not be watered in the mid-day sun because the water droplets would act like magnifying glasses and burn the leaves. I have yet to observe this phenomenon. If the rose leaves appear burned on the edge, it's from too much fertilizer and too little water!

All of my roses are planted at the bottom of a soil basin. All of my roses are hand watered which can take me up to three hours. I usually fill the basins full which is probably about two or three gallons and let the rose absorb all the water. I then return once the water has soaked in and repeat the process. A hybrid tea rose's roots reach to an average of 20 inches below the surface of the ground so it takes more water to reach way down there. Of course, roses growing along the front of a raised bed lose water more rapidly. Their roots maybe much closer to the surface and therefore more likely to dry out.

I can't stress the importance of a good cool drink during the summer and how much roses appreciate it. If you water early in the day, it allows your roses to store a good supply. This allows photosynthesis to take place and the bush to emit water vapor and oxygen.

Good drainage is important to roses as they prefer the soil to be moist but detest soggy roots for more than a day or two. Add some sand to your soil if you have clay and some good compost to keep your roses happy. If you garden in very sandy soil, add lots of organic material. Organic material such as mushroom compost, steer manure, and top dressing will swell up with water and hold onto the moisture content which may just go straight through sand.

Roses like a good drink. I usually give mine five to ten gallons every four days or so during the hottest part of the day. You may have to vary this for your miniature roses and

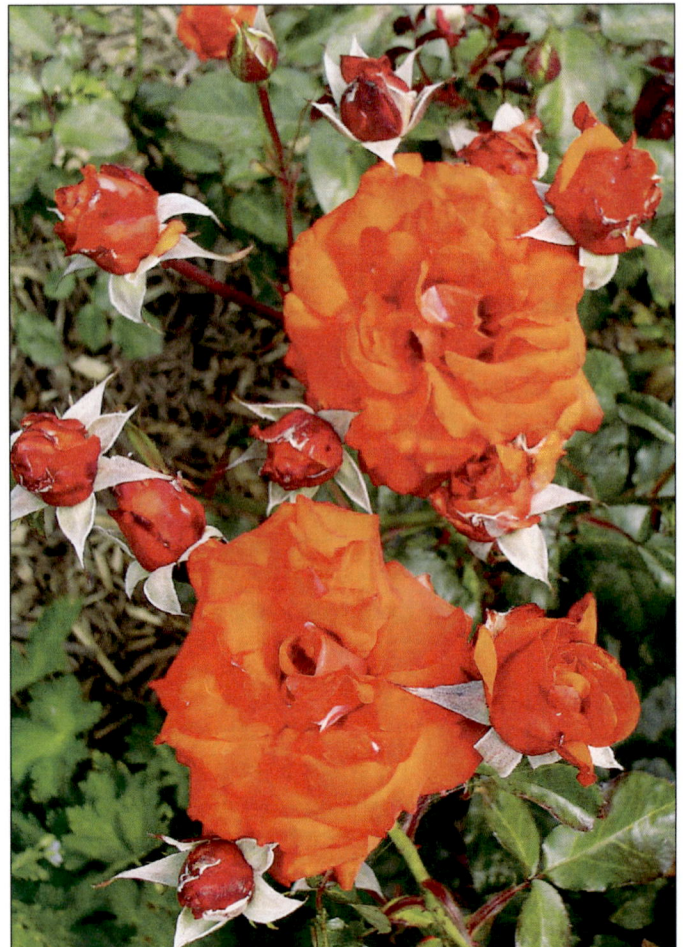

Fireburst, floribunda (1993)

ALLOW NEWLY PLANTED ROSES TO DEVELOP

My desire to pick the flowers of new varieties in my garden immediately is a weakness. Newly planted roses which were part of last winter's bare root crop need at least a year to mature. By cutting a long stemmed rose from them you are reducing the number of leaves they have and sapping their strength. Resist cutting those first flowers of a new plant. Instead, let the petals drop and then deadhead the cane down to the first full leaf as described above.

If you give them time to grow, you will allow the plant to resist diseases better and grow better roots which ultimately will produce more long stemmed flowers for you to cut in the future.

DEADHEADING IS JUST ANOTHER NAME FOR SUMMER PRUNING

The late Chris Rabe, my great rose friend who grew 600+ varieties in Corral de Tierra, taught me a lot about spending the necessary time snipping off spent blooms. She liked to think about how the re-blooming plant will look. When you cut off a faded bloom, find a bud eye on the outside facing part of the cane at least one or two full leaves down from the faded flower. The new growth should always be directed away from the center.

Stubby growth will appear spontaneously lower down on your major canes. Push these sprouts off with your finger when they are still tender. They aren't likely to produce flowers of substance but are likely to impede air flowing through and around your rose bush. Stillness helps blackspot and rust take hold. Thin out your bushes and concentrate on the quality of your flowers and the health of your leaves.

Be sure to differentiate between insignificant growth lower down and new canes or basal breaks. Usually the latter is slower-growing and broader, but once formed moves rapidly upward with real substance. Don't handle or bump this new growth as its connection to the plant is quite fragile. Let it harden before you touch it at all. I celebrate more enthusiastically about the appearance of a new cane than I do the appearance of any single perfect bloom. You do the math.

Don't allow hips to form on your repeat blooming varieties. Hips are fruit and will redirect your plants' nutrients. The plants will need these to put toward a second flush of flowers. The bloom cycle is about six to eight weeks depending on the cultivar. I have four *Joseph's Coats* growing on the side of my house. For visual (landscaping) reasons, I remove all of the spent and nearly spent blooms from these bushes at the same time and keep them pruned to about the same height. They are all flower-less for a period. But, they are all

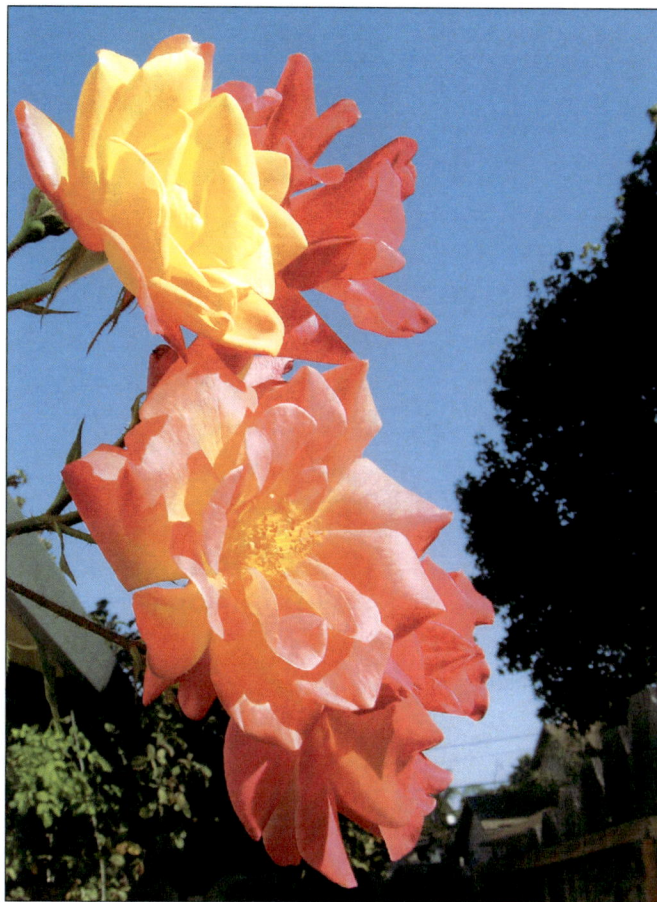

Joseph's Coat, large flowered climber (1969)

on the same re-bloom cycle. When they come on again, it's much more visually pleasing; more so than having some blooms, some buds, some hips, and some dead heads.

It's a big chore to get out a ladder and cut off all of the spent blooms you can find on a repeat-blooming climber. It's a dull task but an important one if you wish to see another full flush of flowers. Don't let your rose start spending its energy on hips. It's too soon for that.

Hybrid teas and floribundas and most miniatures really need a decent trimming after their first bloom. I like to wait a bit and see which bud eye the plant prefers. If it's the first leaf to have five leaflets, so be it. But if that leaf's bud eye faces the interior of the plant, I recommend the next one down.

Trouble in paradise can come with harsh, late year storms. One entire season was set back because of a May hail storm. It did terrific damage to the new leaves and shoots on the roses. Spend time propping up some of the rose canes which could take a tumble under the weight of the blossoms and the force of the wind. If most of the flowers have been spent, I may take one of these toppled canes and reduce it significantly.

Belinda, hybrid musk (1936)

When your beautiful hybrid teas, grandifloras, and miniatures produce a candelabra of buds as many of them do, usually the center flower is the largest and the first to bloom. The other bud stems impede its growth so that you end up with a bunch of buds with a wad of squished together petals in the middle. You may find a wad of squished together petals attractive. I find that if you remove (snap off) the center bud which usually has just a stump of a stem the other buds develop better and open in unison creating a terrific effect. It seems counter productive to remove flower buds but it's worth it in the long run.

One time bloomers, such as most of the Old European roses, species, and ramblers don't need to have their spent flowers removed. In fact, they should be left unattended and allowed to form hips in the autumn. Some OGRs, however, don't have desirable hips and hold on to their spent petals. These petals are soon susceptible to botrytis and look terrible on the bush. Remove all of them when you reduce the size of the shrub at the end of its blooming cycle.

KEEP YOUR EQUIPMENT SHARP

With all the chores that await us, you must invest some time in sharpening your best bypass pruners. A good clean cut is less likely to attract cane borers and act like a repository for the diseases which cause die-back. Sharp, well-oiled shears are also faster to work with and present fewer sore hands. Never use your shears when you need loppers. Never use your loppers when you need a hatchet or saw.

I also remove flowers which I know will start to drop petals unattractively. However, several of the Old Garden Roses look terrific when they have as many petals on the ground as they do attached to the stems. Others aren't so nice looking and the spent flowers hang on in an unattractive beige color. I usually clean out all of these with a pair of vegetable scissors.

Many hybrid teas bloom with a dominant bud and one or more side buds. If allowed to open unimpeded you get a "naturally grown" look. This usually results in a rather lopsided main flower. Sometimes you can't get around to disbudding and that's fine. It won't harm the plant. Do, however, go through your garden and remove the spent dominant blooms as they fade. This redirects the plant's energy toward the remaining flowers.

If you want to encourage a one bloom per stem look which has great aesthetic value, snip off the side buds early in their development and then allow the dominant bud to bloom. After it's finished, look down the cane until you find the first full leaf (with five leaflets) located on the outside of the cane. Snip the cane at a 45° angle about a half-inch above the leaf bud. Your aim is to have the new stem grow away from the bush, not diagonally into its center. Follow this rule for the first half of the summer. Then, use your common sense. If the rose has gotten too tall for you to enjoy the flowers, shorten the canes even more.

Remove the blossoms as they fade and allow each bud on the candelabra sufficient room to open. Cluster flowered bushes are among the most vigorous so you may want to cut off the spent candelabra little bit lower down. Also, the weight of these flower clusters can be quite heavy causing them to topple over in a strong wind. New growth from lower down will give the stem more stability.

Pascali, hybrid tea (1963)

PROBLEMS UNDERGROUND

With some absolutely fantastic weather, I decided I needed to have a few days off from my paying job to work harder than ever in my yard. It took two days to clean up the yard and two days to spread 20 cubic yards of shredded palettes, disguised by the product name of "Forest Floor." The hardest work was weeding and reshaping the garden soil beneath the plants and around the borders.

The miniatures along my front sidewalk didn't seem very hardy. They were all alive. They weren't suffering much from any visible disease. Yet something just didn't seem "happy" about them. So down I went with trowel in hand to investigate. I wasn't quite ready for what I found and hadn't even considered it as an affliction. The culprit in the front yard was the Liquid Amber or Sweet Gum tree the City of Salinas had planted a few years before I bought the house. Its roots had invaded the delicious soil surrounding the miniatures.

I had to remove nearly a 33-gallon garbage can full of roots of many sizes. The largest was two inches in diameter. Why did I find this amazing? The sweet gum grows a good twenty feet away from this bed.

While I was yanking and tugging away, I was also checking out the soil. I was really quite pleased with the loamy nature of the soil, the number of earthworms in it, and the amount of organic material there.

I had applied handfuls of alfalfa pellets about two weeks prior to my digging and was able to work this amendment into the soil. Since I was down that low and actively scooting my bottom from bush to bush, I included a handful of blood meal in my scraping and a fistful of time-release fertilizer.

A SIMPLE MISTAKE

Just prior to the last bit of rainfall we received at the end of one March, I raced about the garden lugging a bucket full of Osmocote that I had left over from the season before. It had been tightly sealed and the application went smoothly. The rain cooperated beautifully and began as I was cleaning up. Later that evening, I was sitting watching a program on the Science Channel when a commercial for some lawn fertilizer came on and a light went off. I had just spread two bags of Osmocote time release fertilizer for lawns all over

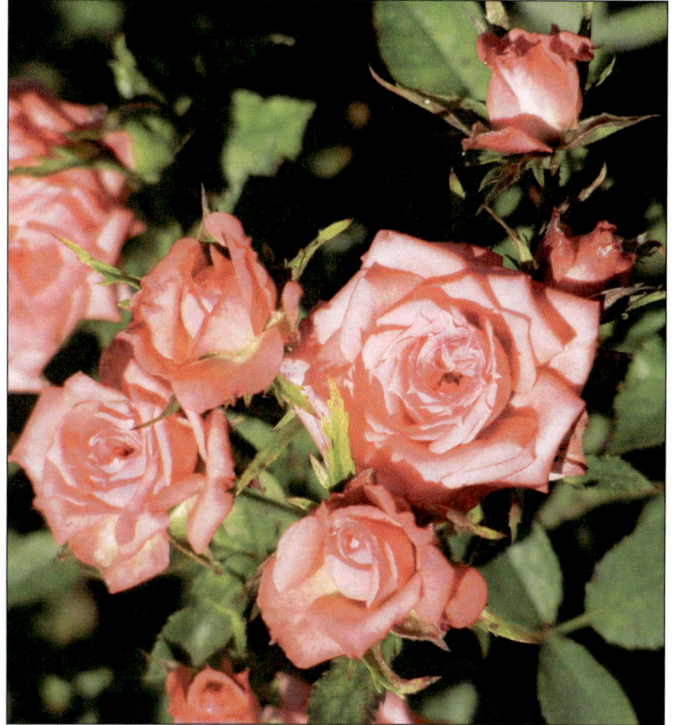

Cuddles, miniature (1978)

the base of each rose bush in my entire garden. I began to laugh hysterically.

Time release fertilizers are intentionally slow to give up their nutrients. There will certainly be ample nitrogen. Indeed, I ended up with the tallest and greenest rose garden on the Central Coast. It didn't hurt the roses, but required extra water all season long. I had flowers thanks to the organic material in the soil, but I also had plenty of blind shoots and vegetative centers.

ADVICE FROM THE PAST

Transplant suckers of roses; it is by suckers from the root that most sorts of these shrubs are increased: these being dug up carefully with roots, will make good plants in one or two years time, and most of them will flower next summer.

Thomas Mawe, London, 1797

June

Your rose garden should be in full bloom at this time, if not a little past it. One great advantage of having a number of different kinds of roses is the variation in their bloom time. My first roses to flower begin in March. By dumb luck I planted a variety of Old Garden Roses, all with differing first flushes from April to July. So my *Climbing Cécile Brünner* (1894) was the first to really pop and my *Newport Fairy* (1908) and *Rosa setigera* (species) will be the final ones. So who cares if they only bloom once in a season, I've had flowers on these various varieties from February *(Madame Alfred Carrière* 1879) to August *(Isfahan* 1832). That's a long season of joy, especially when you consider the length of time that daffodils, lilacs, or irises are flowering. Rosa setigera is also known as the Prairie rose and is native to most of the United States. It is the only rose which truly has male-only and female-only plants. The males tend to have more flowers in their sprays and only the females make hips. It's disease-free and has only a few progeny.

Spring is unpredictable on the Central Coast. A cool, wet one will cause a three- to five-week delay in the bloom cycle. By June though, the first flush of bloom on the hybrid teas and floribundas is usually over and we should have all had fantastic opening displays. A warm spring is great for roses. It can, however, be brought to an end by drizzly mornings followed by scorchingly hot days. One year, spring was crowned with gale-force winds, wildfires, and ash settling all over the Central Coast. Fallen rose petals drifted up into mounds in various corners of my yard.

ROSE CARE WHILE ON VACATION

One of the biggest hazards to summer gardening is a summer vacation. I was gone once from May 30 until June 12. I watered well during Memorial Day weekend and held off giving the roses anything to eat before I left. There's no point in feeding your roses if you plan to be gone. In fact, it could do more harm than good. The extra growth the fertilizer will stimulate in your plants depends on an ample water supply. If you are like me and hand water everything in your yard, then you are certain to court danger. New growth in

Cécile Brünner, climbing polyantha (1894)

plants combined with insufficient water usually results in weaker growth and easily burned leaves. It's so much better just to let the roses sit and wait. Of course, I could have arranged for someone to water in my stead, but I never tied anyone down. Upon my return, I added more water and supplied my bushes with a handful of Triple 16, and then the following day, watered again.

What I lost during my absence were all but two of the roses I started from seed and about half of the cuttings. I was angry about this, but it was my own fault for not making better watering arrangements.

As far as my seedlings go, I suppose this is part of the natural selection process in a amateur hybridizing program. Those two babies weren't any larger than the ten other ones that got fried but they did survive. I only hope they continue to flower and increase in size over the summer. I'm rarely gone that long and now I will be around to inspect them.

Most of the newly started plants got some damage as well but I think they'll survive. It's interesting that I did not lose any of the roses which were in the ground and my ten-day absence did not even phase any of the larger roses which have deep roots. Everyone told me that we had had hot weather and little fog, but they needn't have. I could tell from the parched look of my yard.

If you plan to go anywhere for more than two or three days, make sure someone comes and waters at least the plants you have in pots. Another good idea, if you have the right space, is to bury your potted plants three-quarters down in the ground while you are away. This will lower the soil temperature somewhat and cause less evaporation.

At a minimum, move your potted roses into full shade before you take off on a summer vacation. They aren't likely to need as much water in this location, and the shade is only temporary.

GENERAL MAINTENANCE

If your garden isn't brimming with flowering rose bushes, all boasting healthy, dark green foliage and abundant new growth, something is terribly wrong. You need to call your nearest consulting rosarian and ask for a site visit. We are all happy to lend our various insight and make suggestions on how you can improve your garden.

The trickiest aspect facing a June garden on California's Central Coast is watering. Many of you on drip systems may have solved this problem, but those of us who still water by hand must inspect our beds daily to see which roses need a drink.

The cool overcast mornings may be deceptive. Sometimes they last all day. At other times, the hot summer sun burns through after we've gone to work but the marine layer returns by mid-afternoon before we get back, thereby tricking us into believing the roses don't need more water. Then, all of a sudden, the plants are bone dry. Still other times it's sunny all day. Perhaps evaporation isn't at its greatest when days are foggy, but be careful. Low clouds can

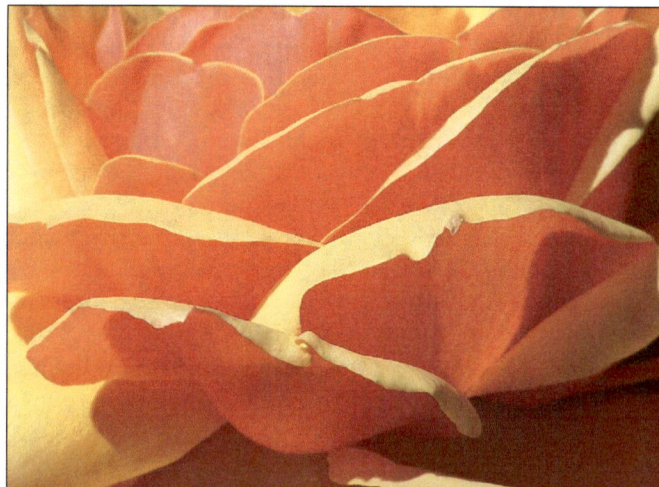

About Face, hybrid tea (2003)

produce heavy mists but we all know that this is not the same as rain. No heavy mist can water a rose sufficiently.

If you grow any plants in black plastic pots, be exceptionally careful. They will need more water than those in the ground. The heat absorbing black raises the temperature of the soil within the pot to levels higher than those on the ground. This is good, as higher temperatures allow bacteria to break nitrogen bearing chemicals down into forms which the plant can more readily use. This process needs more water than normal, not only because higher temperatures result in greater evaporation but also because more accessible nitrogen causes faster growth which takes more water out of the soil and more growth means abundant and healthy leaves on the plant resulting in far greater expiration of $H2O$.

GETTING YOUR ROSES TO RE-BLOOM WELL

Most modern roses need six to seven weeks to produce another flush of blossoms. Much of this depends on sunlight, heat, soil, and fertilizer; much also depends on the variety. The adage "the more you pick, the more your get" is especially true with roses when they are fed, watered, and given plenty of sunshine.

Many of the older repeat bloomers tend to need all of the faded flowers and hips removed BEFORE they will consider a repeat bloom. I find that we can manage to get three good blooms in during the main rose season here on California's Central Coast, sometimes four if we have an early spring. At any rate, it's a good idea to snip off spent flowers before the plant even figures out it's time to set fruit. The exception to this rule is, of course, one time bloomers whose ripened hips add a degree of interest to the plants in the fall. Just leave these alone.

Cécile Brünner, climbing polyantha (1894) close up

Many sources talk about deadheading as if it's a scientific process. They say that one must count down from the spent bloom to the first outside bud growing from a five leaflet leaf and make your cut at a 45° angle about a half-inch above the reverse side of your intended bud eye!

I'd like to advise you to deadhead keeping in mind many of the rules of winter pruning. Open up the center of your bush. Remove insignificant canes and canes which show signs of die-back. Get rid of the entire feeble cane early in the season so that the rose can send up a new, more vigorous, one. Help it use the nutrients you are providing, wisely. If any of your canes are smallish in size and likely to bend easily with a cluster of heavy blooms on top, remove them now.

Also keep in mind the shape of the shrub in the garden. Hybrid teas are the gawkiest of plants. I am amazed at how ugly they are when considered from a distance. It's ugliness is totally forgotten, of course, when you look at a magnificent 7-inch fully open blossom. I'm calling to mind *Oldtimer* (1969). It's the most unshapely rose in the garden and very stingy about setting new canes. But, when it does send one up, maybe every other year, the new cane provides some of the most spectacular flowers in rosedom.

One of the hardest lessons I have had to learn about growing hybrid teas is that you must disbud the flower clusters. This is somewhat variety specific. But, I have found that many of the most common hybrid teas produce a main bud with two side buds. Pinch out or cut off the ancillary side buds. You will get one long cane with a beautifully formed flower on a stem which is more likely to be stronger and larger in diameter. (The nutrients aren't being wasted on the side buds.) Once the one flower on the strong stem is

The Squire, austin (1977)

finished and removed, you are more likely to get two more strong flowering canes from this same good cane.

Floribundas and grandifloras have similar needs. Frequently, these cluster-flowering wonders produce a spray with one dominant bud on the shortest stalk of the candelabra and many other smaller buds on longer stalks. Sacrifice the big bloom to allow the rest of the cluster to develop into an awesome show in the garden. If left to its own, this one flower will open too far ahead of the rest of the spray and mar the impact. It usually clogs up the spray with dead petals and could impair the development of the other buds.

MILDEW SEASON IS UPON US

Cool wet nights and hot dry days are ideal conditions for powdery mildew. It's an airborne fungal disease which hampers the full development of the leaves but will not kill the bush. New leaves, new canes, and blossom stems peduncles are most vulnerable to powdery mildew. It's worth noting that I did not see one bit of mildew during my vacation in Ohio. I'm told it's because of the sulfur dioxide which the steel mills and coal-burning power plants emit. Sulfur kills the mildew by changing the pH level on the surface of the leaves and thereby making the spores disinclined to hatch. It's one un-heralded benefit of acid rain.

I will try to do what organic rosarians advocate and that is spraying the garden (or at least the susceptible varieties) with a sulfur product. I have seen results from sulfur dusts especially on the varieties which mildew only slightly. Summer oils will also interfere with the spores taking hold on the leaves. Others claim that spraying the leaves with vinegar works, still others claim that skim milk will do the trick! Nurseries that use overhead watering systems tend not to be afflicted with powdery mildew.

OILS WELL THAT ENDS WELL

Rosarians can be divided into three camps: those who spray everything regularly as needed, those who never spray at all, and those who spray occasionally with a nontoxic ingredient to solve a specific problem. I'm in the third group—last year, actually, I was in the second group but more for matters of time not philosophy.

I have noticed that sulfur sprayed on certain varieties that mildew a little, curbs it. I have also observed that a mild summer oil, such as Volck® Oil, applied to the leaves of roses that suffer from mildew also helps them look better.

The fungal diseases: blackspot, rust, and mildew proliferate when they literally get a good foothold on a leaf. Oil, Cloud Cover®, and apparently skim milk, all place a residue on the surface of the leaf which prevents the spores from attaching themselves. Of course, as soon as the leaf gets a good

Oldtimer, hybrid tea (1969)

ROSE MOSAIC VIRUS

A number of different mosaic viruses have contaminated the rose industry. They are called that because some of their telltale blotches resemble patterns in a tile mosaic. They can be identified as a yellow zigzag marking on an otherwise healthy green leaflet or they can be pronounced discoloration with showing reds, yellows, and purple blotches on distorted leaves. I've found it covering every leaf on one cane of one of my favorite hybrid teas, *Oldtimer* (1969). I have three of this same variety, all purchased at the same time from a Kmart in 1994. I knew the middle shrub had virus. I'd seen its telltale yellowish white mottled leaves, but this year the white part was more prevalent than the natural dark green on the other two shrubs. The middle shrub is the weakest of the bunch. The two puny flowers it produced on these affected leaves were sickly-looking and misshapen. The sun, during a hot spell, fried the whitish parts. I was about to throw the rose out when I noticed that new growth was appearing from the bud eyes. So I continued to water and feed and the new growth is back to the dark green. Many people who sell virus-laden roses claim it doesn't weaken the plant. But this center shrub is only half the size of the other two.

If you purchase a shrub that shows virus, dig it up and give it back to the people who sold it to you. There's no excuse now for anyone to sell such an inferior product. Action will not happen to correct these sub-standard growing habits until we, the rose gardeners of the world, protest and demand our money back.

sprinkling of water, the benefit is lost. Sulfur is poisonous to fungus and like baking soda interferes with the pH factor on the surface of the leaf.

Spraying not at all is fine by me. By spraying, I am not talking about washing the dust off the leaves with a good hosing down. An occasional bath does wonders and makes the garden very presentable. I would much rather select varieties that are disease-free or highly resistant than try to alter the plant's inherent reaction to our climatic conditions. I have never sprayed insecticides. I can't stand the smell. The same goes for systemic fertilizers. The one time I used them I was sick to my stomach from the odor. Also, I have never had a severe insect infestation.

If I happen to get some aphids, I squirt them off with a strong spray from the hose. They have a slow metabolism and aren't likely to make it back up the cane again. **Remember**. Aphids deliver their progeny quickly. Kill them when you see them. A spray of dish soap and water also keeps them in check. I squish as many cucumber beetles as I see and I make sure there are a variety of birds in my back yard. Many eat bugs. More than one person has told me that the only people who suffer from severe spider mite infestations are those who regularly spray for spider mites. They are also killing the predatory insects indiscriminately.

Spraying belongs in the hands of those carefully trained and adequately equipped to apply it. Use of pesticides in such mono-culture environments as growing fields, hothouses and nurseries is a matter of business success or failure so I don't deride its usage but relegate it to the professionals. I would much rather enjoy the beauty of a naturally grown rose knowing the imperfections give it its unique personality.

Champagne Cocktail, hybrid tea, 1983

THE PH FACTOR

Know something about your water. I received my annual analysis from the water company and sure enough the major RED FLAG that went up had to do with the pH level of my water. Salinas city water has a pH of 7.4 which is well into the alkaline range. Roses love a pH at about 6.5. What to do?

If the water you are pouring onto your roses is pushing the soil pH up, you must work to make the soil more acidic. Make sure you incorporate a sufficient amount of organic material into your soil. Add some alfalfa pellets again. It's a relatively cheap. When the pH factor is high, roses have a more difficult time finding the nutrients that you are providing them. Steer manure is also a cheap supplement, but needs to be worked down into the soil especially around the area where you are working. Blood meal is costly, but it gives the roses a double whammy. It's organic which lightens and loosens the soil, plus it's THE best source of organic nitrogen. Bacteria which break down organic material, such as the wood chips you use as a mulch, feed on nitrogen. It's important to supply the area around your rose with sufficient nitrogen fertilizer for the breakdown to occur and also for the feeding of your roses. The benefit of blood meal, fish meal, and other organics is you can't add too much. Triple 16 or Triple 10 offer the same benefits, but in a highly concentrated form which may burn the roses.

TOO MUCH LOVE

You can identify fertilizer burn easily. It usually occurs on the outer edges of the five leaflets causing them to curl upward and be completely dried out while other parts of the leaves remain intact. Fertilizers can kill a plant so be careful. The leaves will show no other evidence of physical damage. The most affected leaves will usually be the medium aged ones. It's not just chemical fertilizers which are considered too "hot." Big doses of organic material like uncomposted chicken or pigeon manure will also burn the leaves. Pigeon manure, by some curious twist of nature, contains properties which acidify the soil. So if you have access to these droppings, do make a compost pile and let it break down for a month or so, then apply it to the soil.

Feed the bushes you must. Try something new every two weeks. Watch the garden center ads in the local papers. Kmart's version of Miracle-Gro®—"K-Gro" is several dollars cheaper than the original product at its regular price and is basically the same formula. It has the advantage as being absorbed by the leaves as well as the roots so apply it in the early morning. Other products such as Schultz' Rose Powder is frequently on sale at local drug stores. An even stronger chemical formula, Schultz' must be hand mixed so it's

Charles de Mills, gallica (1840)

messier and easier to over concentrate. Read the flyers, shop wisely and follow the instructions printed on the labels.

This is my first season using a time-release fertilizer. So far it's producing great results. I'll add more organics over the course of the summer and another round of the time release stuff probably in late July.

Newly planted roses are more susceptible to strong chemical fertilizers than you may think. The root systems are inadequate to handle the heat of the jolt. The only cure for this man-made problem is water—given abundantly and repeatedly. If you have been overly loving with 16-16-16, you need to flush the soil a bit. Anyway, the only roses bothered by my busy May work schedule were ones which haven't quite hardened their canes to my cavalier feedings as they've only spent two or three months in the ground. They will survive this affliction and grow to be really good roses.

Remember. The plants don't know the difference between organic and chemical sources of fertilizer. They just want water, nutrients, sunshine, and abundant air.

STRAIGHTEN UP AND GROW RIGHT

The big task for me in summer is tending the garden as a whole. The individual health of each plant must be the primary concern of every rose enthusiast, but there are times, such as now, when growth of all plants should be evaluated. Assess their contribution to the design of your garden and ask yourself the following questions: are they in the right spot, are they getting what they need to do their best, are they the right rose for my yard?

In June, differences between the various rose cultivars and their response to locations in the garden become evident. These are serious concerns and crucial to the overall look of your beds and will eventually defeat your plans. When we were planting new varieties in our yards back in February and March, we weren't sure how they were going to respond. Even the roses we thought we knew from last year's plantings behave differently after spending a year in the garden.

Varieties grown on their own roots behave differently than grafted ones, especially in the first few years. There is less of a support system for the newly emerging canes to rest on. You may have to use some props until these new canes harden up. One November, I bought (from Vintage Gardens in Sebastopol) a terrific, salmon/carmine floribunda *Kathleen Ferrier* (1952). Kathleen Ferrier was a wonderful English contralto whose voice I adore and whose life ended—liver disease—far too early. She is remembered not

Ellen Willmott, hybrid tea (1936)

Kathleen Ferrier, floribunda (1952)

only by her remarkable recordings which I highly recommend but also by this truly glorious rose. It's a salmon-pink, semi-double shrub which is quite vigorous. This month, I had to lift up three of her long new canes and secure them to stakes. It appears this is just temporary until the cane hardens into the upright position. The same was true of the cream-colored, single petal hybrid tea *Ellen Willmott* (1936). Eventually, they will have sturdy canes but they may need help now.

One spring several years back, I tore out and discarded an old aluminum storage shed, cut down a plum tree and removed its stump, and pruned back the *Mermaid* (1918), *Rosa woodsii fendleri* and *Rosa brunonii* which over the course of seven years had accumulated on top of the six-foot-high shed nearly six more feet obliterating all sunlight except that at mid-day. These projects took place over the course of several weekends after my ultimate decision was made last fall. The response in the yard has been remarkable. One large flowered climber, *Golden Showers* (1956), emerged as a real champion providing ample dark yellow blooms to contrast with the ruffled purple flowers of the gallica *Charles de Mills* (1840) growing next to it. I had forgotten that I even owned *Golden Showers* it had become so obliterated by the formidable *Mermaid*! Several of the roses, *Electron* (1970), *Portrait* (1971), *Danaë* (1913), *Honorable Lady Lindsay* (1938), and *American Glory* (1991) growing in the center of the bed are at their best ever because of the addition of four more hours of full sunlight.

China Doll, polyantha (1946)

Over one Easter weekend, I extended my back bed into the yard eliminating about a foot of grass but allowing me to weed, feed and nurture along my 23-plant border of the delightful polyantha *China Doll* (1946). With the addition of sunlight, food, weeding, and water, these roses planted in my first year of gardening (1993) are the best they've ever been.

When originally put in, I had hoped that the *China Dolls* would cascade down and cover the slope of my raised beds. I was wrong. Their growth is upright and need the exact same care as other roses. My decision just made them harder to tend which meant they were lower down on my list of things to get to which meant they weren't often got to—and looked it.

Inevitably, I have put taller roses in front of shorter ones and planted wider varieties too close to their neighbors. Some darker colored flowers burn in the hot sun, some many petaled varieties won't sufficiently open because of the lack thereof. It takes time to evaluate; and, as in so many other aspects of life, quick decisions are often bad decisions. Think hard about how the plants will do in their new locations, but don't move them until winter.

Several other new varieties have developed too much growth low down on the plant. I have had to remove this by crawling around on my hands and knees. Many of the new roses, planted on the space left vacant by the now absent aluminum storage shed, big roses, and plum tree referred to above, have bloomed once now. I've tried to guide new growth in an expansive direction and therefore have pruned away inward growing shoots. I've also tried to keep as many leaves on the plant as possible. They are the ultimate success factor in future growth. On the newly planted hybrid teas and floribundas, I only remove the actual flowers and then wait to see where the plant wants to send out its next cane.

Once growth is apparent, I trim the cane and leaves down to above the healthiest new shoots. This practice really isn't necessary after the plant is more than six months old. It seems logical to me that the new plant keep as many of its leaves as possible until it builds a larger, better functioning root system.

Late blooming non-remontant roses are now at their peak. Several ramblers, *Apple Blossom* (1932) in particular, needs to be pruned back. It's a late bloomer and adversely affected by abundant, nonflowering spring growth. In order to make the best show of its huge clusters of flowers, I trim off much of the new spring growth or it will obliterate the flowers. I cut them off carefully so as not to rip up the flowering branches. It's visually much more appealing to see flowers on the top rather than buried among the canes. These old ramblers are so vigorous that after they bloom and get their annual pruning, there will be sufficient new growth to ensure next season's flowers.

The final buds of most OGRs are now opening. Having had most growing for a few years, I know which varieties need to be deadheaded and which will lose their spent flowers naturally. Several varieties don't form decorative hips which I might want for fall arrangements so I don't care about ridding them of past blooms. I also think you prolong the blooming period by eliminating the spent blooms. Having them gone certainly draws more attention to the flowers and buds which remain to open.

Many hybrid teas are in the midst of their second flush of flowers with abundant new growth supplying future blossoms. It's June, high rose tide is ebbing. Take the time necessary to enjoy the fruits of your labor.

Chicago Peace, hybrid tea (1962) a sport of Peace

HIGH WEED TIDE

I hate stooping. I find it much easier to get down on my hands and knees and crawl through the rose garden. I've cracked off rose buds aplenty, tore shirts too many times to count, but I have cleared up, cleaned up, and made attractive the entire garden. Especially important in a year when blackspot has ravaged the roses, circulating dry air will stem the spread of this disease. Remove all leaves and inconsequential growth from the bottom 18-inches of each large rose bush. Expose the bud union or basal portion of the rose to light and air. This promotes the development of new canes, directs the nutrients to places higher up on the plant, and decreases the incident of fungal diseases.

If I described May as "high rose tide," I must describe June and July as "high weed tide." Cans brimming with uprooted grass (nut, Bermuda, Kikuyu, crab, and some errant fescue), several dandelions and their relatives, purslane, sorrels, scarlet pimpernel, baby tears, and bindweed usually await the garbage truck every Thursday morning. I made it through most of the beds and will finish it off in July, when it most likely will be time to start again. The weeds are a byproduct of our extra watering and nourishment. Heavy mulch will stop many of the self sowing weeds. It won't, however, do anything to block the runners from invading grasses and bindweed.

My garden's top priority, after watering and feeding, is weeding. The shredded palette mulch I applied three seasons ago has all but vanished and begs to be replaced. It will save me so much time in the weeding department. A good layer, and I mean, four to six inches ought to take care of weeds germinating from seed. A thick layer of mulch will also cut down on evaporation and allow the rose roots to stay moist.

In the meantime, that is until I replace the mulch, I'm pulling weeds as fast as they sprout. After ten years of spraying RoundUp® on areas infested with nutgrass and bindweed, I've only permanently killed and set back rose bushes. RoundUp® has not killed the tiny bulb that is the source of nutgrass. Nor does it get all the roots involved in bindweed. My only recourse is to dig these invaders out and never let it develop. It's too hard to hoe in most of my garden beds so I have to get up close and personal with my bushes and their neighboring weeds.

The most abundant summertime weeds are nutgrass, a type of spurge which reseeds with a vengeance, several dandelion family members (some suffer terribly from rust but don't suffer enough to not reseed), and Scarlet Pimpernel, a kind of chickweed.

Please be careful to wear gloves when you are pulling weeds. Bindweed sap is an irritant. I discovered this very uncomfortably by pulling a bunch out with my bare hands and later touching my lips and nose. I didn't break out in a rash but it burned and itched like crazy.

Secret, hybrid tea (1992)

DEAD HEAD AND DISBUD

Take time to go through your garden and remove all spent blooms on your remontant roses. This, and a fist full of fertilizer, will encourage them to repeat again soon. Modern roses should be in bloom all the time. Generosity of flowers is a primary trait that rose hybridizers have been striving to achieve.

As summer passes by, many rose bushes have had three or four flushes of bloom. By midsummer, you can have flowers coming from a stem growing out of a stem, which itself is growing out of another stem, on down to the main cane coming from the bud union. When this happens, it's harder to pick a bouquet of long stem roses. So at the end of June, I deadhead the most vigorous hybrid teas much lower down than the first full leaf.

Encourage more blooms by removing all spent flowers before they develop hips. If you see rose hips on your plants, snip them off. Make your cut at least two leaflets down on the cane to the next outside bud eye. For most hybrid teas, if your canes are thinner than a pencil, get rid of the entire stem. Climbers tend to look their best when in total full bloom. After the flowers fade, get up there and get rid of the spent blooms and the nearly spent blooms. If canes are growing in the "wrong direction," remove them or weave it into the bush so that it climbs where it will get support.

Many of the hybrid teas and miniatures send up huge candelabras of flowers. The center most one which is often the largest bud on the shortest stem ought to be removed so that the buds further out will have more room to develop to perfection. Most hybrid teas send up a long cane with a terminal bud and one or two side buds. To get one truly awesome flower, pinch off the side buds or disbud the cane. This is very easy to do when the buds are young. Nothing bad will happen if you let them develop naturally, of course. It's merely a matter of esthetics and heightened visual impact in the garden.

MOVING ROSES IN MID-SEASON

What I advise: Don't dig up and move your roses around in the middle of the summer. Wait until the fall.

What I did: Dug up roses and moved them around in the garden in the middle of summer. I needed to get to the invasive Bermuda grass which took over the front rose bed. I shook the soil off of all the rose roots, pried loose the invading grass and oxalis bulbs, and made sure the roots of my *Old Blush* (1793) were free from entanglement. Then, I plunged the rose into a bucket of water into which I had put some Vitamin B1. I did the same with the companion plants. The day lilies I gave to a visiting neighbor with instructions to go plant them immediately. I divided up the Mexican Snowball (echeveria) to place back in a new and wider border. I discarded *All That Jazz* (1991): too big, too leggy, and too marginally interesting. It's a good rose, but I never did find the right spot for it. *Simplex* (1961) came out of the ground in pieces all of which I potted up for the next rose auction. I sifted and cleaned the soil, added several handfuls of blood meal, mounded it up and replanted *Old Blush* with some time release fertilizer.

Doris Morgan, miniatue (2002)

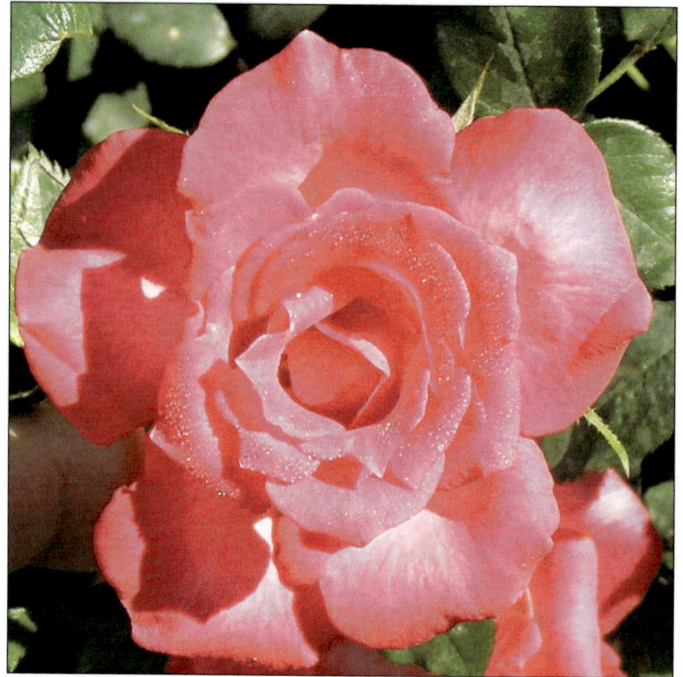

Simplex, miniature (1961)

STORM PROBLEMS IN THE GARDEN

The storm on January 1, 2006 wreaked havoc in my backyard. The west fence blew down completely bringing with it the roses which were tied to it for support. As it turned out, these roses were holding the fence up. The east fence was split in half with several posts sheared off at the base. A local handy man helped me clean up the yard and carry the fence away. In his enthusiasm for his work, four of my large climbers were pruned down to the ground. Ouch!

Later, I discovered when the fence contractors were redigging fence post holes, much new soil (FROM MY NEIGHBOR'S LAWN) ended up mixed into my rose bed. As the weeks went on, I realized that this soil was full of nutgrass kernels and bindweed—my worst affliction as RoundUp® only kills part of the weed. As the prolonged wet season continued into April and May and I couldn't stand up in the mucky rose bed long enough to get it removed, the grass sprouted and the bindweed raced up every rose cane it could find.

My attention was forced into the problem in my front yard. The purple leafed plum tree next to the house was now leaning at a 50° angle and ready to topple over. A two-day early May vacation took care of the tree and gave me a new location to plant two large roses and four miniatures which had been in pots in the back yard. With the tree gone, these new roses in the ground (Hybrid Perpetual *Baronne Prévost* (1842), Hybrid Tea *Apollo* (1972), and miniatures *This is the Day* (2003), *Doris Morgan* (2002), *Ring of Fire (1986)*, and *Sweet Diana* (2001) and the ones that had struggled in the tree's shade *Champagne Cocktail* (1983), *Honorine de Brabant* (1850), and particularly the floribunda *Kathleen Ferrier* (1952) have had their best season, hands down, ever! *Kathleen Ferrier* was repeatedly squashed by falling plum branches—the tree was twenty feet tall—but it didn't mind being misshapen and sent new growth all over. The blood meal also helped the others to produce basal breaks. I'm not missing this tree at all.

There was some blackspot on my roses, especially those that didn't get pruned. It's a lesson to us all. If you have roses that you repeatedly can't get around to pruning, maybe you're growing too many roses.

ADVICE FROM THE PAST

Snails often make great havoc among the choice kinds of wall-fruit, where they are not interrupted: they particularly frequent the apricot, nectarines, and peach trees, and will do mischief to those kinds of fruit, if not prevented.

These trees should be often looked over early in a morning, and in an evening, and after showers of rain: at which time these creeping vermin come forth from their holes to feed upon the fruit, and may then be readily taken and destroyed.

Thomas Mawe, London, 1797

Champagne Cocktail, hybrid tea (1983)

July

An occasionally sunny June will now be replaced by a typically cloudy coastal summer. Cool, wet morning fog burns off between mid-morning and noon permitting the intensely hot desert sun to penetrate and steam things up. Just when you've peeled off your flannel shirt and become adjusted to the hot sun, a sudden gust of wind about mid-afternoon heralds the sea-change and the fog blows back in with temperatures dropping into the fifties.

This is the ideal weather condition for powdery mildew. The absolute best way to avoid powdery mildew in our climate is to select varieties which don't get it at all. Go on a tour of local gardens. Various organizations offer them every spring and summer. If the roses are doing well, they have a good chance of being worth your time, too. Many gardeners have been growing roses for too long to cling to varieties which are high maintenance and low benefit.

I have tried spraying the leaves with vinegar. No change really. The roses that resist the disease, as long as they are well fed and watered, do well. Those that are afflicted by powdery mildew, mildewed just as severely. Those that are in between, perhaps did somewhat better with the acetic acid spray, but not well enough for me to continue.

I plan to spray in the morning with a summer dormant oil spray using the summer formula which puts just enough oil on the leaves to inhibit the mildew spores from clinging to the leaves. There's some sulfur in the oil as well and this also is a remedy for mildew.

COAT THE LEAVES WHEN POSSIBLE

Several practices have been followed since the 19th century that allow us to grow healthy roses and fight back the airborne fungal diseases: rust, powdery mildew, and blackspot—to name the most common plagues in rose horticulture.

I cherish a photograph I found in one of my older rose books of a man about a hundred years ago applying sulfur dust to his roses. He had hung from the end of a long stick an old rag bundle containing the dust and carefully tapped the stick with a shorter one up wind from the rose bush. The vibration from his tapping sent the fine powder inside the bundle out through the material to create a cloud of disease fighting protection which settled evenly on the rose leaves. It does discolor the leaves but the mildew is abated.

Taboo, hybrid tea (1988)

You need to protect the leaves before there is any sign of disease. Other methods of coating your rose leaves in early summer include spraying with a dormant summer oil, Volck Oil, or anything else which will inhibit the fungus spores from attaching themselves onto the leaf surface. Spraying with a solution of baking soda, oil and water has proven to be effective by altering the pH level on the leaf surface making the spores less able to propagate. Cloud Cover, a product developed to help plants in dry climates retain their water, is useful in our climate because its ingredients coat the leaves and make them too slick for the spores to hold on to. The American Rose Magazine reported that scientists in Denmark are experimenting with a once highly secret ingredient which sticks to the leaves, helps prevent disease, and is readily available—especially in Denmark—skim milk. Gregg Lowery of Vintage Gardens in Sebastopol reports that he has relatively little powdery mildew in his growing fields and gardens. He only uses overhead watering applied early in the day. The temperatures in Sebastopol dry the leaves off after a few hours. Down here in the summertime with the marine layer hovering over us, this practice would more than likely promote blackspot.

So what did I do when I saw plant after healthy plant covered in blackspotted leaves? I got on my hands and knees and pulled off all the leaves except the new shoots—of which there were plenty because of my regular feeding and watering. I gathered and discarded all the crumbled and fallen leaves. I tried sulfur dust right out of the can because I was in a hurry and it helped a little. The weather change helped even more though, and I was able to scramble a few entries for the fall rose show.

FERTILIZE AND CONDITION THE SOIL

July is a good time to put out more alfalfa pellets. This inexpensive dried plant product helps roses draw the nutrients from the soil. Toss a handful at the base of each plant and water generously. The pellets will swell as they absorb the water. Water again in a day or so, just to mix the soil and pellets together.

Look for fertilizer bargains. Our local Kmart ran a clearance of its product called Bloom Buster. It's marked 12-55-6 and is meant for a hose-end applicator. The high phosphorous gives flower production a real kick. It also contains all the minor and trace elements and can even be absorbed through the leaves. It's good to alternate it with Triple 16 and fish emulsion. The best fertilizing practice is to make sure your water your roses deeply BEFORE you apply the nutrients. Store fertilizers in air tight containers and give them to your roses regularly.

TRIM UP YOUR ONCE BLOOMERS

My one-time bloomers are now at their peak. I have noticed that many of them especially the big climbers (*Newport Fairy* 1908) and *Rosa russelliana* 1824, to name two), like to send new long canes shooting right up through their flush of flowers. I have no problem cutting this new growth off below the flower line so that the bush presents better. It also helps to contain these guys who want to be as big as they can be—regardless of the size of your yard.

All your once blooming roses should be cut back as soon as the final flowers fade. I now know how large I want the ones I grow to be and I will cut them down significantly. I shape them as much as I can, first. Then, I look them over for any dead, or soon to be dead, wood and get rid of it. If I break any of the green canes in the process, I remove everything above the break and cut down until the next outside bud eye.

I want these grand old roses to spend the rest of the growing season producing new healthy canes from which the flowers of next spring will emerge. Even the few I grow

which I want to continue to climb up into the neighbor's pine tree need some shaping lower down.

One spring, I had to move *Félicité Parmentier*, an alba from 1834 which is THE most fragrant rose in my yard. It isn't the world's most vigorous plant and had ended up being crushed under a stack of piled up broken fence. When I finally dug it up, it was two canes and some peach fuzz roots. It's in a black, one-gallon container, but isn't making a speedy recovery. This bush was eight feet tall and about five wide, once. Several years ago, I dug it out when I demolished a tin shed next to it. I got as much of the root ball as I could and thought I had quite a lot of it still intact when I immediately transplanted it. I trimmed it back so as to make it more manageable and cut off all unnecessary, dead, and broken wood. There were about five or six leaves appearing in alba fashion at the ends of each cane.

That year, we had had a heat wave and dry spell. It sent this bush into severe shock. All the leaves withered despite my watering and misting. I waited two weeks and cut it back again removing all the dried leaves and shriveled up canes. I waited two months and cut it back to within a foot of the bud union. Nothing happened. I wrote *Félicité Parmentier* off and contemplated what might take its place. When I returned from a mid-June vacation that year it had, after four months of petulance, decided to forgive me and sprouted. It did so well I put it against the fence. Again, it withered and looked pretty sad. Alas, it died.

Félicité Parmentier, alba (1834)

USE A GOOD UTILITARIAN MULCH

I spent three days distributing ten cubic yards of fairly course mulch all over my yard. It appears to be partially composted pallets. It's very attractive and heavy enough to be around for a year or so before it disintegrates into the soil. With such raw mulch, I want to make sure that I add adequate fertilizer. Heavy sawdust and wood chips use up nitrogen in the soil as they decompose.

In addition to the attractiveness of its uniform appearance, a good mulch has the following benefits. It inhibits, if not stops altogether, the germination of weed seeds. I've spread the mulch at least three to four inches thick all around my roses. Because of the coarseness of the mulch, it allows water and fertilizer—including alfalfa pellets to sink down into the soil. The larger chips float to the surface, hiding the smaller chunks.

A good mulch also keeps the soil protected from any swings in the weather. Several of my roses planted in the ground were slowed down, if not damaged, by insufficient watering. The burned edges of leaflets usually is an indication that the rose hasn't received an adequate and constant water supply. As I hand water the entire yard, my roses can fall victim to my inadvertent lapses of care.

AT RISK LOCATIONS

Examine your rose garden and decide which areas are "at risk" locations. I've decided that usually good performing bushes which aren't responding well are missing something. Too little light or too little water are often the culprits. Tree roots will also inhibit a plant's growth. Address these problems by finding alternate locations.

I struggled with a badly growing *Just Joey* (1972) for three years. It's a fabulous rose and one that usually does okay in our area. (I caught myself yelling at it one sunny morning. "I've given you food, water, and the best sunshine in the yard. What else do you want?") I've decided that it just didn't like our summertime temperatures.

Then I put it into a 5 gallon pot and lightened up the soil. It put out new canes and two great looking six-inch blousy flowers. As it turns out, I gave *Just Joey* to a friend who was rebuilding her mother's home in Dubrovnik, Croatia. I pruned it down to three eight inch canes and several good roots, wrapped it in layers of thick plastic bags, and sent it to Europe! That Adriatic climate has done wonders for *Just Joey* and compliments, I'm told, abound.

I have two *Belinda*s (1936) which got placed in the worst possible location. (I guess I was tired and just wanted to get them in the ground.) I planted them too close to the north side of a fence and underneath my *Madame Alfred Carrière*

—she a real sun hog. It's time to move the *Belinda*s but I'm not quite sure where. *Belinda* is a hybrid musk and they are supposed to be shade tolerant. This variety isn't really. It suffers from blackspot and just isn't happy. It has remained in its original location. It looks great in the spring and it's down hill from there. But I have no better spot for it except the trash.

A third "at risk" area of my yard is along the rose bed's edges. These outside facing roses love their sunny and airy location. They appreciate the terrific drainage they receive as well. However, the combination of sun and drainage means they must get more water than the rest of the garden. They haven't been doing so well and this, I've decided, is the reason why. They are also what most visitors see and are a testament to my gardening abilities. So I must pay more attention to them.

Just Joey, hybrid tea (1972)

EVALUATE YOUR ROSE BUSHES NOW

The roses planted last season haven't developed sufficiently enough to determine their worthiness. It's too soon to judge most roses after only a few months in the ground, but after twelve months, the rose has had long enough to behave and should give you some indication of its happiness.

A rose will develop a root system during its initial time in the ground. I prevent most of the flowers from developing on newly planted roses so that the bush itself can spend time expanding its root system and multiplying its leaves. All roses which had recently been planted and had long stems cut from them three months later, truly had their development slowed down. Perhaps it's better to pinch off all the buds and let the leaves and roots go to work producing a functional bush before you cut off its healthiest new growth.

I have already placed a few roses on my "to be removed" list. These specific ones are just not growing quickly enough to suit me but they are also suffering from the commonest diseases. I also have planted some roses which are too tall or too wide for where they were placed in the garden and need to be moved to another location.

Surprising even myself, I have removed roses because I just didn't like the color, or the shape, or some other distinctive quality such as repeated production of blind shoots—a cane develops and shoots out leaves but never produces a flower. If you are certain the plant is getting adequate food, light, and water, then this is a definite characteristic of the rose. The best way to evaluate each rose growing in your garden is simple.

Ask yourself the following questions:

- Have I stopped and admired the roses on this bush at least once during the past 12 months?

- Have I picked a rose from this bush and used it as a gift or house decoration?

- Has this rose received everything I could give it in the way of water, food, light, and air AND it still has one or more of the most common afflictions to a severe degree?

- Have I had to cut back canes on this bush because they were invading the roses planted next to it?

- Is there some sentimental reason why I will make an extra effort to keep this rose going?

SUMMER WORK ON ROSES

If your roses are not in full bloom at this time, something is seriously wrong. The long summer days and (perhaps) warm weather should combine with your ample feeding and watering to produce masses of blooms. Your roses should be showing off.

There are always some weather set backs. The summer can be gray along the coast, the evenings damp, and the blackspot a true affliction. On the other hand, now is a great time to amend your soil. So many roses which aren't producing new canes and flowers at this time of year are growing in poor soil. Add some compost or cow manure to underperforming roses. Give your shrubs another helping of alfalfa pellets. Pour some fish emulsion on the roses. All of these items take time to get their nutrients into the soil.

Belinda, hybrid musk (1936)

ROSES GROWN IN POTS

Know the difference between roses you are trying to root and already rooted roses you want to grow in a container. They need different kinds of soil. The former type is coarser with lots of space for air so the baby roots won't rot. This soil has a large amount of Perlite and sand mixed in it with large chunks of organic material. The latter is more loamy. It should have finer compost and some clay which helps to keep the soil inside the container and not washing out the drain holes.

After July vacations, I found that my real problems occurred with the roses which I had recently rooted myself or purchased as rooted cuttings. I had removed them from their original plugs—the square pots used to root them back at the nursery—and put them in somewhat larger black pots. The soil I used was commercial potting mix which tends to have plenty of sand, Perlite, and compost in it. I wanted them to continue to build a root system before I placed them in the ground. Some of these roses were ready for the ground and were just waiting for a spot in the garden bed to open up. Some had been waiting longer than their gardener noticed.

If you water your pots and see the water immediately drain right through, you've got problems. Either the root ball is so tight and constrained that the water can't penetrate it and runs down the inside pot wall or half of your soil has washed away and the plant can't retain any moisture. Whatever the cause, fix it. Add more soil. Add finer soil. Put the rose in a larger pot. Pot-bound plants are at the greatest risk of drought damage.

So I returned home to see all roses in the ground prospering but most of those in pots suffering. Some were totally dried out. The leaves had all gone brown. A normal person would have just tossed out the dead looking things and fired the watering crew.

Danaë, hybrid musk (1913)

However, my crew were volunteers. Ever try to fire someone who has done you a favor? Even my next-door neighbor insisted on reporting to me that my crew hadn't done a very good job. "Stick your finger in and it's bone dry below," he said. "So why didn't you water?" I thought and forced a smile. But I said nothing, of course, and just thanked everyone profusely for their care and concern. "Great job!"

I got my stretcher and carried the dried out potted roses into the intensive care portion of my potting shed. I resisted the temptation of cutting the roses back immediately. Instead, I examined each and replenished the soil where needed. I watered them all intensely and repeated the watering every other day or so. After a week, I noticed that many of the dead-looking canes had been pumped up to bright green and several bud eyes were swollen.

At this point, I gave them some weak fertilizer and some Vitamin B1 and put them into dappled light. Another week saw them produce new leaves in the still living portion of the plant.

I then snipped off all dead canes. I also shaped them up again so that they were growing evenly. I hadn't thought there was anything left alive and am so glad I didn't just pitch them out though they looked bad. Now, there's a renewed commitment on my part to find a more permanent home for them. Really, roses want to be in the ground.

Take a moment to see how roses behave when planted in the ground. You should notice that the roots tend to grow down less than they grow out. Most of us have acquired nursery pots that are taller than they are wide. Roses want containers which are the opposite dimension. The diameter at the top of the pot should be longer than the height of the pot. These containers are available but hard to come by. You can find halved wine barrels and redwood containers which are the correct shape and which show off roses best.

PRUNE OLD GARDEN ROSES NOW

I spent a full day pruning back my *Charles de Mills* (1840, gallica), *Henri Martin* (1863, moss), *Kazanlik* (before 1612, damask), *Salet* (1854, perpetual moss), *Danaë* (1913, hybrid musk), and *Duchesse de Brabant* (1857, tea). Most had not had a good cane-cut in two or three years and it was way overdue. The more I pruned back the more deadwood I found and removed. I also cut back all of the inconsequential growth and many of the ground-level, lateral canes.

I discovered that a couple of these horizontal canes had been close enough to the soil and covered by mulch that they had rooted. I dug them up, gave them some shape, and potted them to give away. I also thinned out these bushes.

The yellowing canes which will eventually be deadwood are now gone. The older canes which didn't look like they had much left in them are pruned away. What's left are the healthiest canes trimmed back to just below the fence, instead of three feet above with more falling over. I think that that neighbor likes me more now. There is no harm in keeping a rose bush which could grow larger kept down to a more suitable size. I care about these plants. They are genuinely healthy and produce flowers abundantly when it's their season. But, I don't want them to be the only roses in the yard. Having done this bit of trimming up, I have identified others which I want to tackle later today.

July and August are great times to trim Old Garden Roses because time exists for these beauties to put out fresh growth which will produce flowers next spring. The yard bears its newly shorn roses well. It looks sparse but will fill in quickly.

Salet, moss (1854)

I made the decision earlier this year to remove several larger roses in my yard and replace them with bushes which will bloom more frequently, behave better, and not grow so large. The telling moment was when I heard a chain saw coming from the neighbor's yard. Then I saw its vicious blade coming up over the fence trimming back all of the trespassing old rambler. The rose was *Apple Blossom* (1932), a terrific but very large arbor rose developed by Luther Burbank. It was stunning when I saw it in full bloom up at Heirloom Garden Roses in Oregon—a massive display. Its blooming period is rather short though and arrives on California's Central Coast at about the time when wet summer fog becomes the daily weather pattern. In another location it fills an important niche because it does bloom later in the summer than most of the older European roses. It also wasn't a good candidate for a north facing wall. Its lower canes were naked and covered in green moss. While removing it, I realized it had sent several long canes into its neighbor, the disease-free moss rose *Henri Martin* (1863). Trying to separate the tangle was a chore and I ended up ripping *Henri Martin* away from the fence as well. I used the opportunity to prune this terrific moss rose and secure it tightly back onto the fence while there are still some months of growing time left. It only blooms on year-old wood, so I was very selective about which canes fell to the shears. But now, its shape is greatly improved. I hadn't really done anything to the plant since it went into the ground about six seasons back. It isn't a fast grower like *Apple Blossom* but its display this year was spectacular. (I also won the Dowager Queen Award at the Rose Show with it.)

Do spend some time looking over your Old Garden Roses. It's past the time to prune them back hard. But if you find a spare moment, it's good to get rid of any dried up flowering stalks and insignificant growth.

FERTILIZE IF YOU ARE HOME TO WATER

About two weeks prior to my July departure for back East, I stopped all fertilizers. There's no point in encouraging new growth if you are not going to be around to provide the essential element of water. What's more, you could run the risk of fertilizer burn.

When I returned, I noticed the yard had some flowers and generally looked very nice. With the addition of some Triple 16, however, it sprung back into action. The color of the roses was more intense. More new bud eyes were sprouting and canes were growing longer and healthier looking.

Many of the leaves produced in the late spring have now yellowed. Only half have gone the rest of the way and dropped to the ground. So I spent some time while deadheading pulling off the ugly yellow leaves and the leaves showing signs of blackspot. **Remember.** Dispose of these spore-bearing hazards immediately and discard the refuse away from your rose bed.

I took advantage of the trimming up time to replace some of the jute twine I used to secure the Old Garden Roses to the fence or to the post they grow on.

ELIMINATING POOR PERFORMERS

I had an *Iceberg* (1958) growing next to a fence. Its leaves—those that survived the blackspot attack—were yellow and sickly. Something was suddenly wrong with the plant but I hadn't figured out what. So I took my shears and pruned it way back leaving it leafless. I had been watering it and feeding it like all the other roses. Perhaps it was just too crowded growing between a very healthy *Lavender Lassie* (1960) and a *Climbing Chrysler Imperial* (1957). This severe pruning is a test. If *Iceberg* responds with a new set of healthy leaves, it stays. If it just sits there, barely alive, it goes.

Update. The badly treated *Iceberg* did not want to be in that spot. So I put what was left of it in a black five gallon pot and set it aside. Set it aside for five years! I just couldn't find the right spot. Then I forgot its existence, in spite of its occasional flowering bursts. It nearly fried twice when I went on vacation. But it came back, twice. In 2010, I decided to put it back in the ground. A spot had opened up and I didn't

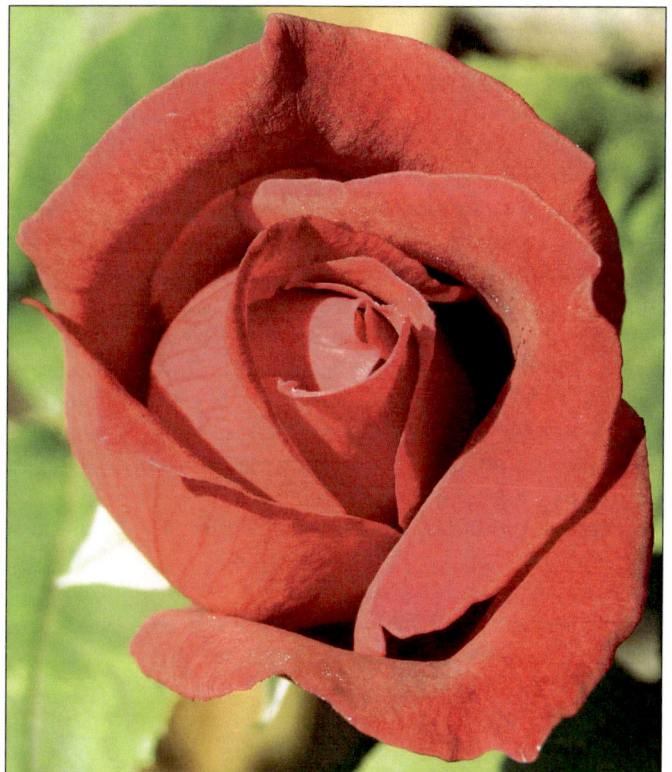

Chrysler Imperial, climbing hybrid tea (1957)

Disco Dancer, floribunda (1984)

have anything sexier to go there so I planted it, fed it, and watered it. *Iceberg* bloomed once. Dropped its petals and spent the rest of its time moving in. It doubled its size in two months sending out luxuriant apple-green, pointed leaves. I dusted it with some sulfur and it never developed its characteristic July powdery mildew. It's now set to bloom its heart out. Roses are indeed a remarkably easy plant to grow, especially *Iceberg*.

Pride 'n' Joy (1991), a terrific orange miniature, was getting overcrowded so it went to a pot, as did *Golden Halo* (1991), a yellow miniature which also needed to get out of the way of a larger hybrid tea, *Abracadabra*. Both spent two seasons in pots until I found spots for them. *Golden Halo*, by the way, is not one of the "Halo" miniatures developed by Ralph Moore. *Halo Today* (1994) is and I just rediscovered her growing beneath a prominent fiery-colored *Disco Dancer* (1984) which has two-stepped all over that part of the garden. Also hidden underneath is *Secret Recipe* (1995). This is one of Ralph Moore's novelties. It's a modern moss, striped miniature. I love it and should find a more accommodating spot. While I'm on the subject of Ralph Moore's great creations, let me put a good word in for *Chic-a-dee* (1990). It's a pink lightly variegated, multi-petaled miniature which has a sweet scent and happy personality. It's very disease resistant and stays quite small.

It's harder to remove occasional performers. I don't spray chemicals on my roses, and even this season if I were a sprayer, I wouldn't have got around to it. Therefore, many of the hybrid teas I grow (and they are mostly the ones which were introduced more than thirty years ago) have suffered from powdery mildew. The fungus grows beneath the leaves and results in crinkly, wavy leaves, extraordinarily long canes between the leaves, and poor flower production.

All three problems are reduced light and variable humidity issues. September and October's warm sunshine will change it all. Look to the future and we'll make it through the summer doldrums.

GET RID OF YOUR BAD ROSES

This will mean different roses to each of us. But I wielded my shovel mercilessly and went after roses which just weren't for me. Many of them have had multiple stays of execution. I removed *French Lace* (1980) and *Johnnie Walker* (1982); both for different reasons. *French Lace* wanted more heat and *Johnnie Walker* didn't bloom enough or show sufficient vigor. It spent too much time in a drunken stupor.

After three weeks of minimal care, these particular specimens looked their worst and I decided to remove them. You can't call me totally heartless. Most of the ones I decided to discard had been moved about in the garden, which can be a remedy. Most had been in my possession for at least four years. Sometimes it does take that long for a rose to demonstrate its full worth.

It's so important to plant suitable roses and now is a good time to plan for next year. Many nurseries are running clearance sales. These plants were potted up back in January or February and will be so happy to be in the ground. If you plant them now, they'll have a great time developing a strong root system to tie them over the winter. Next year's blooms will be spectacular.

You may even get them to put out a full flush of fall flowers, if you buy them now and get them in the ground before Labor Day.

I dug up *Remember Me* (1984)—a rose which originally held such promise and replaced it with *Julia's Rose* (1976)—purchased while on the MBRS Memorial Day tour to Sebastopol's Vintage Gardens. I decided that *Remember Me* had to go (it mildews and rusts in North Salinas and its interesting orange/russet colored flowers fry in the brief intense mid-day sunshine!). I thought that a new rose—one that was on its own roots ought to use the rest of the summer developing a good strong root system and some healthy, long canes. My thoughts are already on next year's roses!

Walk through your garden with a pair of newly sharpened pruners and snip away the spent flowers and hips. Toss the discards in a bucket. Don't let hips form on hybrid teas, floribundas, or any other repeat blooming roses. They reduce the flowers in count and size. Rake up dropped petals, leaves, and pulled weeds which might be littering the ground around your roses. Keep the top of the soil free of plant refuse. It harbors too many disease spores and insect eggs.

Now is the time to examine your garden. It should be at its peak. If your hybrid teas, miniatures, and floribundas aren't blooming, feed, water and deadhead.

Summertime Checklist

WATER

❑ Each bush needs water once or twice a week. This can sneak up on you, especially in a period of heavy fog when everything seems perfectly wet. The roses are growing in full force and they need deep watering.

❑ Larger bushes need more water than smaller ones. This seems rather obvious, however, the reverse can also be true. A well established (four to five-year-old bush) planted in good sandy loam can actually go for a longer period between waterings than smaller plants. In fact, some rose growers stop watering and feeding their established plants after the rose shows and garden tours end. Established roses won't grow without water, but they aren't likely to die. Smaller roses will suffer and die as their roots don't go down as deep.

❑ Roses in black plastic pots need more water than those in the ground. The roses that I have lost have truly been ones in pots that didn't get watered enough. Black absorbs heat which causes the roses to grow more and need more water. It's a double whammy. So water the pots well. Also check to make sure that the soil hasn't washed out of the drainage holes. The top of the plant may look like it has plenty of soil but actually the soil has been gradually washing out the bottom. If you find yourself watering a plant in a pot too frequently, it's probably time to put that bush in a bigger container!

❑ Roses in terra cotta pots need constant observation as do roses which are in containers they have outgrown. If you can't keep up with this water monitoring process, you probably are growing more roses than you should.

❑ Roses given large amounts of fertilizer need large amounts of water. The tell tale signs of this are burned and dead leave edges. When dying of drought and dehydration, the outer most parts of the plant suffer worst. Drooping rose buds and cane ends are clear signs the plant is dying of thirst.

❑ Overhead watering done in the early morning tends to reduce powdery mildew. The spray on the leaves interrupts the toeholds of the spores, so to speak, and they slip off. Oddly, the molds hate being wet.

❑ Leaf surfaces which remain wet for more than seven hours and then dry off will likely suffer from fungal diseases. Good air circulation helps the rose dry itself faster than the spores can sprout. There should be sufficient space around your roses to allow you to get to all sides of them. The bushes will be better shaped as well.

DEADHEADING

❑ Good pruning starts with sharp shears. Spend the money on a good sharpening tool and quality shears with changeable blades. Felco tools are the best and are the most expensive. They are available at high-quality garden centers. They are worth every cent you pay.

❑ Removing spent flowers from repeat blooming roses stimulates more flowers. The faster you do this, the faster the blooms will reappear.

❑ Carry a five-gallon pail with you to deposit all spent petals, trimmed canes and dead leaves. Don't let these fall to the ground and re-infest your plant with disease spores.

Matangi, shrub (1978)

Incognito, miniature (1995

❑ Many one-time blooming Old Garden Roses want a good pruning after they finish blooming unless you are interested in the hips providing fall color.

❑ Hybrid teas want to have their flowers removed down to the first five-leaflet leaves with an outside facing bud eye. The three exceptions to this rule are very vigorous plants which are blooming up too high, bud eyes sprouting from more than three stem-on-stems, and newly planted young roses. Go ahead and prune the vigorous ones down further to a more manageable height and merely pinch off the spent bloom and hip on newly planted, younger roses. The idea here is that these bushes need every green leaf they own to help them grow big and strong.

❑ Remove the side buds from your hybrid teas allowing only one bloom per stem. This creates a more attractive flower shape, larger flowers, and a quicker repeat cycle.

❑ Floribundas want to have their entire candelabra of blossoms removed. If you do a mass removal, even before some of the flowers are completely finished, you will have a mass repeat of bloom in six or so weeks.

❑ If you wish to allow hips to develop on one-time bloomers, pick off all of the spent petals and discard them. Depending on the variety, brown and drying petals usually aren't the most attractive feature of an OGR. I will sit and carefully pull off the spent petals on the varieties which are most visible. It's not hard and looks so much better.

❑ Shape your plants now for ultimate health. Open up the inside of each bush. Remove weak undergrowth often caused by extra rainfall and darker, cooler days. Many roses produce blind shoots. Greenery which didn't end in a flower. Remove all such growth. They are useless and won't ever produce flowers.

NUTRITION

❑ Apply an all purpose fertilizer such as MiracleGro® which has the minor and trace elements plants need to grow at least once every summer month. MiracleGro® has gotten a bad rap for killing some insects and worms beneficial to the garden ecology. Don't worry about it. Use it and dilute it. Water aplenty. Life in your garden will not end because of chemical fertilizers.

❑ If you can reach the soil beneath your roses, now is a great time to add blood meal. It's an intensely good source of nitrogen. Don't overdose and always work it into the soil.

❑ Hit your freshly deadheaded hybrid teas, floribundas, and climbers as well as your pruned Old Garden Roses hard with a handful of handful of Triple 16. Water it in well and repeat in two or three weeks. Stand back as they produce the flowering canes of the future. They need it especially after you've completely deadheaded a bush.

❑ Bury your steak bones down in the soil at the feet of your roses. The nutrients they contain take months to be depleted and the rose roots will use them on an as needed basis.

❑ Bury your banana peels and fish scraps. Both rot away quickly and as long as you don't have critters interested in playing in them, you won't have any worries.

❑ Give some fish emulsion to your plants and some extra alfalfa meal. Earthworm castings are a great way for your plant to strengthen its nutritional intake. All organic fertilizers seem to intensify leaf color and help the rose store energy in its canes.

❑ Cat kills bird, rat, gopher. Gardener buries bird, rat, gopher beside large rose bush. Rose bush loves cat.

WEEDING

❏ Pull out weeds before they flower, the most important weed rule.

❏ Never pull out bindweed, second most important rule. Never, ever let bindweed bloom. After knocking several roses for a loop with my RoundUp® spraying and still not clearing the garden of bindweed, I'm revising my statement to read: pull out bindweed just to keep it from flowering. If all you can manage is to pull it out, that's better than giving up.

❏ Spray nutgrass, Bermuda grass, and bindweed with RoundUp® or other herbicides only if growing close to but not in the rose bed. Make sure that you choose the version that kills broad leafed plants and grasses. Protect your roses from the over spray. It really does them damage which won't necessarily show up immediately. Use a piece of cardboard as a barrier to protect neighboring plants. Spray on a windless morning.

❏ Dig out plantains, dandelions, and crab grass.

❏ Pull out anything and everything else.

❏ Save time weeding by using four to six inches of dense mulch. No weed seeds should be germinating underneath your roses.

Climbing Talisman, hybrid tea (1930)

❏ Cheap mulch like shredded palettes lasts two or three seasons and gives your garden a professional look.

❏ Put a barrier between lawns and rose gardens. Grass is hard to remove from underneath roses. Best advice is don't let it get near. Dig a one foot deep trench. Take the ashes from your barbeque grills and fireplaces and spread them about where you do not want anything to grow. A line of dense wood ash will definitely prevent anything from growing. This is particularly useful as a barrier between the garden and a wild field or beneath a fence to prevent what your neighbor is growing on the other side to cross under.

SPRAYING

❏ Wash your leaves down with a hose at least twice a month. Do it early in the day and let the leaves dry off. It will clean the dust off the leaf surface and make the plants look and act healthier.

❏ Apply a summer dormant oil on the roses which get powdery mildew. I find a little bit of sulfur helps them resist this disease. Dusts are available. Roses with severe issues with powdery mildew or rust or botrytis (never have their buds open fully) need to grow in a place other than YOUR yard.

❏ Good gardeners learn to throw out non-performing plants. This past spring, several roses were eliminated from my garden, *French Lace* (1980), *Double Delight* (1977), and *Tribute* (1983). I will most likely dig out my *climbing Talisman* (1930) and *Maiden's Blush* (before 1400). Both have been in my garden from its start in 1993—but that's not a good enough reason to keep a plant whose size is great and whose other attributes are not. My taste in roses has moved toward plants which keep their petals, don't grow to unmanageable sizes, have healthy green foliage and lots of flowers and readily open in hot or cool weather.

❏ Use dish washing liquid in a spray bottle on roses hit by aphids. Use pyrethene which is a chrysanthemum extract on the severest cases. Use neem oil on combination problems. I have seen very few insect pests in my garden during the past several seasons since I've stopped spraying any pesticide. I haven't yet even seen a cucumber beetle. Those look like green lady bugs but they put holes in the flowers. If you see them, kill them. I had some thrips earlier on but they were eaten by minute pirate bugs. I had a case of leaf cutter bees, but nothing to worry about. White flies show up at the end of the season and hover around the *Rosa eglanteria* (before 1554) but aren't much of a concern as the garden is shutting down anyway. If they arrive sooner, spray them with neem oil.

❏ Squash snails whenever you encounter them. With a cold winter and relatively dry spring, I was hoping they wouldn't be such a problem. Seems like there's a enough watering going on in the neighborhood to keep them reproducing with no end. I have killed buckets of these nasty devils. They slime all over the roses—not to mention the garden, the patio, the outdoor furniture, and the picture windows. They use some of the lower leaves on roses to hide from the dry times. It's another reason why I pull off all the growth from the lower ten inches or so. (In wet seasons, I've even seen snails scaling up the canes and attaching themselves onto rose petals!)

COMPANION PLANTS

❏ Choose companion plants carefully. Avoid anything that will spread too much, too quickly. Roses hate the competition and really don't want anything else growing close to them, especially down by their bud union.

❏ My favorite companions are spring bulbs. They bloom without interfering with the roses as the roses are all pruned down. The leaves of most bulbs have dried up and gone away by the time the roses are getting all the attention. I also like *Echeverria*. It blooms in spring and makes quite an attractive foil. When it gets too big, you can easily thin out the succulent rosettes.

❏ Companion plants can hide more invasive plants such as bindweed and Bermuda grass. You won't notice that the grass is growing underneath the species geranium until it shows up tangled in your rose bed.

PUT YOURSELF IN THE GARDEN

❏ If you do not have multiple spots where you can actually sit among the roses and admire your work, you need to create some. There's no substitute for personal observation. This year, my garden bench which has been a portable treasure and constant companion finally gave way beneath me into an unrepairable pile of fire wood.

❏ My broken bench did not have spindle legs, but instead had a flat board end which was less likely to penetrate soft soil. I replaced it with a curiously strong, black plastic step stool from Kmart. Its base is a broad and continuous rim which does not sink into the soft bed. Buy one.

❏ Make sure that you have sources of water in your garden. Birds love a good drink. Standing water allows insects to breed. Make sure you drain and refill the containers every two or three days. Most birds will snack on insects and spiders at this time of year and deposit fertilizer in the ground. If you put a bird feeder in your yard, keep it out in the grass and away from the rose bed.

With the final flowers of my *Rosa setigera* (1810), the prairie rose, finally fallen, the last evidence of our spring time bloomers has ended. Most of the hybrid teas, floribundas, and other repeat bloomers have produced three beautiful flushes of bloom and have never been completely void of a flower. In August, I try to shape up the plants and get ready for the fall blooming cycle. I usually have flowers through to December, but the last really heavy bloom will take place in September and October.

Escapade, floribunda (1967)

August

Having given my roses some extra special care to make sure the garden showed as well as it could for the summer rose tour, I've now cut back on the frequency of feeding. I've gone from a little something every week to something less every couple of weeks. I'll keep this practice up until mid-October. I'll continue to spray every couple of weeks, too. I use a commercial dormant oil spray which contains calcium polysulfide.

With the extra amounts of food, there's lots of new growth and in our cool coastal summers that part of the plant is ripe for powdery mildew. The sulfur changes the pH level on the leaf surface, increasing its acidity which inhibits powdery mildew from getting established. The oil also sticks to the leaf and spores can't get a foothold, making the plant further resistant to fungal diseases which can't get established. Once the leaves get a bit older, they get tougher and are more resilient.

CARING FOR ROSES WHEN YOU FEEL YOU COULD CARE LESS

Gardening from June to August on California's Central Coast is often a challenge. When you wake up and it's cold, cloudy and damp, you don't feel much like going outside—let alone standing around and hand watering. And yet, the chores are there waiting and won't go away.

After opening my garden for various tours this past spring, traveling on several trips for the rest of the summer, and dealing with at-home weekends of foggy weather turning suddenly into scorchingly hot and humid mid-days then blowing away again by the approaching marine layer, I wasn't much motivated to be in the garden tending to the needs of my too numerous roses.

When your activity and interest levels are in a slump, don't despair. Better weather is coming soon. Here are some absolutely imperative tasks that you just can't overlook.

WATERING POTTED ROSES

I've probably killed more roses this way than any other. With my excellent care when the season is young and my extraordinary ability to put roses in pots which are way too small, the young, new roses have spread their roots and pretty

Tahitian Sunset, hybrid tea (2007)

much used up all the available space in the can. They need to be put in the ground, but I haven't decided where yet. They must get MUCH more water and I'll find a brief moment to get it to them. I really like to drench potted roses, but you also have to monitor the bottom of the pot to make sure the soil hasn't washed away.

Another problem I've encountered involves the soil I use to root a cutting and the soil I use to plant a cutting that takes. Too frequently, the sandy soil washes out of the pot and hasn't enough organic matter to hold the moisture. This is a double problem easily taken care of by repotting the entire bush into a better soil medium.

WEEDING NEVER ENDS

Although my various visitors saw nary a noxious weed during my open gardens, I pooped out entirely on this onerous task during the summer.

Do you remember me talking about the heavy mulch and how that was going to save me? Well, it works well to stop weeds sprouting from seeds. But, I now have huge sections of my rose bed covered by bindweed and nutgrass. Both of which emanate from the soil and had no problem finding the light of day through six inches of shredded palettes. I may just pull up some of the more visible ones so I don't have to look at them again. I will dig out those plants like callas, arums, and stray gladiola bulbettes which I know I can.

DEADHEADING IS ALL ABOUT THE FUTURE

When September and October roll around, we can get a really nice repeat bloom from all of our roses. But, we must deadhead during the summer to get the new growth. If you have the time and the weather permits, it's important to do a methodical job in removing all spent flowers and hips.

My circumstances haven't provided ideal conditions. I have a fairly large *Joseph's Coat* growing outside my kitchen. Its second flush of flowers and growth nearly covered the window and bloomed beautifully in July. For the past three weeks, I've watched the petals turn brown, gather cobwebs, grow walnut-size hips, collect spider webs, and totally embarrass me into stopping what I was doing and go trim them back. But I couldn't quite ever get there. I just kept forgetting. Thank goodness I didn't have house guests.

Joseph's Coat, large flowered climber (1969)

What the four *Joseph's Coats* (1969) got wasn't deadheading in the text book sense, like I usually advise people. I had to get the yard waste container out to the street one morning so as I was dragging it past these roses, I took my gloved hands, gathered up bunches of flopping canes, and hedge-cut them with a pair of shears. It took about ten seconds and I was done. I did wonder as I approached the curb with the can why I hadn't done this sooner. I'll give them a good drink and I'll get another great bloom from them in October.

SUMMER PRUNING

With a fantastic rose spring we can have and the time release fertilizer I put out, I've seen really good growth on most of my roses. As a result, I've had them invade the roses planted next to them, the walkways and pathways, and shoot straight up to the sky.

I made a pact when I first started gardening that I wouldn't allow a plant to grow onto a sidewalk and cause me to move into the grass to get by. I've kept my word and pruned many of my miniatures growing beside my front walk and some of the Old Garden Roses growing in my rose bed severely. Part of gardening is shaping plants to conform to an overall design, whether stated or not.

My *Kazanlik*, an old damask rose from before 1620 and one that is grown for the scent market throughout the world, had become an enormous plant; way too big for where it was. So on one day in July, I took advantage of a few minutes of sunshine and trimmed it back by a little more than half. It was a desperate act, but I got rid of the leaves with rust, spindly growth, and canes growing through the middle of the plant. It's a one time bloomer but has already produced ample new growth so that next spring's flowers will be assured. The remontant roses growing around it have responded with the best flowering they've had since *Kazanlik* became a neighbor.

RE-STAKING ROSES

With the weight of summer growth and the use of wooden stakes I've had to go about the garden and replace stakes which have rotted. The roses lost a few canes in the process but at least they aren't lying in a heap anymore. I'm slowly replacing the stakes with plastic ones available at Orchard Supply Hardware. They are more costly but do last much longer.

Again, once you start reorganizing living roses, you will notice canes which need to be removed. I particularly like to get down on the ground and clean up the area at the base of the bush. Over the growing period lots of spent leaves and petals accumulate down there. It's a horrible place where all manner of spores congregate. Make the effort and get rid of the clutter now.

DRASTIC MEASURES FOR DRASTIC TIMES

Life, as we know, deals us challenges. As soon as that climbing rose that's been nurtured along the side of the house gains its magnificent height sporting abundant, sweetly smelling sprays of roses and its arching grace calls attention to the skilled pruning ability of the rose grower, the window that it has so artfully framed turns out to have a severe case of dry rot and needs to be ripped out and replaced. What to do?

Mike, the house painter, took advantage of a dry spell last February and painted my house. *Belinda*, a hybrid musk from 1936 growing along the far side of my home, had been a marginal rose. I had settled upon its ultimate eviction, but the timing never seemed quite right. Mike, with a painter's disregard for pruning methodology, took my sheers and cut *Belinda* so severely that it was entirely out of his way and he could paint the house unencumbered.

Of course, I had been gentle with her over the years and complained about my results. Mike's approach, however, produced the best flowering that particular rose had ever had. Food and regular water helped, but sometimes a good root system would rather produce some newer canes than waste energy re-supplying an old one.

The dry rot in the window frame was dealt with but not before good old Mike had secured some rope, lassoed the tall climbers and pulled them *en masse* away from the house. He secured them with some stakes, circus tent fashion onto the side lawn.

These two experiences led me to my decisions on July 10 immediately after the Tour of my Garden by the Society. Major window work had to be done on the east side of my house coinciding with the remodeling of my kitchen. For thirteen years, four climbing *Joseph's Coats* have grown along that side of the house. It's a good rose, suffers from some mildew, some

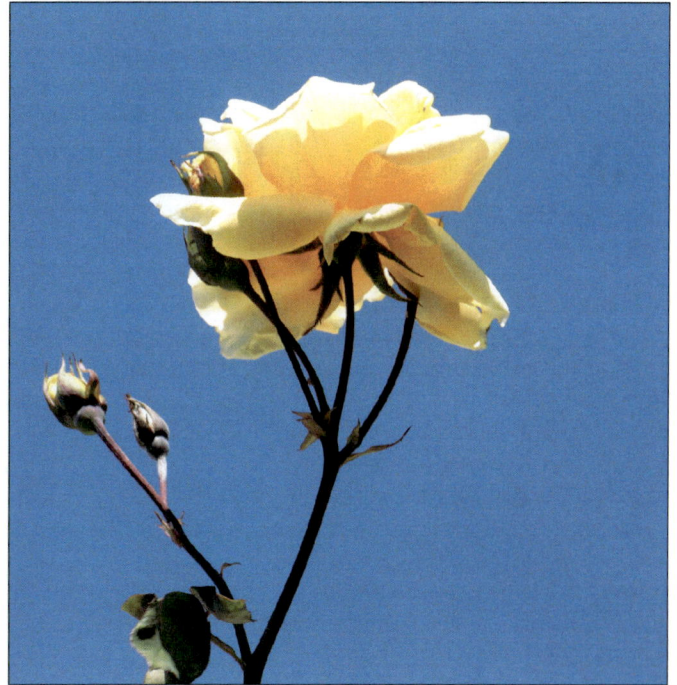

Lady Hillingdon, climbing tea (1917)

rust, and springtime aphid infestations but recovers well. It's been stingy with its new canes which has always made me think something just wasn't right with this rose.

So the workers were scheduled to begin and I wanted them to have as much room as possible. I pulled out one of the *Joseph's Coats.* It showed lots of mosaic virus this spring and was growing too close to my *Climbing Lady Hillingdon* (1917). The other three I decided would probably be safer if I merely removed all canes down to just above the bud union. If that killed them, so be it. Six weeks later, I reported that all three of the plants had sprouted new canes and taken on a new vigor.

Growing Roses in Times of Drought

When the annual total rainfall in our region is less than normal, our communities have to deal with the fact that there just isn't a sufficient amount of water for business as usual. A drought isn't anyone's fault. It's nature's way of placing stress on marginally healthy plants and animals—cleaning out the gene pool, so to speak.

Water company fines and restrictions are also very real. We all have to do our part in conserving our most important natural resource. Roses, as we know, absolutely love water. Many of us have spent lots of money and time planting dozens of these thirsty plants and must now confront this new challenge in growing them. Let's not despair. There are better ways to spend time, use less water, and save our roses.

ESTABLISHED HYBRID TEAS AND OLD GARDEN ROSES

- Reduce the size of your bushes. By now, they have finished their initial flush of flowers and should be sending out new growth. Examine each bush carefully. Remove any and all lateral growth coming from the first 12-18 inches or so of the main canes. Prune away any inconsequential growth and any blind shoots (canes which produce leaves but no buds). Any canes which clutter the inside of the bush or have grown diagonally through the center of the shrub should be eliminated as well. If some of the leaves look old and tired, help them along by pulling them off the plant now. When deadheading your spent flowers, we normally advocate that you snip just above the first five-leaflet leaf with an outside facing bud eye. In times of drought, make the cut further down.

- July is the appropriate time to trim back your one-time bloomers. I took advantage of drought conditions to reduce by half several of the ones which have been growing untrimmed for three seasons. My old damask rose, *Kazanlik*, will rebound over the summer and produce flowers on the year-old wood. It never truly defoliated last winter so it carried over some rust and mildew. All the more reason to trim it back and discard the sick leaves. It might take it a full season to regain its glory, but it's well established and will be back with a vengeance!

Tournament of Roses, hybrid tea (1988)

- Cut down the number of flower buds by half. Pinch them off with your thumbnail and forefinger. Get rid of any side buds. Most hybrid teas should only be allowed one bloom per stem. As the roses bloom, do not remove the spent flowers. No more deadheading for the rest of the season once you have reduced the size of the bush. The petals will fall, the hips will form, and the rose will slow its growth. Some blooms will continue to appear on hybrid teas until the amount of daylight signals autumn, but these flowers will be fewer in number and slower to develop. Chances are the size of your blossoms will actually be larger because there is less competition from other buds.

- Pull out any and all weeds growing anywhere near your roses and other specimen plants. Eliminating the competition for water will allow them to use every drop you can spare.

- Stop feeding the roses any chemical fertilizers. Triple 16 and the hose-end fertilizers are very dependent on water. Since we don't have much, we shouldn't use these strong potions. Instead, switch to a diluted fish emulsion (one or two tablespoons per gallon of water). This way, the water you provide contains some nutrients and soil amendments. These organic materials work over a long period of time. Since it isn't likely to rain until November, we are in for rather a long haul, anyway. Add what water you give them no later than 9:00 a.m.

• Apply a thick layer of mulch (5-6 inches) on the top of all of your garden beds. This is the easiest way to conserve water. Heavy mulch keeps the moisture in the soil by insulating the earth and subsequently keeping its temperature cool, thus further slowing down the evaporation process. It also prevents many weed seeds from germinating. With a lower soil temperature, the roses won't grow as quickly. Shredded palettes are cheap. Ground up pine trees may be available for free from municipal sources. Rice hulls might also be had in the Central Valley. Only use lawn trimmings if they are from your own yard and you are confident they contain no seeds or residue from Weed and Feed chemicals. These herbicides are formulated to kill broad leaved plants. (Read: plantain, dandelion, and ROSES!)

• If you follow the above procedures, you can water established roses perhaps just once or twice more this season. Seriously, many roses grow around the Central Coast of California in abandoned lots and fence rows without being watered. They survive. You may not want to look at them up close, but they don't die.

• You may have one or two roses that have performed only marginally for you and you thought you might give them one more season to prove themselves. We're in a drought, remember? Stop being wishy-washy and dig them up. It will give the plants around it more room to spread out and get more ventilation.

POTTED PLANTS AND MINIATURES

• The darker the pot, the more the soil heats up in the sun, and the more water the plant will require. Terra cotta pots naturally shed water. You should not have put a rose bush in a terra cot pot anyway. Move your pots out of full sun and put them into areas of dappled light or heavy shade. The shade won't kill the rose, but will slow down growth and water usage.

• It isn't wise to transplant anything in the middle of a drought. Pot-bound plants are an exception. Place them into larger surroundings full of fresh soil being careful not to disturb the root ball too much. Once in their larger home, water them well once. Then, not again. The extra soil and a shady location should insulate them.

• A layer of mulch placed on the top of the soil of a container grown plant will also help conserve water. It will prevent weed seeds from sprouting and maximize the amount of water consumed by the rose.

• Stop feeding potted roses anything. Even organic materials will be absorbed faster by plants in pots. You are essentially putting them on hold until more water is available.

• Don't ever let the soil in which a potted rose is growing completely dry out. The majority of roses I have ever lost have been in insufficiently watered pots. Get them out of the sun. Put them in a large pot. Keep them cool and they will survive the drought.

• When watering a potted plant during a drought, it's better to add water in small amounts slowly. Put a little water at the top of the pot and wait. If the water runs right through the pot, there's something wrong with the soil and you may have to change it adding more organic material which absorbs and hold moisture longer than just dirt. If the water quickly runs up and over the rim and takes a long time to sink in, your plant is probably pot-bound and needs a larger home. Don't keep watering until you see the pot start to drain. You've given them too much and are wasting what comes out of it. If you can't seem to help this problem, place the pot under a tree or large shrub so that any excess water goes into the ground to nourish the tree or shrub.

• Miniature roses deserve a word of caution. They are not blessed with the long and spreading root systems of established hybrid teas, climbers, and Old Garden Roses. Their root system is quite near the surface. If they are long established roses, they should be fine as long as the mulch is kept well mounded up around them. Treat them with caution.. Trim off inconsequential growth and allow their hips to form. Hold back all forms of fertilizer.

ROSES PLANTED THIS SPRING OR LAST WINTER

- Perhaps you have been contemplating buying a new rose bush this season and haven't quite made up your mind, please continue to contemplate, study, and review catalogues. Don't plant any new roses during a drought. They need extra water when they are establishing themselves and the probable sunshine and heat will exacerbate the circumstances. Decide what and where and take on the task in November.

- If you planted some new roses this past spring, keep a watchful eye on them. You probably won't have to trim them down that much because their growth is still so new. Keep them well mulched and watered with the weak fish emulsion. You may have to give them a season or more to judge their garden quality.

Oldtimer, hybrid tea (1969)

DRIP IRRIGATION SYSTEMS

- If you reduce bush size and place mulch around the garden, you can also reduce the frequency and duration of your irrigation.

- Check to make sure the nozzles are located properly and that the rose is absorbing the water directly.

- Set your timers to begin watering at about 3:30-4:00 a.m. and be finished before the sun is up.

- Disconnect the water system from any of your older, more established roses. Watch their progress. If you need to give them some water, use a hose and do so sparingly.

A FINAL WORD

During my years of growing roses in Salinas, I've discovered the locations of several old and species roses growing in the most inhospitable environments—alongside highways, adjacent to parking lots, behind abandoned buildings and in the middle of open fields. These bushes seem to get enough water during the winter to keep them blooming and gaining in size. Then, once the rain stops and the sun bakes down on them, they stop growing. But they don't die. The coastline's lower temperatures are less likely to cause as much stress as inland locations. While walking in Pinnacles National Monument in August, I discovered several lush thickets of *Rosa californica*. I know those bushes hadn't seen a drop of water in months.

My bet is once the rains begin again in the late fall, the garden roses will respond happily. They may even squeak one more decent bloom cycle in before Christmas. Your January pruning chore will be somewhat lessened because the roses won't have grown much this season. Save your water, do your part in conservation, and you'll still be able to smell some roses this season and many more in wetter years ahead.

September

As fall approaches, significant changes begin to take place in the rose garden. Many of the roses have a great bloom in the spring, occasional flowers in the summer, and then a final, almost as great, display in the fall. Some produce their best flowers. The warmer temperatures and shorter days often promote exceptional color and size.

Chores mount up but a significant slow down is happening in many ways. Fewer weed seeds seem to germinate after August. Grass, which was dead for most of the long dry summer, starts to show green again. Annuals begin to look tired and need to be removed.

The rose bushes sport plenty of wearied and yellowed leaves. But, they also have ample new growth, marvelously productive new canes produced in early summer from basal breaks and plenty of flowers. I hope your roses are now quite showy and that you feel rewarded from a summer of tending to their needs.

The non-cultivated parts of our gardens or yards are now very dry and dusty. Please make use of this great opportunity to clean out your garden, rake up the dead leaves, clear out your gutters and drains, and get ready for the onset of heavy rains and strong winds.

It's a perfect time to give each and every rose in your garden a once over. **Remember.** You don't have to wait until January or February to get rid of deadwood, canes growing into the center of your bush, blind shoots (ones with pretty green leaves but no flower at the end), and all the insignificant and scrappy growth especially growing from the lower portion of your otherwise healthy canes. Deadhead through September and you will still have roses for Thanksgiving and hips for Christmas.

A great year in the rose garden begins after a cold winter with several consecutive nights below freezing in Salinas and a slight frost or two in Carmel and ample rain coming steadily through March and stopping in April or early May. So the roses that developed weren't marred. The summer along California's Central Coast will be foggy from June to September. Some years, however, we get lucky. Roses love our beautifully clear warm summer days with their accompanying heat and light especially when you keep up with the blooming cycles; deadhead; water; and feed the roses all summer long. Now, it's fall, and everyone should be getting terrific repeat flushes of bloom. I expect to have roses until the frosts come again at the end of November.

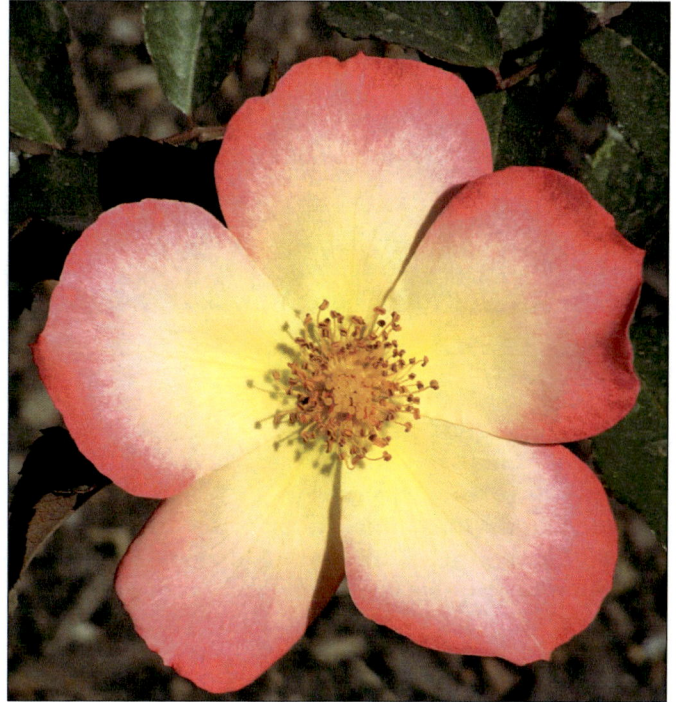

Watercolor, shrub (2006)

FALL FERTILIZER PROGRAMS

Stop applying any commercial fertilizer which has a double digit nitrogen count. Days are becoming too short for roses to convert large amounts of nitrogen into plant matter. It will produce spindly and inconsequential growth. What is more, winter pruning will only lop off this new growth in a matter of three months or so. Although some of our best weather arrives at the end of September including days with highs in the 80s, the duration of these days is shorter than the length of night. It's best to let the roses use what nutrients are in the soil and bloom their hearts out.

The manufacturers describe their products' potency by using three numbers: 20-20-20, 23-0-0, 0-10-10, 5-1-1, 18-19-30. They represent the mix of Nitrogen-Phosphorus-Potassium, the three essential elements plants require. The five mixes above are for: general summer growth, lawn fertilizer, autumn nutrients for fruit bearing trees and

Ballerina, hybrid musk (1937)

shrubs, fish emulsion, and (because it was on the shelf, marked down really cheap) tomato fertilizer. Nitrogen provides nourishment for the plant to produce green leaves. Phosphorus aides the production of flowers. Potassium helps set fruit. All three provide general maintenance for the entire plant from root to fruit. I prefer to give the plants organic food. Sea kelp and fish emulsion, cow manure, alfalfa pellets or meal, and any other well composted material.

Fish emulsion is down in the 5-1-1 range. It stays in the soil and will provide some nourishment, mostly for the plant to develop a stronger root system. Use perhaps a little more water than what the label calls for. Steer manure and good compost will also help your roses at this time. I like to make sure some exists at the base of each rose bush when the winter rains begin to fall. The heavy rains will help the nutrients percolate down to the rose roots. Chemical nitrogen is water soluble. After four months of rain, the roses primary growth nutrient will be leached out of the soil. Organic nitrogen is likely to "stick" around.

I add a fist full of blood meal again in September. As I've mentioned, it's my favorite organic material. I give each bush about half of what I do in the spring. Water them well, then water them again to mix it in. It takes a while for the blood meal to be absorbed by the rose and roses don't need that much nourishment in the fall. Include it especially if it looks like your rose leaves are on the yellow side. Greening them up not only makes the plant look better but it helps to put more sugar in the cane (so to speak) for next spring.

PLANT YOUR SPRING BULBS NOW

Advice is much easier to give than take. One year, it wasn't until April—APRIL!—when I got my spring bulbs interred. It wasn't a very showy display at all. In fact, about half of the bulbs never came up that summer. The ones that showed green never flowered. I had to wait one entire year for them to get back on the correct schedule.

My great combination plants for roses are daffodils. The daffodils make February when all the roses are pruned to their lowest so much more cheerful. They are basically finished blooming and nearly all dried up by May when the rose garden peaks. Then they go away until next spring. The other wonderful trait they possess is their slow and steady ability to multiply. Each spring they look better than the previous year.

Select some key spots in the rose garden. Put them where you can see them bloom from the house. It's where we usually are during the windy and rainy winter months. This may or may not fit the best garden design but it fits your sense of joy! The objective of all your work in the garden, as I've mentioned before, is for your own satisfaction. It's meant to be your paradise so plan for it and build it.

Daffodils are toxic to gophers which won't eat them, but they might move them about underground.

ROSE FRUIT... MY, WHAT BIG HIPS YOU HAVE

If you make flower arrangements, by all means, start fruiting your rose bushes now. Remove the spent petals throughout the fall but leave the hips. *Altissimo* (1966) makes some of the best large orange hips. They look like miniature pumpkins. The sprays of smaller hips found on roses such as *Ballerina* (1937), *Newport Fairy* (1908), and *Rosa woodsii fendleri* (1888) also add contrast to fall flower arrangements. Speaking of contrast, rose hips also include black to burgundy on burnet species, miniflagons on *Rosa moyesii* (1933), and prickly orange pods from the eglantine roses.

Assess your roses on the type of hips they produce. The Old Garden Roses offer a really wonderful assortment. Some modern roses also serve well in this area. So do many of the ramblers. It's fine to leave some rose hips on your bushes, as they do look nice on the plants when the rains start to fall. The rose buds will rot with botrytis, but a few orange-red hips will add some color when it's lacking elsewhere.

Fall's the time to watch your hips grow!

WHICH ROSES NEED RELOCATING?

Now is the time to start thinking about which roses need to be eliminated from your garden, which merely need to be trimmed back, and which need to be moved to a better location. I like to move my bushes in late October and early November. By Thanksgiving, we have had in north Salinas a frost which has killed the impatiens. We haven't yet had the nourishing heavy rains of winter which turn my Salinas adobe soil into thick pudding.

If you move your bushes try to keep as much of the soil ball around the main root cluster intact. To ensure this process, water the bush deeply two or three days ahead of the move. This will allow the plant to absorb into its canes as much water as possible before some of its nutrient-providing roots are severed. You may lose much of the soil around the base as you hoist it up and cart it away. If this happens, replenish the soil with a good mixture of sandy loam. Before you replant the bush, trim it down about a third and remove anything that is thinner than a pencil on a hybrid tea. Let it keep as many of its leaves as possible. The frost is likely to damage the most tender new growth.

I am a strong believer in adding some form of root hormone to transplanted roses. The hormones were developed for starting cuttings, but they will give your rose help recovering from the move. By the way, if you damage a cane or a

Altissimo, large flowered climber (1966)

root, remove it from just below the break for a cane, above for a root. You can do great harm by allowing insects and disease to enter into the plant from a badly tended break. Trim it back. Next year, feed it well and it will grow strong replacement parts!

If you dig out a rose bush now, you can add some organic material to the hole and give it four months to prepare for a bare root variety coming to that spot in January.

DEADHEAD DIFFERENTLY IN THE FALL

Many of our rose bushes will produce flowers right up until Christmas, if we continue to snip off the spent blooms down to the first leaf with an outside bud eye. In fact, several of my bushes—*Climbing Talisman* (1930), *Oldtimer* (1969), *Climbing Chrysler Imperial* (1957), *Climbing Étoile de Hollande* (1931), and *American Glory* (1991)—seem to enjoy the drier, cooler, sunnier, and shorter days of fall.

The flowers on these bushes are extraordinarily beautiful at this time of year. The slower development of the blooms gives them more body, a higher petal count and thicker petals. The color is more intense. The fragrance is headier. The overall beauty is high, even though the overall number of flowers is going down.

Fall deadheading is a bit different than that of the spring and summer. Because we are trying to make the plants go dormant, we need to encourage them in this direction. Let some of your better looking flowers stay on the bushes. When the flowers fade, simply grab the petals from the top and pull them off. Leave the hips attached. If new growth should appear, let it develop but be sure to pinch off any side buds. We want the bush to spend its nourishment on developing hips.

New growth at this time of year tends to be weak because of the shortening daylight. It's helpful to allow roses to complete a more natural life cycle and the hips have their own beauty and uses.

BOTRYTIS IS JUST ROTTEN

As wet weather approaches, many of the blossoms will fall victim to botrytis—another word for rot. In rose growing, when blossoms do this it's referred to as "balling." Many of the Old Garden Roses and older hybrid teas are particularly susceptible to botrytis because their petals are thinner and contain lesser amounts of chlorophyll. When the outer petals of the buds stay wet for more than seven hours or so, they rot. Then, they get gluey and prevent the flower from opening. You can sometimes peel the outer petals back and save some of the flowers as the inner petals will force the bloom open. Other times the botrytis has hit the entire bud at the base of the petals. Just touching the bud will make it drop off the bush, half-formed and useless. Remove the petals and put them in the trash. Don't let balled rose buds stay underneath the bushes.

Good sanitation at this time of year is very important. Our bushes are much larger after a season of healthy growth and all the green leaves are pumping even more energy into the plant. It's tougher to get around the plants because they are at maximum size now. Make sure any leaves that have fallen to the ravages of blackspot, rust, or just normal aging are removed and discarded. Don't ever put rose leaves and buds into your home compost. The risk of spreading rose diseases is too great.

Perhaps you have noticed that many rose varieties have a tendency to hold on to their faded blossoms. The petals just don't fall off. Instead, they cling in an unsightly way to the bush. With wet weather coming, these faded petals need to be pulled off. They too will fall victim to rot which produces spores. The spores are carried by the air and spread to the rest of your garden. You can't eliminate rot but you can significantly reduce the amount by removing any clinging petals. Besides, the garden looks better with spent flowers eliminated.

Popcorn, miniature (1973)

KEEP AIR CIRCULATING

Many of us grow too many roses in too small a space. What with all the tender loving care we heap on them, these plants get too big for the space we have allotted them and that causes more problems especially with fungal diseases. If you look at each plant separately, you will find insignificant growth cluttering up the bush. Spend the time necessary to remove any canes thinner than a pencil. Eliminate any growth that has not produced a flower. Open up your bushes center and allow for more air.

LOTS OF NEW GROWTH AND CONSTANT CARE

Some of the blossom cycles were great. I had to cut back the roses to keep the blooms down at eye level. Throughout the growing season, I discarded deadwood and dying wood. I got rid of canes which dissected the plant and snipped off inconsequential growth at the base of the shrubs. When pruning time comes again in January, I will have had a lot of the work out of the way. **Remember.** It's much easier to get around your roses now (and I mean on your hands and knees), when the garden bed is generally dry, than it will be when the rains start falling again and wetting everything up.

SOMETHING IS TERRIBLY WRONG WHEN THERE ARE NO ROSES

After weeks of rumination, I finally acted. Two large roses, original ones that I had planted when I put in the garden in 1993, had to go. They did not produce enough flowers. They did not bloom for a long enough period. And the plants themselves were misshapen and clunky-looking (that's a technical term used a lot in garden club circles).

The first was a *Climbing Talisman* (1930). I selected it for the wrong reason. It was the first rose that I ever grew. That was back in Virginia where it did very well and produced well. (Come to think of it, perhaps my expectations have changed in twenty years of gardening.) The long canes were gone in a few minutes. The shoveling took a bit longer but eventually I got the bud union and roots out. Not surprisingly, the roots snapped off quickly and I noticed that at some point the drainage wasn't good. A lot of the roots were rotten. It was no wonder things weren't going well for this climber.

The second was a great Old Garden Rose, an alba, known as, *Maiden's Blush* (before 1400), (in French, *Cuisse de nymphe emué* — translated as, "Nymph's Blushing Thigh") Okay, I kept it for so long because I liked telling people what the French name was! Its canes took a little longer to remove

Gourmet Popcorn, miniature (1986) a sport of Popcorn

This year, I stopped. I spent hours throughout the summer on my hands and knees pulling up the shoots. Figuring, if I can prevent it from growing at all. It won't be able to regenerate. I don't think I was that successful, but I tried.

I sprayed a front garden bed with RoundUp® several times to kill the Bermuda grass. I didn't plant anything in this bed until midsummer. Impatiens, I planted Impatiens. I watered and watered. Soon, the Bermuda grass was back and the Impatiens—Impatiens, mind you, looked awful. They would not grow. Clearly the poison in RoundUp® stays in the soil after the weeds have long succumbed to it.

Bindweed was more prevalent this year than ever. I suppose if I stopped feeding the birds, I'd have less of it. They eat the fruit around the bindweed seeds and pass the seed. My birdbath which has a beautiful ring of Gourmet Popcorn planted around it, is totally engulfed by bindweed. I've sprayed it and pulled it and will pull it again.

FALL IS A GREAT TIME TO PLANT ROSES

I prefer to plant roses at this time of year. I believe it really makes a difference when the rose has several months to add to its root structure before it's expected to produce flowers. Roses planted in the fall won't produce that much new growth as the sunlight has diminished. They can spend time putting out lots of feeder roots. Just make sure they have good drainage, as these tiny roots are susceptible to rot. Plus most garden centers have them for half off and if your favorite nursery gets similar conditions as you get in your yard, you can tell which roses are likely to do well. Another advantage in planting potted roses now is that they really want to be in the ground and push out their roots.

because they are thorny and were entangled somewhat in a few of its neighbor's. When I went in with the shovel, it took much longer to get out. It liked where it was growing. But this variety just hadn't produced enough flowers. Its bloom cycle is far shorter than other albas. Its leaves are characteristically grayish and healthy, but the canes are coarse and the leaves too far apart. It wanted to take the shape of a wild raspberry bush.

Maiden's Blush came up in telltale crumbly pieces. CROWN GALL! I had moved it to this great sunny location about eight or nine years ago. I must have damaged a root at sometime which allowed the gall to grow. Crown galls are a form of "plant cancer." A bacterium in the soil invades the cells of a plant and reconfigures their growth patterns producing this great mass of spongy flesh. Roses will last for a while with crown gall, but eventually they suffocate. I carefully removed as many of the pieces as possible and washed off the shovel. You can spread the bacteria to other rose roots if you aren't careful. The bacterium occurs naturally in the soil and is not at all a problem as long as the rose has healthy roots.

PROBLEM WEEDS AND INSANITY

Albert Einstein is quoted as saying, "Insanity is doing the same thing and expecting different results." For ten years, I sprayed RoundUp® on nutgrass and this year I have just as much of this weed in the same spots as I ever had. I stunted the growth of surrounding roses, losing some entirely to the over-spray—which, believe me, was minimal.

Honorine de Brabant, bourbon (1850)

Isfahan, damask (1832)

The first rule in planting a new rose bush is digging a hole big enough for the new plant. It's important to dig deep. The more you break up the soil beneath a rose bush, the sturdier it will grow and the more drought resistant it will be. Deeper roots can go down further to keep cool and absorb moisture in the hottest days of the summer. The rose will eventually get down there, but you can make it happen sooner by breaking up the soil to a depth of three feet.

Amend the soil now. Stir into the broken soil around your roses some steer manure. One third of a bag per rose is more than adequate. It's cheap. It's rich in nutrients. It's easy to do. Make the effort to turn the soil several times. Then, re-dig the hole. Put some old steak bones or ham bones beneath the rose. Cover with an inch of soil and then place the new bush on top.

I've never liked breaking up the root ball. Some people say to do it. I suppose it is okay and probably necessary if the rose roots were circling around the bottom of the pot, but shame on you for waiting for so long to repot the plant.

 Rosen Resli (1987) got placed where the Maiden used to blush, *Elina* (1984) took a spot a bit further out from where *Talisman* grew, and *The Gift (1981)*—a modern polyantha landed on the other side of the old Talisman. None of these roses were planted in the exact same spot, by the way. Every time you plant a new rose bush, try to locate its successor in a somewhat different location. It only makes sense that the soil will be less depleted elsewhere.

MY BIG PROJECT

The last time I mentioned MY BIG PROJECT, the person I was with said, "Joe, either cut down all the roses growing on the top of your potting shed or don't cut down all the roses growing on the top of your potting shed, but please STOP TALKING ABOUT CUTTING DOWN ALL THE ROSES GROWING ON THE TOP OF YOUR POTTING SHED!"

The project is necessary as the roof of the potting shed is made of that translucent green corrugated fiberglass. Over the twenty plus years it's been up there it has cracked in several places and drips like a sieve. It makes a total mess during wet weather. My potting shed had once been a friendly refuge in the winter, a place where I could be busy doing gardening projects even when it was raining. I want those times back.

So I happened to find a carpenter who looked it over and gave me a bid. It's not just the roofing material but a few of the beams have rotted and need replacement. Otherwise, the frame of the shed is solid and ready for more use.

Once I knew I had found someone to do the labor I couldn't do, I began doing what I could do. On Sunday, August 17, I started clipping off the roses at the roof line. I was pulling at the *Phyllis Bide* (1928) and *Climbing Cécile Brünner* (1894) canes and dragging them onto the lawn where I sat with a sharpened clipper and cut them into manageable pieces.

I've netted three large size green trash bins, courtesy of BFI, and twenty construction material strength black plastic bags which I also carried off to a "friendly" local dumpster. Off and on, it took five weekends.

Climbing Cécile Brünner is really a weed. This vigorous rose bush had actually sprouted roots up in the decomposed leaf litter sitting on the roof! It has one great flush in the spring and then only occasional flowers, here and there, the rest of the time *Newport Fairy* (1908) is still only about half gone. Its wood isn't as dense as the *Cécile Brünner* so it chops up much faster. *Phyllis Bide* was struggling as *Cécile Brünner* was smothering it. The fourth large rose is the famous damask rose, *Isfahan* (1832). It's a great one, but it only blooms on year-old canes. Fortunately, it has long and very flexible canes which (unlike *Cécile Brünner* and *Newport Fairy*) didn't get too tangled up. So I was actually able to extract it from the clump of roses on the shed and lay the individual canes down. When the new roof is on, *Isfahan* will have its old place back without competition this time. I'll try to bend the canes horizontally and secure them for the winter. This should give me a breathtaking bloom once it re-flowers in the spring. Isfahan will send out its first flowers in early to mid-March and keep them coming through the end of July.

Of course, once such a mass of greenery is eliminated, much more sunlight hits the ground. My *Ballerina*, a hybrid musk rose from 1937, has been growing in the shade of *Climbing Cécile Brünner* from the get go. I love *Ballerina*'s simple clusters of flowers, their delicate pink color, and their tiny little red, jewel-like hips. Well, with some great sunshine, *Ballerina* is dancing her little heart out with her new canes, new flower clusters and much healthier, happier leaves. It's kind of a thrill to watch.

With a good pruning, *Phyllis Bide* has sent up lots of new growth. I'm now committed to keeping it trimmed up.

QUICK ASSESSMENT TOOL

You can bet your life that while I was sitting and chopping up those monster-size rose bushes until the muscles in my hands went numb, I was evaluating every other bush in the garden. Separate past memories and associations with the roses you grow from how well they do for you. Look at each rose bush individually with a keen eye and a predetermined set of criteria.

Here are some of the questions I asked of each rose bush in my garden:

• Did I cut one flower from this bush and bring it inside to enjoy?

• Did that flower last more than two days in a vase?

• Did I ever stop in front of this bush and admire what it was doing?

• Did I lean over and see what kind of fragrance it had as I passed by?

• Did I ever notice rust, mildew, or blackspot on this bush?

• Does this rose bush clean itself? I mean after it blooms, does it drop its spent petals and expose its hips or does it hang onto the old dried up petals until they turn chestnut brown with mildew and look like a smear of rotten compost?

• Has anyone visiting the garden stopped to ask me a question about this rose bush?

• Does this rose fulfill a specific purpose in the garden, i.e., provide flowers and greenery to decorate the fence or provide a barrier from unwanted visitors, or serve as an edging or border plant?

• Do I spend more time cleaning up after or corralling this bush than loving its roses?

• Is the rose only really attractive at one stage of its bloom? Great buds, and that's it.

• Can this rose hold onto its petals for more than a day or two in warm weather? in the wind? in the rain?

• Is this rose a magnet for aphids, thrips, spider mites?

• Does this rose have any personal significance that makes me overlook its faults? For example, is this the rose I grew from a cutting I took from my long departed grandmother's neighbors' house.

• Will this rose ever be worth much at a Rose Show, if I ever have time to exhibit it?

• Do I enjoy the taste of this rose's petals in a mixed green salad? I've sampled every rose petal in the garden and do have a favorite one to eat! (OKAY, I'll tell you. I find the taste and color of the hybrid perpetual *Black Prince* (1866) to be delicious. Well, maybe not as good as butter lettuce but at least an enjoyable surprise and conversation point at a party. Taste your petals!

• Did I even forget this rose was in the garden?

GONE FROM THE GARDEN RUNWAY

"As you know in fashion, one day you're in and the next day you're out.," so says Heidi Klum. With all due respect to television's hit show "Project Runway," I made my decision. "One hundred and fifty-nine of you can stay. Seven of you are out."

Frau Dagmar Hastrup: You are essentially a hedge rose. Your flowers with their great clove fragrance last barely six hours. Your hips are attractive but only when they're new. Your leaves are interesting and cover you from top to bottom. But you act as a barrier to the roses growing behind you. I can't weed them and they can't get sunlight on their bud unions. You're right for someone, but not me. *Auf wiedersehen.*

Salet (1854): You have been around a long time and are one of the few perpetual moss roses. But, you mildew. Your coarse leaves are never attractive. You have a great fragrance but rarely have open flowers. You are wrong for the garden and you are out.

Portrait (1971): You were created by an amateur. You have an interesting bloom, but there are never very many of them. It's been ten years I think since I ever picked one. Bye. Bye.

Rosen Resli (1987): I had such high hopes for you and gave you a great spot. You just sent out extra long canes with three or four flowers on the end and they were gone before I knew they were even there. So are you.

Brother Cadfael (1995): With such ancestry, I would think David Austin would have given you more to work with. Your leaves are rubbish. Your flowers never open fully and you hardly have anything positive going for you. I think the kindly monk whose name you carry would feed you to a goat.

Maman Cochet (1893): You are a tea rose. You have great potential but you never took advantage of your location. When you sent out flowers, which was not often, they never opened fully and were dead to botrytis in a day or two. And what a nasty *Maman* you were! Your prickly canes grew out in the most angular fashion and interfered with every bush around you. *Au revoir.*

NEW ROSES IN THE GARDEN

I took advantage of the rose sales usually occurring at garden centers now and came home with the following new selections:

Bewitched: A medium pink hybrid tea that's been around since 1967. It holds its head up high and lasts a week in a vase. It looks vigorous, clean, and healthy. (RUNWAY UPDATE: Or so I thought then, after a month of typical Salinas weather, it contracted everything and was yanked up from its prime location. YOU'RE OUT!)

Smoky (1970): It's been in a pot for nearly two years and by relocating the pot into the sunshine it's taken on a new life. It hasn't any sign of mildew and has flowers. (RUNWAY UPDATE: I went on a trip and it was put in the shade and forgotten. It happens. When I next remembered it, it was down to one green, leafless spindly cane. Could it have been that quick a fizzle? My philosophy is that a rose should have the vigor necessary to blend with my life. I can't sit next to it everyday and hold its cane! YOU'RE GONE)

Tournament of Roses (1988): Considered a bicolor, it doesn't ever seem to be without a bloom which opens. (RUNWAY UPDATE: After two years it finally bloomed in two great sprays of flowers and showed good disease resistance. The flowers last a long time on the bush. I'll give it more time to develop its root system and get even stronger. YOU'RE IN.)

Midnight Blue (2003): Every garden should have a show stopper for visitors. This is a clean little **PURPLE** rose which looked terrific at the nursery! (RUNWAY UPDATE: It's taken it a long time to develop and was without flowers for the entire summer. It has lots of new growth now and produced a flush of blossoms. Alas, when a hot spell blew in, the flowers literally fried in the sun, but YOU'RE IN.)

Morden Blush (1988): I'll keep a watch on this one. It was developed for cold climates but seems happy here. (RUNWAY UPDATE: It blooms in great flushes of smallish pink old fashioned flowers. It doesn't clean itself at all and requires deadheading as the dirty brown spent petals cling to their stems. Once removed, the bush responds with another set of flowers. Leaves are resistant. YOU'RE IN.)

Tahitian Sunset (2007): It comes highly recommended for its vigor and attractive color combination. (RUNWAY UPDATE: Fantastic in every single way! YOU WIN.)

ADVICE FROM THE PAST

Rose suckers may be occasionally planted in a hedge border along the front or back edge of a border to be trained in a dwarf or low hedge to produce large supplies of flowers for medical domestic occasions, or other purposes.

Thomas Mawe, London, 1797

Morden Blush, shrub (1988)

October

October brings such great weather to the Central Coast. Repeated picture perfect days from dawn to dusk will cause the roses to respond with wonderful flushes of blooms. The summer has slid into fall. The mornings are cooler, the days warmer and sunnier but shorter, and the cat less interested in being out all night. Soon the rains will start and winter will be with us again. This should be a sufficient heads up to get some chores in the garden taken care of before the rose beds get too wet and messy.

Your garden should be in the middle of its fall repeat bloom. After a long season of feeding, watering, and deadheading, and of cutting roses for shows and demonstrations, of indulging myself by bringing perfect blooms to the folks at the office, autumn has arrived. I love this time of year, always have.

My *Newport Fairy* (1908), a rambling rose from 1908 which was one of the highlights of the garden tour this past June, has produced the most incredible harvest of hips! There are hundreds of them on the 15-foot plant. Each spray has about 15-20 pea-size, orange hips. I can't wait to get in there and snip away. I think I can probably produce an entire, front-door-size wreath made of nothing but *Newport Fairy* hips.

I was even tempted to harvest my *Rosa eglanteria* (species) hips and cook them! Rose hips make good preserves which have a distinctive fruity flavor. Rose petals can also be used for jellies but may be too perfumey to appeal to the American palate. The petals on the hybrid perpetual *Black Prince* (1866) are quite peppery with a trace of perfume. Their deep burgundy color is quite attractive on the top of a mixed salad. The rose hips remind me of the taste of crab apples which we used to pick in the woods back in Ohio. I have a very fond memory of picking a peck of them and presenting them to my grandmother who made us a batch of jelly to go with her homemade bread.

Roses are deciduous plants. When September arrives and turns quickly into October, roses start to lose their lower leaves. Even the most disease-free ones will show their age—yellow leaves. Simply pull them off the canes. They won't ever go green again. Doing this allows the upper leaves to produce the chlorophyll needed to make the plant continue to grow.

By the end of November, we are likely to have a frost. The harder the frost in our area, the better it is for the roses. It helps them drop all their leaves, go into natural dormancy and thus stop producing new growth and begin to store up energy for spring. I'm now letting all the roses form hips. I

Snowballet, shrub (1977)

will still get some blooms, but it's time for the roses to move toward dormancy. It's quite easy. Simply pull off the petals from spent flowers and keep the rest of the flower intact.

AUTUMN IN THE ROSE GARDEN

Take a walk in your garden. Do so BEFORE the fall rains begin. Make your final decision on the worst performing roses this season. Is it time to try something else? I have become particularly fussy about the roses I look at up-close all the time. I really don't want black-spotted, rusted, mildewed, botrytis-afflicted plants in clear view of me or my guests. (It's such bad publicity for all of us rose enthusiasts who know it's really not our fault the weather was ideal for spreading blackspot all over the garden.) In fact, I intentionally grow *Rosa russelliana* (Old Spanish Rose, Russell's Cottage Rose known before 1826) right alongside my garage where everyone enters my back yard because this tough old plant is DISEASE-FREE. A good spray with the garden hose rids it of its insect pests and spider webs and makes it look like the healthiest thing in the yard. It only blooms for four weeks in late spring, but it's an attractive shrub, especially if kept trimmed to a tall hedge.

I've also learned to avoid plants which may look terrific initially but produce seedlings everywhere. Beware of Jupiter's beard, forget-me-nots, alyssum, nigella, and others. I will continue to grow these annuals because I love their flowers, but I fully understand I'm going to be pulling their seedlings out from underneath the roses.

Rose hips are one of the most concentrated sources of Vitamin C. Wash the hips, remove the dried sepals and stems, cut lengthwise in half, remove the seeds, and spread on a clean cloth or drying screen. Place the hips in a cool but dry place and allow them to harden. By including several dry rose hips in your tea pot, you'll increase the nutritional value of your tea and not really change the taste noticeably.

USE ONLY ORGANIC FERTILIZERS NOW

I calculate the amount of sun on October 20 to be the same amount as on February 20 which means not a lot. Roses simply can't grow sufficiently well in gradually diminishing sunlight. The growth they will put out when given double-digit doses of nitrogen, simply isn't quality growth. Some good steer manure can be used as a top dressing. Its nutrients will leech down into the soil during the winter.

The fish emulsion I used just two weeks ago and the resulting slowly developing rose buds have given me an incredible treat in the garden. The color of the roses is consistently deep and complex. Many of the undertones are more pronounced. Roses with color blends seem to show their contrast more. The dose of organic fertilizer helps to produce these fantastic color variations.

Tiffany, from 1954 for instance, is usually a pink rose with a little yellow at the base. At this time of year, however, the portion of the petal which is yellow is greater and more intense. A rose such as *Matangi* (1978) which has orange on the top of the petal and a white underside is incredibly more vivid in the fall. Throughout the summer, my *Climbing Chrysler Imperial* (1957) has produced nice blooms. They suffer from the intensity of the sun and frequently fry on the edges. It has produced such a stunning display this past month I couldn't believe it was the same rose bush.

DIG OUT YOUR UNWANTED ROSES NOW

Each year, I feel liberated when I can begin to thin out and trim down the size of my rose collection. I love many of the Old Garden Roses because they have an extended blooming

Tiffany, hybrid tea (1954)

period and then an even longer resting period. Many of them produce colorful hips at this time of year and will again show some color. I don't mind the fact that they are not ever-blooming because I find their healthy green leaves attractive. They provide a very nice backdrop for the hybrid teas, floribundas, and miniatures I have planted in front of them.

It's a good idea to remove bushes you don't want now and fill in the hole with some steer manure. It will have a few months to incorporate into the soil over the winter. If you have a rose in a pot, make sure you keep the root ball together when you transplant. Pack the soil in around it, but don't squash it down too heavily.

On the other hand, I look seriously at the roses which don't have a particularly long blooming period and produce abundant canes with diseased leaves and no hips. Several of my roses were planted in the wrong location; just not enough sunshine. I will move them in the winter to adjust for the size. It's very simple. Plant your taller roses in the back and your shorter ones in the front.

At this time, I make the final decision on several bushes (triage), two or three will move to new locations in the yard (curable) and others will go into the trash (R.I.P.). Perhaps I will put some of the roses on the raffle table (rooted cuttings and offshoots), but I won't pass anything along if I know the plant is not a healthy or happy one in our general climate.

I will toss out some rose bushes which have been poor performers. If I once liked a particular bush, and it has been in the ground, I may put it into a black pot with fresh soil and see if the extra heat on its roots brings it around.

When digging up an established rose, I generally get rid of the top of the bush quickly leaving only enough cane to grip. Use a sturdy lopper. Remember my philosophy? More results from less work. Cut low down on the plant and chop up the big piece later. Then, dig a circle around the bush about a foot and a half from the bud union lifting up the soil with the shovel. That's usually all it takes to dislodge the plant—typically a sign that its root system isn't very well developed which may be a reason for discarding the bush. Pull the rose out of the ground and shake as much of the earth from its roots as you can.

For more established plants, you may have to remove some soil and repeat the method until you've cut a sufficient number of feeder roots. Grab the stub at the bud union and pull up. This usually will give you an indication of where you might have to cut the next root. For very large roses, I use a hatchet on the roots until I get the bulk of the bush out. Loosen the soil and pluck out any odd bits of rose root, especially if the bush had been grown on root stock.

Most grafted roses sold in California are grown on a rose called *Dr. Huey* (1920). It's the preferred understock because it roots easily in a variety of soils, produces a healthy set of roots within a growing season, and stores well as a bare root product at 33° F. This said, I continue to find it sprouting from unextracted root bits the following season. Get as much up as you can. If it does sprout again next year, it's easy enough to get rid of—but don't let it ever become a mature plant. You won't like *Dr. Huey*. It's a one-time bloomer with a brief flowering period. Its semi-double, dark red flowers are attractive enough but they burn in our hot springtime sun. The bush grows too large and mildews quite readily. Some of the species roses I've moved around in my garden have also sent up new roses in the spring from the root fragments. Make sure you turn over the soil and remove as many of the root pieces as possible.

Blueberry Hill, floribunda (1997)

Once the soil is loosened up a bit, add some cow manure into the hole where the rose once grew and mix in a couple of handfuls of sand to make the soil texture more friable (if you are growing roses on clay, of course). I also recommend that you bury some old steak bones or beef knuckles in the hole. They take a long time to disintegrate and are genuinely good for the soil. Usually bury them 18 inches down directly where the rose roots will find them and deeply enough so that any nighttime marauders won't get to them.

I suggest you shovel prune your garden **now** for a couple of reasons. It's not raining yet and the ground won't be muddy. Most people have a limited number of days that can be spent in the garden. If those turn out to be stormy ones, the rose will live on. It's good to add all the soil amendments now so that they can have a few months to break down and blend a bit more.

Spread the used soil on top of the mulch in a hidden area of your garden. The soil will probably contain sufficient bacteria to help break up the mulch and turn it into fresh soil. Mulch will not and should not last forever.

If the rose you are removing has been growing in that spot for more than five years, you should probably consider replacing a good deal of the soil altogether. Roses, as you know, are hungry critters and the former tenant of the spot has probably depleted it of most nutrients. It's much easier to grow good roses in fresh soil. Buy a sack of top soil and add it to the spot along with some cow manure.

GET RID OF YOUR TRASH

If there is a recurring theme in this *Manual*, it is get rid of your garden trash. Don't let leaves which have dropped from blackspot and rust winter over beneath the bushes. Start raking them up now and finish the job once you have pruned your bushes in January. If you manage a compost pile, don't put your rose trimmings into it. There's just too much risk that you are passing around your spores from season to season.

If you find you just can't get at the dropped leaves, you are definitely growing your bushes too closely together. That's probably also the reason why you are losing your leaves to disease in the first place. Roses really want good air circulating around them.

This is also the time to trim back other plants in the yard. Most have been growing quickly for about eight months. If they've poked me or tripped me or clung to me or caused me to walk off the path during my normal garden prowling, I clip them back. It's my yard and they'll grow where I want them to. It's a control issue, I know, but who is in charge? Depending on the variety, they take my corrective measures well.

CONDITION YOUR SOIL BEFORE THE RAINS BEGIN

Spend time covering your entire rose bed with cow manure. If you are lucky enough and countrified enough to have a fresh source, all the more reason to add it now. The nutrient value isn't high and the time it takes to break down into the soil is aided with time and winter rain. It will be easier to work it into your soil once you have pruned your bushes. For now, just get it spread around.

In your travels about the garden, pay particular attention to your drainage. Now is the time to make sure that none of your roses will be standing in water for more than three days. I lost about four roses once when the rains were ceaseless and the drainage insufficient. Where there is a serious problem you may have to consider a porous drainage pipe dug between your bushes or even a crude ditch. Each yard is different.

Remember. A rose's natural habitat is a broken area such as a river bank or the edge of a clearing. They can tolerate a good soaking but their roots must breathe air within a few days.

Elina, hybrid tea (1984)

RETIE OR RE-STAKE YOUR CLIMBING ROSES

I can't emphasize to you enough that it's much easier to secure your climbing roses when it's not cold, windy and raining. My early morning rescue missions trying to prop up a fallen 12 foot *Madame Alfred Carrière* (1879) have taught me that certain problems should have been avoided. I may also suggest that some of these climbers fair better with a light autumn thinning before the rains set in. It's too soon to prune them back severely because they will want to grow and will only be able to produce inferior canes. Yet, lightening the load will relieve some of the burden when early winds start to howl. I recently bolted *Mme. Alfred* to the back eave of the house. She's torn out nails and bent eye screws straight.

Most of my climbers on the house are now secured to it by nylon cord and hooks in multiple locations. The days of using a nail and some plastic binding are over. Roses are heavy especially when wet and growing sixteen feet into the air.

Those roses which grow up into trees seem to secure themselves better. It also helps to have the rose growing on the windward side of the trees. When the wind blows, it blows the climbing canes against and into the tree, not out of and away from it. Not usually a problem, but do consider it.

ADVANCE PRUNING SAVES TIME

With this great weather comes a fantastic opportunity to get a jump start on your pruning. I've already identified canes which I will eliminate when I prune in mid-January. I've also noticed some deadwood in among my Old Garden Roses. There's no point in waiting for pruning time to get rid of deadwood. It's already dead and can only be collecting the falling leaves from the roses. It will be just as dead three months from now so get rid of it.

Yes, it's way too soon to prune any of your roses and it's too late to prune your one time bloomers. But, it's a perfect time to get rid of the inconsequential growth coming out of the lower twelve inches of your roses growing on standards. You will only have to prune this away in January. Why not save some time and improve the sanitation in your garden by getting rid of any growth coming out on the bottom eighteen inches of your hybrid teas or floribundas as well?

I also look my roses over, up and down, and try to spot soon to be deadwood and spindly canes which aren't dead yet, but are certainly in Heaven's waiting room. I'll whack them this weekend. It's so much easier to clean up the garden now when everything is dry.

By removing these twigs, you allow the rose leaves to fall to the ground and not get caught on their way down. It's also

Crazy Dottie, miniature (1988)

If the weather remains dry and you continue to water your bushes, there's no reason why you shouldn't have roses on the table for Halloween and even Thanksgiving, especially if the rains hold off. In fact, the roses which bloom in the fall are slower to develop and not likely burned by the hot summer sunshine, thus usually resulting in deeper, richer colors, and larger blossoms of greater substance.

In addition, many of the insects which damage petals and leaves have also shut down for the season. You may be rewarded with your finest flowers of the year. If the weather is wet, however, expect to lose most of your blooms to botrytis. The flowers won't get enough heat to burn off the damp petals and the rose buds will simply rot before they open.

I start in the back corner and work my way around the yard. I want to clear away as much refuse as possible. Weed carcasses zapped by RoundUp®, rose trimmings fallen to the ground, and dropped leaves all should be raked up and discarded.

At any rate, I love the dryness of the garden now, before the rains begin. I scoot along beneath the roses pulling out weeds, scraping up the dead grasses and leaves, killing sleeping snails, and with a garden claw reshaping the ground around the each rose into an easily watered basin.

a good idea to keep tabs on what's happening at the bud union, supposing you have grafted roses. Sometimes I find that the decaying organic matter in my soil has caused the soil line to fall below the bud union. Now's a great time to throw some composted cow manure around the base of the plant. It's important to keep that bud union moist.

Investigating this crucial part of most roses will also give you a heads up in spotting any crown gall. If you find it, dig out the rose and throw the plant and the soil immediately around it away. Then wash your shovel and any other tools which have come into contact with the gall with bleach or Lysol. A rose bush has its own defense against invasive galls. The layer of bark surrounding all roots and stems is an adequate deterrent and you should not have to worry about this affliction too much.

However, if this bark is broken or cracked, usually during shipping or by accident—I've stepped right on top of rosebushes busting off most of their canes and damaging the bud union—you could have a problem. Galls love to invade split crowns and will eventually kill the plant as they sap it of energy and steal the nutrients. You can't kill the bacteria as they are in the soil and air, but keep an eye out because once developed, they will multiply.

CLEAN YOUR GARDEN BEFORE THE RAINS BEGIN

The shortened daylight will curtail the growth of most of your roses. Whatever new canes are produced at this time of year are apt to be spindly and chlorotic (chartreuse leaves with dark green veins).

Tribute, hybrid tea (1983)

Baronne Prévost, hybrid perpetual (1842)

DON'T FORGET TO GIVE ROSES A GOOD DRINK

I was surprised by how much water a rose bush can draw up when the days are getting so short. There is still plenty of nourishment in the soil from my intense summer feeding. I notice this by the continuous growth and flowering I'm seeing after a month of only giving the roses water.

Water is the medium of growth. The more regularly you provide it, the better your roses will grow. I hand water my roses, so they are stuck with having to wait for my schedule to free up so I can get them some water. It's good to check the drainage of your roses now and make any adjustment necessary. When the rains start falling in earnest, you could lose any shrubs growing in spots that don't drain properly. If you have some heavy clay mix some compost with sand and add it to the soil. It's important that your roses grow in somewhat raised beds. You can achieve this by digging a ditch around where your roses are growing and by adding soil onto the top of the bed. Roses really do prefer growing higher up than what's around them. It comes from their natural habitat of broken land and river banks.

PLANT YOUR NEW ROSES NOW

Catalogues are coming my way and it's wonderful to think about all the new roses I want to plant. Let's hope we again have a great Annual Rose Raffle!

I'm also excited about the shrub form of *Mme. Cécile Brünner* (1881) which I have attempted to grow in the past and killed, one by drowning (It was 1995—the Flood of the Century, for goodness sakes.) and the second again by neglect. This one likes its spot and has already produced a few buds on its seven little stems. I know that this is a vigorous plant. I have seen several specimens in Salinas and Monterey which have been pruned into cherry tree looking entities with eight-inch diameter trunks and the top a bushy shrub rose. It's one of the very best roses to grow on the Central Coast and can be found surviving in many yards. I've also seen it pruned into hedges along a sidewalk or front window.

The little flowers will dry perfectly on your dashboard in the summertime and keep their beautiful pink color with a hint of yellow in the center. Everyone reading this *Manual* should find a spot for this bush.

WATCH OUT FOR RUST

Rust is one of the main airborne fungal diseases which infect rose bushes. Rose hybridizers have also made the greatest amount of progress on breeding resistance to this disease in modern roses. Unlike blackspot and powdery mildew, most roses introduced in the past thirty years have shown a good resistance to the disease. It does afflict many of the Old Garden Roses.

This was the first year that my hybrid perpetual *Baronne Prévost* (1842) was in the ground and it has given me five-inch, old rose, dark pink, deliciously scented flowers and endless joy all summer.   Last week, however, I noticed how susceptible it is to rust. It's the end of the year. My work schedule is intensely busy so I don't let it get me down. I will continue to water and weed it and perhaps throw some sulfur its way in the form of rose dust.

FALL NEEDS TO BE THE SEASON OF RESOLUTIONS

It's not New Years, but I'm making some resolutions. I want to remove a few more rose bushes from my garden. *Double Delight* (1977) is going. It's a real winner in areas with warmer, drier nights but only marginal here. *Roter Stern* (1958) [German: red star] is going. It might have earned a red star when it was introduced but there are healthier and more floriferous reds available. *Tribute* (1983) which I brought back from the brink a few years ago, is going. It's likely to be a forgotten rose which is sad. When *Tribute* has the right conditions, it's a noteworthy specimen with a gorgeous flower form and intense color. *Capistrano* (1949), which I so wanted to grow in my garden because it's a rose I remember from books I read as a boy, is going. It never could produce flowers that lasted and leaves that stayed mildew free.

Removing these poor producers might give me some extra room to move around and tend to weeds. Don't know about your yard, but mine is plagued all summer long with bindweed and some type of spurge. I want to spray RoundUp® less. It kills some plants better than others. Oxalis, arum italicum, nutgrass are never eliminated. Only their leaves and stems get fried.

I really did a number last summer on my *Matangi* (1974) which was down wind from where I was spraying. When spring came this year, a full half of this specimen shrub rose suffered from spring dwarfism induced by the RoundUp® AND the weeds I sprayed were back in force.

Let's hope this year's rainfall will again be ahead of average.

GOOD COMPANION PLANTS TO ROSES

I have decided my favorite companion plants with roses are those that are very slow growing and self-contained. I love the varieties of *geranium phaem* and *geranium sanguiem* and any of the *erodiums*. These are commonly called cranesbills.

Duchesse de Brabant, tea (1857)

Betty Boop, floribunda (1999)

They are terrific border plants. Many come in whites, pinks, and BLUES, complimentary to roses. I also love the *scabiosas*, especially when I keep the spent flower stocks removed.

Now is a terrific time to plant daffodils, crocuses, and other spring flowering bulbs. I am particularly fond of using them in a rose garden. They flower when the roses are dormant and pruned down to bare canes. They fade when the roses are at their best. They are absent entirely through the summer and fall where, if you need color, you can plant annuals.

Daffodils, especially the variety known as *Ice Follies* has naturalized in my garden. The *King Alfred* daffodil, I think, needs a slightly colder winter than what we get in North Salinas. It's okay, but nothing quite like Ice Follies.

The Miniature daffodils also do really well. I grow them both in the ground and in large containers. They bloom when the roses are dormant and disappear as the roses come in season. My favorite miniature daffodils are: *Tête a Tête* (blown-back yellow petals with yellow trumpets), *Jet Fire* (yellow petals with orange trumpets), and *Jack Snipe* (white petals with yellow trumpets). They come other sizes and shapes as well. Again, if left undisturbed, they will increase in number and beauty year after year. They also appreciate the season long rose feeding schedule although they spend two thirds of the year totally dormant.

I've had no luck with any of the alliums, better luck with some of the scillias, only so-so results with the grape hyacinths, tulips just don't work here, but I've had great seasonal growth with *Society Garlic*.

HOW TO PLANT BULBS

I mention daffodils now because good selections of them are available at local nurseries and through mail order catalogues. The last batch of *Ice Follies* (creamy petals and yellow trumpets) I won on an Ebay auction!

Graceland, hybrid tea (1988)

To plant daffodils or any other spring-flowering bulbs, dig a hole about four times the height of the bulb. Pick a place that is not likely to be disturbed in several years so that they can multiply comfortably. Place a handful of bone meal (or hoof and horn—which has both organic nitrogen and phosphorous) in the bottom of the hole. Do not mix it in. It lasts longer if it's concentrated. Place the bulb point-side up, root-side down and secure it in the hole so it doesn't tip sideways when you add the soil. Pack the soil firmly on top so that the hole doesn't become a drainage basin. The bulbs will rot if the soil doesn't drain properly. There's no need to stomp on it either. The bulb needs to send out roots in friable soil.

Arrange the holes in a line or some pattern separating each bulb by at least four widths of each bulb being planted. Sit back and wait.

Plant your bulbs before the first weekend in December. I've planted them as late as mid-January, but the results have never been good that first year.

Another great way to acquire cheap bulbs involves shopping at grocery and drug stores just after Easter. Many of these establishments are stuck with leftover pots of daffodils that have already bloomed. (People buy flowers, not plants.) Talk to the store manager and ask to buy each pot for a $1 instead of the full price. He is likely to just toss them in the trash because the flowers are gone. You can easily plant the bulbs in the garden while thinking of how great they'll be next spring. Do let the leaves naturally wither.

The one important lesson in growing great spring bulbs is allowing the plants to go dormant. I always deadhead spent daffodil or narcissus blooms. Don't let the plants spend energy developing seeds and seed pods. Clip them off with your pruning shears. Then, let the longer and hotter days of summer send the leaves' nutrients back down into the bulb. My best displays are a result of the leaves drying up so dry that I can easily gather them up.

I have also braided spent daffodil leaves and it adds a curious touch to the garden and puts some order into a chaotic spent display.

By the way, all jonquils are daffodils, but all daffodils are not jonquils. All daffodils are narcissuses, but all narcissuses are not daffodils. The terms are all confused now, so don't spend time worrying about what's correct.

ADVICE FROM THE PAST

This is now a most eligible season to plant almost all sorts of bulbous and tuberous flower roots, which were taken up when their leaves decayed . . . the beds wherein the fine varieties of these roots are to be planted must be well dug a proper depth and let all the clods be broken: the beds should be moderately highest in the middle, and laid somewhat rounding: this form best throws off the wet, and looks better; the beds should be three or four feet broad and raked even.

When the beds are ready, choose a dry and mild day to put in the roots; the best roots should be planted nine inches distant every way. Plant them in rows nine inches asunder, and not less that six inches in each row, by three or four inches deep; performing it either by dibble or drilling, or bedding in.

Thomas Mawe, London, 1797

November

Walking through the garden, I surveyed the damage from short, dark days and drizzly foggy weather. I have blackspot on a few roses. I found some aphids on a few others. I found some botrytis on hybrid tea buds and I found a lot of tired old leaves. Clean up is just about all you should do now. I want to have some flowers for Thanksgiving and maybe even Christmas so the best candidates for these were deadheaded. Other roses, which I don't use as cut flowers, had their petals pulled off. There's no point in encouraging new flowers on them as they'll do better getting some rest.

The roses will get a good chill in November. Typically, the porch thermometer at my house in Salinas records lows in the 30° range but the intensity of the cold isn't prolonged enough to send the roses into deep slumber land. What will do that is a longer spell of below 32°. Impatiens and other annuals are ready to be yanked. Take advantage of our warm sunshine for these chores. If the sun lasts through Thanksgiving, we get a lot done in the yard before it's just too cold and too wet.

Check your roses for their need of water. The showers we get now may or may not be giving them a sufficient supply.

Ferris Wheel, miniature (1984)

Miniatures are particularly at risk of drying out quickly because their roots are near the surface. A few afternoons can be in the 70s and the surface soil gets parched.

I have made heavy reference to my *Climbing Cécile Brünner* (1894) throughout this *Manual*. It is the large single rose in my entire garden. Why my sudden interest in this (I almost said "carefree") rose?

Had you visited my garden on the MBRS July rose tour, you might have noticed the *Climbing Cécile Brünner* that grew up the side of my potting shed, across its roof, over the fence, and up about ten feet into the neighbor's pine tree. On November 12, our first winter rain storm arrived. It was accompanied by powerful gusts of wind blowing up from the southeast. On my second trip to the kitchen for coffee, I noticed something was not right in the back yard. I was as busy as I could be and late for work, but I found time to let loose one long sigh. The entire *Cécile Brünner* had blown down in the storm and was lying in a 15' x 15' mass of tossed leaves, cracked canes, broken trellis, and rotting debris right in the middle of my back yard. I surveyed the damage and had no choice but to let it stay that way for a week.

I should have known better from the start. The neighbors cut down the pine tree in August—which was a good thing. Its roots were discovered beneath my old patio. I did not want them invading again—after having paid a considerable sum to replace the entire patio. But, I didn't do anything to the *Cécile Brünner* because I thought it was so large nothing was going to bother it. Wrong.

PRUNING DICTATED BY CIRCUMSTANCE

Where to start? When the weekend arrived and the day was an outdoor one, I inspected the cracks in the main canes. Not all were broken off, but some were. I pulled apart the severed canes and dragged them across the yard. I then looked at the amount of deadwood which had been hidden underneath the massive climber. That went, too. As I pulled apart the good canes, I snipped away any awkward or inconsequential growth. Then, I kicked out the ruined ladder trellis and nailed in a replacement. Cane by cane I lifted *Cécile Brünner* back onto the potting shed. Several of the canes remained long enough for me to tie them to the other side of the shed and with luck prevent a similar reoccurrence.

Phyllis Bide (1923) and *Isfahan* (1832) planted on either side of it had also come down in the storm. Phyllis needs a good pruning every year anyway. So I removed the cracked canes and deadwood and brought it down to a manageable eight feet.

Isfahan has an entirely different growth pattern. What I did for it was interesting. It's a damask rose and thus once flowering. I should have pruned it back in August, but I didn't. It was late in the season to prune one-time blooming roses. However, circumstances being what they were, I had no choice. Its canes were not nearly as brittle as the two climbing polyanthas. They were flexible and unbroken. My cane removal method focused on eliminating the oldest (most barren) canes and preserving the newest and strongest canes. Isfahan, too, had amassed a considerable amount of deadwood which should have been taken out a year ago.

It was a lot of work which produced six 33-gallon trash containers of chopped rose bush. But, my three big roses ought to be in great form for high rose tide.

THIN OUT YOUR CLIMBERS

Stormy, rainy weather is about to arrive and I need to get up and thin out *Madame Alfred Carrière* (1879). All the summer's growth combined with wet leaves and gale-force winds spell big trouble for your climbers. The stress on their fasteners is at its greatest now. Even if it's too soon to prune, I find there's no harm in thinning out some of the growth now when it's relatively easy to work with the bushes.

Always be extra careful when you are using ladders in a garden. The ground is uneven and its firmness is always questionable. Please make sure that someone is around and knows what you're doing. If you have an accident—heaven forbid, at least you won't be down for too long before help arrives.

CLEAN YOUR GARDEN BEFORE THE RAINS BEGIN

It's time to shut down the garden and I like this time of year a lot. It's refreshing to clean out all that's been and make room for all that will be.

If you have been religiously removing spent flower petals but allowing the hips to remain, your rose bushes will spend their remaining energy on developing hips. Many of my one time bloomers are in full display of their hips. The *Rosa eglanteria* or Eglantine species rose (also known as the sweetbriar and Shakespeare's Rose as the great playwright included it in Oberon's speech in *A Midsummer Night's Dream*) has produced a bumper crop of the brightest red-orange hips! They are elongated and covered with prickles.

Rosa californica, species, hips

WATER YOUR ROSES SUFFICIENTLY

Be careful of these misleading cool damp days. Check your roses carefully. They may need water especially those in pots. I just tossed out four of my healthiest cuttings, dried to a bone through negligence. I forgot to water them. The showers we will start to get may or may not give them a sufficient supply. Miniatures are particularly at risk of drying out quickly because their roots are near the surface. If the soil surface below the rose is dry to the touch, water!

REMOVAL OF OTHER GROWTH

The grocery outlet was selling daffodils and other bulb plants eight for $1.99. That's a deal knowing that they will multiply. I trim my hydrangeas to the ground. This year's flower crop was particularly attractive so I may tie the flower clusters upside down in my potting shed for a dried, fall arrangement. The trumpet vine gets a major haircut. If not contained, it gets too wild. It also has the power to split concrete so you can imagine what it will do to a redwood fence if given a chance. I shape up here and trim back there.

If I manage to have a spare hour or two and don't feel like doing anything brainy, I sit on a stool in front of an Old Garden Rose and help it go to sleep by pulling off all of its leaves. Now is not, repeat, NOT the time to do any trimming of one time blooming roses. They should be pruned back after they have bloomed in midsummer. By pulling off the leaves, however, you may find some weak or dead canes. Now IS a good time to extract deadwood.

LEARN TO LOVE THOSE BIG HIPS!

As many of you know, I'm a fan of rose hips and the bushes which produce them. I'm particularly interested in plants which offer bright orange hips just in time for Halloween and Thanksgiving and bright red ones for Christmas and New Year's.

When I grew *Altissimo* (1966), a fire-engine red, five-petalled pillar rose, I looked forward to the fall because it produced magnificently large pumpkin-shaped hips. As a plant, *Altissimo* was stiff and leggy and not always generous with blooms, but oh those hips! In fairness, I grew this rose on a north facing wall and it clearly wanted a little more sunshine. It's a great rose and if I had right spot, I'd grow it again.

Honorine de Brabant, a bourbon rose which has been around since the 1850s with striped lavender and mauve petals produces continuously through the season offers just wonderful oval, bright red hips at Christmas. These look so beautiful with a December bouquet of *Iceberg* blooms.

Rosa californica produces great red cherry hips in large clusters. *Rosa woodsii fendleri* offers a different type of hip, large sprays of red, pea size beauties with prominent sepals dangling below. The fantastic noisette *Jeanne d'Arc (1884)* sports large clusters of elongated orange hips. There are many more. The burnet roses produce large mahogany hips. Eglantines offer spiny orange hips on prickly stems. The hips of one time bloomers showing color is an added treat mostly enjoyed by rose lovers only. Much education needs to happen.

SEED HARVEST IS NOW ON

My Novembers are spent harvesting seeds from some of my favorite annuals. These usually have been hanging in my shed for several weeks and offer a bountiful quantity of seed. I use a colander and a sieve to separate the chaff and store the seeds in glass jars for next year. I keep nigella (Persian Jewels), blue thimble flowers, and one of the spurges—perhaps gopher. The snails don't like any of these and therefore allow them to grow beautifully.

GET YOUR ROSE CATALOGUES ORDERED

Now is also a great time to think about and order new roses. If you have access to the Internet, sources of roses are easy to find and there are some promising new varieties being toted. They're great to look through while digesting turkey, stuffing, mashed potatoes, gravy, cranberries.... Happy Thanksgiving!

ADVICE FROM THE PAST

Now clear the borders from all dead annual plants pulling them up by the roots; such as African and French marigolds, lavateras, China asters, and all other of the like kinds, for these never survive to flower again.

Cut down all the dead stems or decayed flower stalks of perennial plants, and let the borders be well cleared from leaves of trees and all sorts of rubbish and litter.

After this, let the surface of the borders be gone over with a Dutch, or common hoe in a dry day, cutting up all remaining weeds, and loosen the general surface, and then rake them smooth.

This prevents the growth of weeds, and renders the borders clean and decent for the winter season.

Thomas Mawe, London, 1797

Jeanne d'Arc, noisette (1848)

December

Often during December, we experience a warming trend which totally confuses the roses. I have recorded a few days of 70° weather. For the roses which still had buds on them, I got several beautiful blooms. The fall flowering roses seem much more vividly colored than spring and summer blossoms. The foliage, where it exists, is really not too bad. A few holes here and there but, considering the lack of attention, rather presentable if not downright showy. It's a bit of a chore to walk about the garden as I just can't believe they have grown so much since Labor Day.

Because of these warm and sunny afternoons, I have had to stretch out the garden hose and give my roses a hearty drink. The miniature roses are especially susceptible to drought because their roots are mostly near the surface.

The rainy days we had in November were ideal for blackspot and botrytis to spread everywhere. My miniatures are now often totally leafless except at the end of the canes where the warm weather has started the growth of more leaves.

GET READY FOR WINTER

The days are at their shortest now so any growth attained in such minimal sunshine won't amount to much. Although my advice is not to prune until mid-January, when I'm down on my knees beside a bush and notice ultimately doomed side growth and deadwood, I get it gone.

I will also do early pruning if two things have happened. One, there have been several nights when the low temperature has fallen below freezing and, two, there are free, sunny days to work in the garden. The cold weather causes the roses to go dormant and the short, cool days keeps them from starting to grow. Pruning too early puts the new shoots your roses will produce at risk of freezing should the January or February storms be extremely cold ones.

My second reason why I might have to prune now has to do with wind storms. During the past many seasons of growing roses in Salinas, I've had horrible wind damage. Twenty feet high *Cécile Brünner*'s have come crashing off their trellises and laid in a heap in the back yard. When the weather cleared, I trimmed them as heavily as I dared, lifted them up over my head and back onto their supports—the hardest work in the rose garden, in my opinion, as the bushes are heavy, damaged, full of hard, sharp thorns, and soaking wet.

Apricot Twist, miniature (1993)

Fortunately, I also cleared out all of my drainage ditches and the roof gutters which run beneath several climbing roses. I dug out much *Arum italicum* which I have managed to spread all over the place. Don't ever let this near your garden. It produces tiny little bulbettes which snap off and show up in several months as mature plants. My means of ridding the yard of this nuisance is to dig out the bush and throw away the bulb soil and all.

I also like to spend some time in December and January removing the leaves from many of my roses. It's wet and I can't really get going on more serious projects, but I do want to be in the garden. I usually get a small stool, position it in front of a rose and pick it clean of leaves. This too will help the rose go dormant and keep the leaves, infested with fungal spores, from overwintering in the garden. I did this Christmas Eve morning in the middle of a fierce wind. Old leaves will fall anyway. Why put more weight on the canes when the leaves get wet. I'm always afraid of snapping canes off in the wind at unattractive spots.

This past month, we can experience it all; record setting hot temperatures, short days and cold, dark nights, and our first rainfall of the season. It's always amazing how nice my garden and the general neighborhood looks after a shower has rinsed the dust off the leaves. More rain is certain to fall and the coldest temperatures of the year will be upon us.

TIE UP YOUR CLIMBERS

A large rose bush can be very heavy when it's soaked with rain and tossed about in the wind. I like to use clothes line which has an inner core of wire, an outer layer of plastic and a filling of nylon cord. This is a bit unsightly as I can only find it in bright white. During the rose season, however, the leaves mostly hide the cord. Make sure whatever you are tying the rose to is also secure. I've been through two or three of those wimpy (but attractive) trellises sold in the Garden Department of a big box store. They do look nice and they don't rot. They just aren't quite strong enough to support a really BIG rose.

MOVE AND REMOVE YOUR ROSES NOW

The roses I am removing, I cut down leaving just enough cane at the bottom to grip and yank once I've loosened the soil around the rose. Because it hasn't rained too much, the soil in my garden isn't too heavy yet. The roses I pulled out of the ground were ones which I've had for about eight years. I never once got a really show stopping bloom from

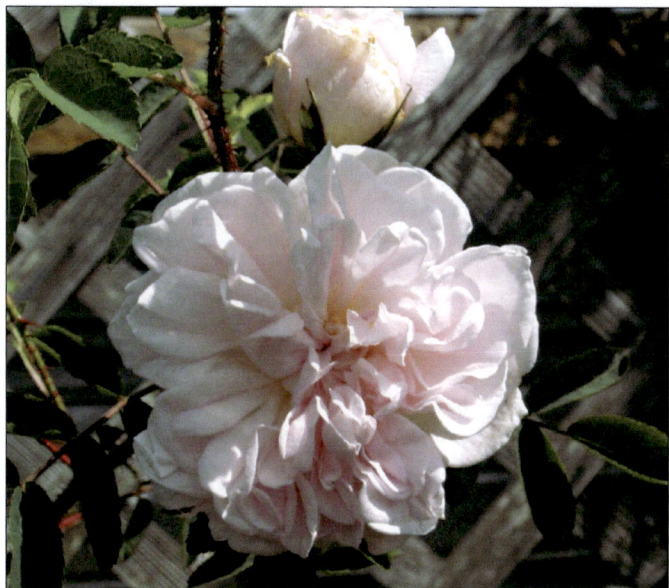

Lady of the Mist, shrub (2002)

Stanwell Perpetual, hybrid spinossisima (1838)

either of them. When some nutgrass invaded the garden bed in their area and I sprayed a good dose of RoundUp® on it I missed my mark and got it on these two roses. They were the polyantha *Chatillon Rose* (1923) and the miniature *Cri Cri* (1958). I didn't even use a shovel, just got a good grip and pulled upward. The soil in that part of the bed is really friable. I also removed a fuchsia called "Fanfare" which I bought as a shoot at the UCSC Arboretum two years ago. I decided I'd had enough of Fanfare when it reached ten feet and invaded all of its neighboring roses. What a mess!

I have a wonderfully slow growing *Viburnum davidii* which I noticed needs a good reduction plan. My trumpet vine and *Climbing Cécile Brünner* had to be trimmed up in order for me to work on the no-plants-land between my fence and potting shed. It's too dark for roses and too hard to get to for much else.

A few years ago I wrote that my big relocation job was *Stanwell Perpetual* (1838). It's a hybrid spinnisissima or Scotch briar—one of the very best Old Garden Roses. It's nearly disease-free, when given plenty of room, and never without a fragrant bloom. I'd had it in three different places and can't quite find the right one. I planted it at my office in Carmel where it was never happy. This past summer I brought it back to Salinas and it has just come to life again. Now I want to move it up against my potting shed and hope to get it in the ground (it's in a black pot) before Christmas. *Stanwell Perpetual* is really prickly. I bought a new pair of goatskin gloves specifically for this effort.

Margaret Merril, floribunda (1977)

AMEND OR REPLACE USED UP SOIL

Too many of our yards have one (or a few) perfect places left to put a rose. Once it's time to remove that rose from its perfect spot, discard the soil that it was growing in and replace it with fresher stuff. If that's not possible, then add ample amounts of cow manure and some sand (only if you have heavy clay soils). I like to pull out the rose and its roots in a clump. Then shake the rose free of soil. I usually stand in a different part of the garden and let the used up soil fall on the top of the remaining mulch.

I then pour into the hole about three cubic feet of cow manure and a gallon of sand. I mix the soil, sand, and the cow manure and let it rest for a week or two. This isn't necessary but, if I can't get back to work in the yard for a couple of weeks, the rain will help the cow manure to decompose further, make its nutritional content more available, and allow microbes and earthworms to circulate through the new mix.

In the spot where I yanked up the two roses that I mentioned above, I decided to bury a dead bird and two dead rats, a donation from Buddy, my ever-present garden companion. The decaying animals will add a variety of nutrients to the soil and won't likely be disturbed until they are reduced to their essential elements, dust to dust.

CHECK YOUR GARDEN'S DRAINAGE NOW

Don't repeat my mistake of waiting too long before I made sure that my garden would drain quickly. I've spent several rainy mornings out in my yard getting soaked, opening up my drainage ditches. You can expect several days of heavy downpours. The water must go somewhere. That's a fact. And if you live in a flat neighborhood, you had better make sure that your garden beds are slightly higher than the rest of your yard and that your entire yard is able to expel any excess water. Point the downspouts on your house and garage in a direction where the rain water they drain won't erode or flood your garden beds.

MAKING CHANGES IN THE GARDEN

As promised, I dug out six roses. Five of these came out without much strain. The plants were underperforming and, not surprisingly, the roots were seriously underdeveloped. Essentially, some roses are more vigorous than others. The five I had no trouble digging out were in good locations and growing in friable soil. There's not much you can do when the rose variety itself is an under performer.

The sixth rose caused a bit of a sweat. It was the very decent modern climber *Golden Showers* (1950). It was too big for the spot I put it in. Why did I do that? Well, I didn't know it was *Golden Showers* when I planted it. That's what I told myself as I tried to extricate it without damaging its neighbors.

I took it as a cutting from my mother's yard where it got terrible attention, was subject to frigid winters, nibbling rabbits and too little sunshine. I thought it was a lemony little thing called *Betty Compton*. Not sure how I thought that but someone back home must have told me. I've never found any reference to a rose named *Betty Compton*. So I got the cutting to root and once rooted stuck it in a then empty corner of my back yard. It was a good private laugh—not quite an epiphany—when the first bloom opened and I realized that mom was growing *Golden Showers*, a rose easily identified as it matched another that was growing on my back fence.

I'll repeat, *Golden Showers* is a highly recommended, disease resistant medium size climber. The only fault I have with it is it wants to be too big for my yard and the flowers don't last as long as I'd like them to. It's a nice deep yellow, too, and doesn't fade.

NOT TOO EARLY
FOR SOME PRUNING

Although I don't recommend you start pruning your roses now, if you are down on your knees and notice some cleaning up you could do, by all means start now. I grow about 165 rose bushes of varying sizes. That's still too many to give the care that I would like to give.

GARDENING TIPS FOR
THE END OF THE YEAR

Here are some ways to make your garden chores easier:

- Walk your garden and look carefully at each and every rose bush you grow. Spend at least a minute or two looking inside and around each one. Bring your pruning shears and a bucket for the scraps along with you on your tour.

- Cut out any and all dead and dying wood and discard the trimmings.

- Prune away all blind shoots and inconsequential growth.

- Remove any larger canes which are growing through the center of the plant.

- Leave intact any and all rose hips that have developed. They help the rose bushes to stop growing and go dormant.

- Cut some of the nicer hips and decorate your house for the holidays. You should have an assortment to choose from. If not, make some changes so that you do. If you make a holiday wreath of rose hips, don't save it in the attic. Rats love hips and might find them.

- Deadhead the spent roses that don't produce hips. Modern roses will continue to flower in our mild winter so feel free to keep harvesting those blooms for your holiday table.

- Pull off the petals of roses which are likely to rot in the rain. I don't even let them open. I hate it when I look out at the garden and all the rose buds have botrytis and turn into disgusting looking gray wads.

- Give garden sanitation your highest attention by raking up all dead rose leaves and petals.

- I once warned against pulling out the oxalis, but now find that if you get it removed before it gets too established, it takes it longer to return. I like to think if I can't poison it, then I'll frustrate its growth habit. White Vinegar works for this purpose.

- If you have any standing water in your garden, make an effort to drain it away immediately. You won't want to see your roses drowning and the garden too soft and muddy for you to do anything to help them.

- Watch out for quickly sprouting weed seeds. It's easier to hoe them under when they just emerge than it is to wait until they grow and pull them out.

- Invest in a potting shed. I just love mine and find myself sitting in it as the rain beats down and ruins my plans to work in the garden proper. I tossed out so much junk: old rotten baskets, broken hand tools, ruined leather gloves, busted up garden pots, broken stakes. I sat outside and read my rose catalogues. I looked at the progress I've made over the years and am almost satisfied with the result.

- If you ARE watering and feeding your roses and still not getting great results, there's something wrong. Take a trowel and poke around underneath the rose. If you find something invading roots, you may have to lift the rose out and get rid of the invaders. You may have crown gall. You may have rotten drainage. If everything seems in order, the rose bush may not be right for this area. A rose without flowers is useless. Eliminate it without regret.

- Don't eat watermelon in your garden. More specifically, don't spit the seeds in your rose garden. I had no idea they would like my soil. Same goes for cherry tomatoes.

- Clean your garden tools regularly with Lysol floor detergent, especially during the season when you're deadheading. It will help eliminate die back on canes.

- Scrape your fingernails across a bar of soap before you start working in the garden. When it's time to clean up, it will take much less scrubbing.

- Wear old, loose clothes in the garden. Manually remove the prickles from the canes of roses in high traffic areas.

Scentimental, floribunda (1997)

ADVICE FROM THE PAST

Take care now, if frosts should set in, to protect the roots of the more curious new planted shrubs and trees, by laying strawy mulch on the surface of the ground: but this is more particular to be understood of the more curious or tender kinds; but would also be beneficial to all others.

Thomas Mawe, London, 1797

Common Rose Challenges

*A*lthough I mention various obstacles all gardeners encounter on the Central Coast throughout the *Roses By Month* section, I thought I would provide some additional information in this chapter on the most prevalent challenges you'll face. A few articles were special interest ones published in *The Bay Rose* over the years, so they run a bit longer.

Maria Callas, hybrid tea (1968) in detail

Disease and Pestilence

BLACKSPOT

Diplocarpon rosae

This airborne fungal disease is persistent and is spread by splashing water droplets. Once infected, the leaves produce the plant hormone ethylene as a means of healing itself. High ethylene content in leaves causes them to yellow and drop off. So once you see the telltale blackspots or splotches, it's too late. The leaf will die. The dropped leaves are storage containers of spores waiting for more water droplets to catch a ride on. Rake the base of suffering plants thoroughly.

Blackspot which is not a pathogen is easily misdiagnosed as downy mildew, a parasitic fungus. Both are prevalent on the Central Coast. The edge of the spot in blackspot has a feathery margin. Downey mildew on the other hand usually develops a straighter edge to its spot, often has a dead spot in the center, and the underside mycelium though tiny stand up like down directly below the spot.

Blackspot

As the roses lose their leaves early, they'll look bare but won't die. Blackspot also affects many species roses growing in the wild which recover when the weather changes. Take advantage of the bush's misfortune though and prune off any inconsequential growth coming from the lower half of the bush. Open up the center of the plant and remove any little canes that might catch and hold on to dead leaves. If you use overhead watering, do so only early in the morning or when you know that the leaves will dry completely within an hour or so. The growth cycle of the fungus is ready to begin again within 10 to 18 days after first infection. Ideal conditions are rainy periods with temperatures between 50 and 80°F.

Good air circulation is the best preventive measure for controlling blackspot. Make sure you have plenty of room to walk around each of your rose bushes. Spraying your garden with a dormant oil spray after you have pruned and raked your garden helps to kill any overwintering spores. The spray will also cover and therefore suffocate insect eggs.

Roses hybridized in the past few years are proving to be much more resistant to this common rose affliction. Check out hybridizer Bill Radler's family of *Knock Out* roses. He's expanded the color range and petal count of this tough-as-nails member of the species.

POWDERY MILDEW

Sphaerotheca pannosa

The Central Coast's notorious and discouraging summertime affliction, powdery mildew is an airborne fungus which thrives when the weather is hot and dry during the day and cold and damp during the night. It's the typical weather pattern we live with from late-May to mid-September. The practice of "big box" venders ordering their roses from a central office in the United States and marketing them heavily without regard to local climates is a further wrinkle to unknowing gardeners. Only a few varieties of the thousands of available roses are truly immune to powdery mildew but some are more resistant than others. Because of this long period and the accompanying disappointment, many novice rose growers just throw in the trowel.

Powdery mildew

Select the varieties recommended in this book. Look about your neighborhood and see what is prospering. Find out the names and grow those roses.

Several varieties I grow suffer from powdery mildew. I keep them in the garden because I like the flowers. A little sulfur dust sprinkled on the leaves will help them get through the summer and keep them growing. I get good spring and autumn blooms from them and know the weather will change.

Overhead watering will keep the leaves clean. Make sure it's done in the morning so the leaves can dry off quickly. Otherwise you create the condition for blackspot to attack. A summer dormant oil will coat new leaves and make it harder for the fungal spores to become attached. In a similar fashion, anti-desiccants such as Cloud Cover coat the leaves with a polymer which allows the plant to hold onto its moisture and prevents the spores from gaining a toe-hold. These products must be reapplied regularly as the plant develops new growth which is also the most susceptible.

Home remedies include spraying the leaves with Epsom salt or baking soda or even skim milk. The recipes for deer repellents will also coat the leaves with substances which should block the spores from growing. Rest assured. Powdery mildew is a seasonal problem and is specific to certain varieties. Choose well, feed well and use some inhibiting practices. This should allow for good blossoms all summer long. You also have to face the fact that roses that did just fine for you in Baltimore or Tucson or Mobile may not be happy here.

RUST

Phragmidium mucronatum

In the past thirty years, much progress has been made by rose hybridizers to make their new introductions increasingly resistant to this airborne fungal disease. It's easy to recognize. The spore packets are rust-colored and cover the underside of a rose leaf. Rust afflicts specific varieties of rose when the temperature is right.

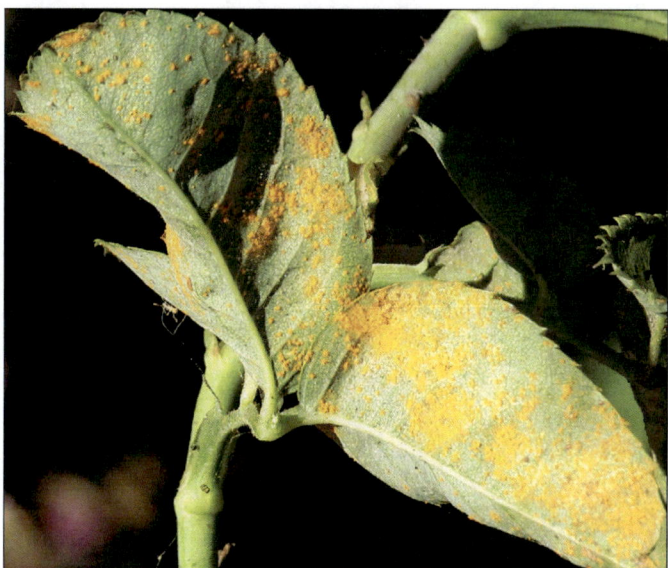

Rust

Like its cousins, blackspot and powdery mildew, it flourishes when there are wet cool nights and hot dry days. It too runs rampant in congested areas where the spores aren't carried away by the wind and moisture remains high.

Best controls for rust are selecting disease resistant varieties, planting them with sufficient room between the bushes for you to move 360° around them, and keeping the centers of the bush open. You can do the later by clearing out dead leaves and removing inconsequential growth.

BOTRYTIS

You may also know this fungal parasite by its many other common names: Gray Mold, Flower Balling, Water Spot, Gray Ghost, or just plain Rot. Its botanical name is *botrytis cinerea* and it's a terror to numerous non-woody plants worldwide. In agriculture, it's a particular hazard and can wipe out a harvest of grapes, strawberries, apples, and lettuce in no time flat. Cut flowers are also susceptible. Commercial growers must always have controls in place.

With November storms comes the rain we need so badly. It's likely to be the first precipitation since May and is welcomed by all. With wet weather, however, comes the primary ingredients for a massive outbreak of *botrytis cinerea*: temperatures between 60° and 72°, dampness on the leaves and petals for more than 7 hours straight, abundant spores in the air, less air circulation around our individual roses (they've had the summer to get larger and fill in the empty spaces) and a shortening day.

On roses, *botrytis cinerea* manifests itself first on open petals or the outer petals of a rose bud. It's most noticeable on the white and pink petals as little red circles or spots. On red or orange petals, you may notice some brown, dead patches on the outer petals. The mycelium or spore is blown onto the petal surface and with the aid of water droplets adheres itself to an area of broken or damaged cell tissue. It sends out its equivalent of roots and begins to invade healthy cells consuming them to fuel its own growth.

As this initial infestation occurs on petals, you can limit damage by pulling off those petals and allowing the hips to ripen. Frequently, a change in the weather might bring drier, calmer air and this will halt further growth.

The next stage is even more visible and irritating. Many roses with petal counts of 25 or more, especially those with thin petals, are very susceptible to botrytis. The fungus attacks the outer five petals of rose buds days before they would have opened and spreads. It destroys the large outer petals and begins to work on the inner ones. If there is a change in the weather, however, and the air and petal surface dry, these dead outer petals become a type of sealed paper which the still healthy inner petals don't have the strength to break through. Usually, the fungus has also eaten through the petal base and the whole wad falls off.

Botrytis

Many older books describe this phenomenon as "balling" because Old Garden Rose buds with the rosette or quartered shape are quite globular. Sometimes you can just peel open these buds and they will stay on the bush a few days as blooms.

The final stage of this fungus is its spore-producing period. As the mycelium ripen, they turn a medium gray to black. If disturbed, these rotted rose buds will send out a cloud of spores ready to infect the next plant. Don't let your afflicted rose buds get to the stage when they are covered with the ripe gray mold.

Several fungicides exist which control the disease. I don't recommend applying them in home gardens and certainly not at this time of year as weather conditions will promote botrytis growth and the spores are airborne. The best control is to remove spent or nearly spent roses before the onset of the wet weather. At the first dry moment, go back in the garden with pruning shears and a bucket and get the dead and dying flowers, shoots or canes removed. If you can rake off all the spent petals and leaves which have fallen to the ground, this will eliminate further hiding places for the spores.

Botrytis cinerea is not a total malady. Even the wine industry which can be afflicted by grape bunch rot near harvest time, if the conditions are correct, ultimately benefits from it. The presence of *Botrytis cinerea* adds to the flavor of the wine. In fact, sauternes derive their characteristic taste from it. In the cycle of life as well, *Botrytis cinerea* aids the decom-

position of plant materials and thus contributes to the garden indirectly by being a compost catalyst. A good spray of dormant oil on your pruned roses and the mulch surrounding them in late January is a proven way to decrease the number of spores.

As research on botrytis and its symbiotic relationship with other molds and bacteria continues, botanists are discovering that the nature of this common affliction is quite complex.

GALLS

Agrobacterium tumefaciens

In one January pruning frenzy, I noticed that my *Climbing Étoile de Hollande* (1931) [French: star of Holland], originally one of the most vigorous of my large climbers, had sent out no new canes the past year and many of the older canes displayed substantial die-back. I pruned it heavily and thought I might, when spring finally arrived, give it some extra nutrients (blood meal, Epsom salt, and a little more fertilizer).

Spring arrived, and I got some new growth with many rose buds appearing on "The Star of Holland." But the vigor was definitely gone. A plant that once was covered in canes, leaves, and flowers produced a bare minimum of new growth. *Flash back.* Last season really wasn't a showstopper either for this bush. The flowers are somewhat smaller this year and the shape of the climber has lost its grace. Something was up.

At first, I thought I might have been too sloppy with my RoundUp®. Nutgrass grows in that area and I have to spray

Etoile de Holland, hybrid tea (1931)

heavily to control it. But, *Étoile* didn't look like it suffered from that affliction.

As I was preparing the rose bed for a huge application of mulch by pulling weeds, rearranging the soil beneath the rose, and clearing out old dried rose leaves from last season, I got a trowel and dug around the base of *Étoile*. I suspected it but didn't want to see what I saw. A grapefruit size gall had formed around the base of the rose and was staring up at me in all its vulgarity. It wasn't as if this teenage rose was hiding its condition! After all, it was MY fault it got this trouble.

Quickly, to the Internet went I. What I found was absolutely amazing. Mother Nature is so much cleverer than we can imagine! Crown gall is an infliction of many woody garden plants including all members of the rose family (apricots, apples, cherries, almonds). It afflicts a wider range of plants than any other disease. The culprit is a soil-borne bacterium, *Agrobacterium tumefaciens*, which has some absolutely incredible characteristics.

Agrobacterium tumefaciens is a non-sporing, rod-shaped bacterium related to *Rhizobium* which causes nitrogen fixing nodules on clover and leguminous plants. It's present in soils all around the world. It enters a plant through an open wound and once inside begins its evil magic.

Flash further back. While I was pruning *Étoile de Hollande* three seasons ago, it started to rain. It was the last rose I needed to prune and I was tired and getting wet. My loppers were on the other side of the yard and I had no idea where my pruning saw was. So the dried up old stub of a long since dead cane was sticking out of the bud union, and I just kicked it with my shoe.

Sure enough, it cracked off. When I went to pick it up, however, I realized it hadn't been a clean break so I pulled at it and tore some bark down along and under the soil line. Three years passed and now, the crown gall.

When a rose root is damaged, it seeps its invisible fluids into the soil, similar to the milky sap a poinsettia oozes when a leaf is broken off. *Agrobacterium tumefaciens* senses this sap being released, like the Real McCoys heard their ole' dinner bell. The invasion begins.

A. tumefaciens multiplies itself and enters the rose. But, it doesn't just stay there as a parasite like mistletoe—two separate plants, one living off the other.

No, *A. tumefaciens* is much shrewder. It invades the cell structure of its host and places within that structure an independent set of chromosomes called a plasmid. Most of the genes involved in crown gall disease are not borne in the chromosome, but are contained within the tumor-inducing plasmid. This plasmid then alters the host's cell structure convincing it to do something that its parents hadn't intended at all. It essentially re-programs the host's genetic instructions.

The tumor-like appendages we see visibly choking the life out of the rose bush is actually the rose itself gone crazy. Its signals confused, roots and bark divert the smooth

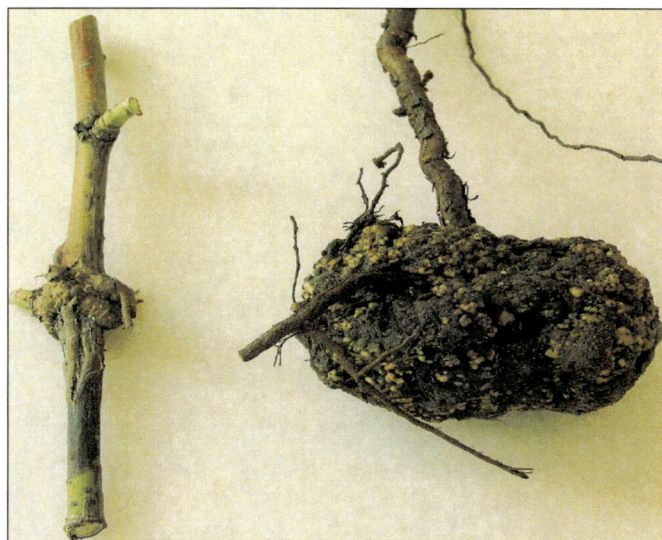

Galls can develop on injured portions of a bud union, stem, or root and cause a lack of vigor, and eventual death of all or part of the rose.

progress of nutrients up from the roots to the plants into the galls. These tumors appear at the spot of the injury and alter the growth habit.

Older galls are not necessarily horrendous repositories of *Agrobacterium tumefaciens*. The bacteria is abundant in the soil around the rose and around the outer surface of the gall which has contact with the soil, but not necessary inside the gall.

A relatively new biological control agent for crown gall developed by Australian Allan Kerr in 1973 is available for apple, pear, stone fruit, blueberry, brambles and many ornamentals. Kerr essentially discovered that a nonpathogenic strain of bacterium (*Agrobacterium radiobacter* strain 84) can protect plants against infection. By dipping plants at the nursery in a suspension of commercially prepared *Agrobacterium radiobacter* strain 84 before planting will give them natural resistance to crown gall. *A. radiobacter* strain 84, however, acts only to protect disease-free plants from future infection by the crown gall bacterium. This procedure cannot cure infected plants.

It was once felt that applications of copper could treat the disease, but the build up of copper in the soil is ultimately detrimental to the roses.

There is no cure for the disease. You may be able to take cuttings from the infected rose and grow new plants. Usually in roses, the gene altering plasmids stay close to the soil where the bacterium lives and don't migrate to all the cells in the plant as a rose mosaic virus will. However, it's important for you to proceed methodically and remove the entire bush and the soil it was growing in.

Cut the rose bush down to the bud union leaving only a few six-inch long canes to serve as handles. Dig the soil

Rose mosaic virus

18 inches from the center of the bud union with a spade. Take your spade and dig away from the rose until you have a healthy moat encircling the condemned bush. Then, proceed carefully lifting up all the soil, gall material, roots, and bud union of the bush. Keep a large trash can nearby and throw into it all materials falling within the original 36 inch diameter and 18-inch depth. Do not attempt to move the soil elsewhere unless you have lots of land and don't care what grows where you dump it. For most of us in the city, put it in the yard waste and get it out of your life forever.

Follow sanitary gardening rules. Use a bleach solution (1 cup per gallon) to rinse off your shovel, pruning shears, leather gloves and anything else that may have come into contact with *A. tumefaciens.*

Anyone claiming that man must not alter the genes of other living things certainly doesn't know much about *A. tumefaciens.* That's exactly what it's doing to your rose. It has the remarkable ability to incorporate itself into a plant's life and meet little resistance. The incredible properties of this bacterium were not lost on genetic engineers. The basis of genetic engineering using Agrobacterium is that the DNA contained in the plasmid of A. tumefaciens integrates into the plant genome as part of the natural

infection process by this bacterium. So, any foreign DNA inserted into the plasmid will also be integrated.

Scientists were quick to use this bacterium to do the following things: alter tomatoes to give a more vine-ripened flavored and extend shelf life; provide enhanced insect resistance to cotton, potatoes, and corn; and make cotton, soybeans, and canola impervious to the effects of RoundUp®.

Genetic engineers are working on placing enzymes which degrade the cellular walls of fungal diseases into these plasmids. Instead of creating galls, the rose bush will be able to muster its own forces and destroy the outer walls of fungal diseases such as powdery mildew, blackspot, and rust. The future is very promising for rose growers.

ROSE MOSAIC VIRUS

Rose mosaic virus is an indication of sloppy propagation practices in the growing fields. Several varieties of mosaic viruses exist. They manifest themselves by causing discolored blotches, lines, or patterns, often yellow or combinations of colors on rose leaves; often on the first set of leaves in the spring, often after heavy applications of Epsom salt. This virus is not contagious, just unsightly, but it arguably weakens the plant. Please note that you did nothing to acquire this condition. It already existed when you bought the rose bush.

The mosaic virus was used by horticultural firms to cause leaf variegation in commercial house and garden plants. Somehow, the virus was transmitted to the roses used for root stock in the growing fields. The infected root stock was propagated year after year in the field. Year after year, it transmitted the virus to the grafted roses.

The only practical cure for mosaic virus is to rip the rose out of the ground by hand and run it over to the nursery where you bought it, slam it down on the counter, point out its presence and demand your money back. Unless WE ALL protest, growers will not change their ways.

My backyard allows for a variety of birds and predatory insects.

Pests, Marauders, and Friends

APHIDS

Aphidoidea

Aphids are the most common rose pest. This is true because varieties of aphids are present in the spring, summer and fall. The eggs which hatch in the spring are all female and they are born pregnant. This form of reproduction is called parthenogenesis. Babies emerge in a matter of days. They cause damage by sucking the juice out of buds and tender shoots of roses. They are easy to spot as they cluster together, usually at the tips of new growth. During an aphid's life cycle, it molts its outer skin and leaves its former carcass behind on the top of rose buds and leaves.

Aphids

Formerly called "plant lice," aphids tend to appear early in the season, but can be found clustering on sweet new growth at anytime in our area. They also seem to target roses which receive a gardener's inadequate attention. They can almost sense whether the plant is already in a weakened state and then attack it. They can be black, green, pink, brown or almost colorless. The changes in light in the fall or an over population can trigger the aphids to produce winged male and female versions which mate, fly off and establish new colonies by depositing eggs in the nooks and crannies of your other roses. They find new growth delicious and will cluster around it. After pruning your garden, spray the canes, bud unions, and the soil around them with dormant oil. This will safely reduce their population. A covering of summer oil on the leaves and canes will also slow their attack as well as inhibit fungal diseases.

Victorians used a very soft bristle brush to sweep them off plants. The bristles caused serious damage to the aphids' soft bellies but didn't affect the canes or new leaves. In my Salinas neighborhood, we are blessed with flocks of bush tits averaging about six to eight birds in a group. They enter the garden seemingly from nowhere chirping happily, flitting from bush to bush, pecking at any insect that happens to be on the canes and leaves. They prefer a variety of plant elevations from which they will move up and down controlling the aphid population. They disappear as abruptly as they appeared.

Several varieties of ants, on the other hand, will actually "farm" an aphid colony. The ants feed on comicle or honeydew, a substance secreted by the aphids. The ants will actually use their antennae to "milk" the aphids. It's one of the best examples of mutualism in nature as the ants will ward off any predatory insects as shepherds do guarding their flocks.

Aphids' slow metabolism will work in your favor. Squirt them with soapsuds, rinse them off with a hose, or prune off the deformed growth and discard it. Every aphid you kill means you've killed hundreds.

BLACK WIDOW SPIDERS

"What did I get for Christmas?" I'm waiting to be asked, "I got bit by a black widow. That's what I got!" Yes, I spent part of Christmas Eve in Natividad Hospital. I met Dr. Michael Solomon who explained to me that, in fact, even if I had been bitten by a black widow which I couldn't prove, there wasn't anything he could do. "We can give you something for the symptoms. Come back in three to four hours," he said, "if your arm gets really cramped and painful. But, black widow bites only run the risk of being fatal in infants."

I guess it was all those action movies I watched as a boy which made me think that anytime somebody was bitten by something poisonous, death was near. Although I don't consider myself to be a hero, I was sure as I sat in my garden watching my left thumb get increasingly sore and stiff that I was going to die. I talked myself into believing that my left side was shutting down and, perhaps, I better get to Natividad before I started foaming at the mouth.

Christmas Eve had been mild. The first bit of sunshine we had seen in several days. I went out to my potting shed and started picking up things which had blown to the ground during the last wind storm. I reached down and grabbed a gopher trap—one of those effective shoe box shaped killing machines with a bar that snaps up and cuts the varmint in two. As soon as my bare hand laid hold of the trap I felt an incredible sting—like a hypodermic needle—and flung the trap down. There may have been some scurrying but I wasn't sure. It could have been one of those sharp prickles found on the underside of some rose leaves. That's what I thought at the time. Anyway, dumb as I was, I picked the trap up again and hung it back on a nail. About ten minutes went by before my thumb reminded me that it had just suffered an injustice. I have occasionally seen black widows crawl out of some stacked clay pots I keep in the shed so I knew that a likely culprit could have been this deadly spider.

Once I focused my eyes, my reference library reported that the black widow found in Salinas is probably *Latrodectus hesperus*. The female, as most people know, will eat the male after they mate. It turns out she only does that if she happens to be hungry after procreation. (Once again, males need to take their partners to dinner, just to be on the safe side; admittedly sexist but intended to be funny.) The female black widow is poisonous. The male and juveniles are not. She reaches sexual maturity in 50-70 days and lives for about a year and half.

Female black widow poison is 15% more toxic that the poison of the prairie rattlesnake. But, usually the amount injected is minute. It's a neuro-toxin so it will affect the nervous system and could cause respiratory failure. Female black widows use it as a preservation method. They inject a little bit into their victim so it will be paralyzed, but not dead. Then they bind the poor soul in their crackling web. When they start feeling a bit peckish, they go to their storage shelf and have something to eat. Black widows are not hunters. They let the prey come to them.

Female black widow spiders, at about an inch and a quarter long, are twice the size of the male. They have long, angular, shiny black legs and a very round shiny black abdomen with a characteristic red hourglass marking on the underside. She usually hangs upside down in her nest making the hourglass visible. Species variation occurs. Sometimes they are chocolate brown. Sometimes the hourglass is more like two red blotches. Juvenile coloration is a lighter brown with red-orange, orange, or even yellow and white mottles.

The three-dimensional nests the females build are loose and irregular mesh-type webs, located lower down in wood piles, undisturbed areas, bottom branches of thick shrubs, and unfortunately sometimes behind furniture, in closets and crawlspaces. If you hear the webs crack when you destroy them, you've probably just torn up a black widow's lair. Their silk is the thickest and most brittle in spiderdom. Females only attack if they are protecting their nest. The eggs of black widow spiders are laid in a pear-shaped sack.

At this point, I dropped my *Handbook of American Insects and Spiders*, ran out to the potting shed, pulled on leather gloves, and investigated the gopher trap. It was full of cream-colored, pear-shaped egg sacks, attached to a mass of stiff, irregular webs. I drove myself to the hospital.

When I was discharged an hour later, I came home and read more on this pest. About 200 eggs may be laid in a sack and females produce several sacks if conditions are favorable. Normally, only 1 to 12 young survive after the 14 to 30 day incubation period due to cannibalism. The spiderlings disperse themselves by spinning a little web which acts like a kite and carries them off. They prefer to nest near the ground, in dark, undisturbed areas. Before indoor plumbing, bites were fairly frequent in outhouses, particularly on the genitals of seated male users. (!)

Although extremely painful and temporarily debilitating, fatalities from untreated black widow bites are uncommon. The very old, very young, and those with a history of high blood pressure are at greatest risk. Death usually results from respiratory paralysis, but no reported deaths have occurred in decades. Muscle and chest pain are the most common reactions, but there could also be abdominal cramps and nausea, restlessness, anxiety, breathing and speech difficulty, and sweating. Swelling may be noticed in extremities and eyelids but rarely at the bite site. Often there is a general sense of discomfort shortly after the bite. Acute symptoms increase in severity during the first day, but usually decline after two to three days. Black widow bites can also be fatal to small dogs and cats.

Spiders bite using a pair of fangs known as chelicerae. The bite can go unnoticed, although it often produces an immediate sharp, pin-prick pain. A slight swelling and redness may develop at the bite site. Before going to the doctor, wash the wound thoroughly, treat it with a mild antiseptic to prevent infection, and keep the patient quiet and comfortable. The toxin moves quickly in the body. Trying to suck out the poison would be ineffective.

Teach everyone in your family about the potential danger of black widows so they can readily identify and avoid them. It's always a good idea to wear gloves and a long-sleeved shirt when working in spider infested areas. Periodically check spots in and around the home where black widows may occur. When discovered, crush them or vacuum them up. You can discourage their reappearance by periodically moving furniture and providing additional interior lighting. In protected places such as fuse boxes, plug entrance ways with steel wool. Insecticides can be useful but seek professional help as these chemicals are toxic to you and to mud-dauber wasps which will hunt down and kill black widows all on their own.

Four hours passed and no further symptoms occurred. I had read that the black widow doesn't always transfer venom with every bite. She must have figured I was too large for supper. I opened a bottle of champagne and celebrated another Christmas.

CUCUMBER BEETLES

Diabrotica undecimpunctata howardi

The spotted cucumber beetle is a common rose pest. It feeds on rose petals and stamens and lays its eggs on the underside of protected leaves or in the soil. When they hatch, its larvae tunnel into the soil and will feed on the rose's roots. Good clean up of fallen leaves is essential in rose gardens as it removes possible wintering over larvae and unhatched eggs. It's a winged invader so it will fly into your yard from your neighbor's property to take up residence in the center of your rose devouring it.

Cucumber beetles don't move very fast. So if you see one, catch it and kill it. A simple squeeze should do the trick and prevent it from procreating. This pest is a serious threat to cucumbers and melons because it also transports a form of wilt which can devastate a field in no time flat.

Cucumber beetle on a chloritic wild rose

CURCULIO

Merhynchites bicolor

Rose curculios are weevils which attack rose bushes in a most savage fashion. Symptoms include unopened rose buds which have fallen over and shriveled or blossoms which open full of tiny holes, like they've been shot with a machine gun. The rose curculio is about a ¼ inch long and dark red to black in color with a very long snout. It lays its eggs in rose buds or hips which hatch into destructive larvae. The larvae fall to the ground where they pupate over winter to emerge as these long-nosed devils. Check out information on these critters on the Internet and be able to identify them. Always give any new roses a careful once over. If you see a parent, you can pretty well guess eggs and juveniles are about. Always inspect any new rose bush you bring into your garden for possible marauders. Curculios love multi-flowered shrub roses and wilder portions of your garden. If you see one, kill it. Another way to catch them is to place a shallow pan of water beneath the infected bush and shake the shrub gently. The curculio should fall into the water. Larger infected areas and large shrubs may have to be sprayed with neem oil. Take extra care to rake the ground beneath an infected bush frequently. Give the affected rose plenty of good food and water.

DEER

One summer at a Monterey Bay Rose Society garden tour, forty of us arrived at a house in Soquel to find an entire hillside with nothing but healthy green rose leaves and not one flower. Deer had gotten into the garden and eaten all new growth and anything showing color. It was too late to get the word out so we sat and commiserated with the disappointed host. We also discussed several methods to protect roses from deer. Lack of forage at this time of year will make the deer much bolder. Most rosarians who must deal with these unpredictable foragers use a combination of the following techniques.

Frightening Smell: Several hardware stores and nurseries offer potions made from mountain lion spray which when regularly applied are purported to make Bambi seek out other pastures fast. Home remedies include multiple placements of moth balls around the edges of the garden. Panty hose segments knotted at the end and hung like grapes at nose level work well as holders. You can also string lines of Fels Naptha soap chunks a la Christmas lights throughout your garden. Dial and Irish Spring also work, but avoid anything that smells flowery! Mounds of human hair secured from barber shop sweepings, some report, will scare the deer away at your garden's threshold. Still others extol the effectiveness of regular applications of first-thing-in-the-morning human urine around the edge of the garden. To spare the neighbors, I don't recommend direct application. Use a relief station inside the house or garage and, for application purposes, carry the result outside in an old coffee can.

Unpleasant Taste: Deer will eat almost anything, but they prefer new shoots, buds and hips. Mix up in a blender until smooth a solution containing three large eggs (shells and all), 1 tablespoon of ground cloves, 2 tablespoons of cayenne pepper, 2 tablespoons of Epsom salt, 2 tablespoons of lemon or orange scented dish detergent, 6 cloves of fresh garlic, and ¼ cup of bacon drippings or used cooking oil. Add sufficient water to make spraying this concoction possible. Coat the leaves, stems and buds especially at deer grazing height. Repeat with a good coating regularly throughout the spring, summer, and fall. Don't believe me? Check out www.deer-departed.com for additional recipes. The dried substance will wash off if you want to cut flowers and bring them inside.

Startling Sounds: Check out www.talkingpresents.com. They offer Big Mouth Billy Bass, the talking fish. He works by a motion sensor, sings a variety of irritating tunes, delivers groan-able punch lines, and slaps his tail onto the mounting board. Place several in the garden. They will frighten the deer with such annoying gems as "You can tune a piano but you can't tune a fish." There are also motion activated croaking frogs, noisy car alarms, and false breaking windows. If you search hard enough, you should also find recordable warning systems enabling you to deliver such messages as "Get out of my garden before I shoot" and "I love roasted venison with a glass of bold merlot." The unexpected noise startles the deer.

Douse with Water: Do a Google search for motion activated sprinklers. There are several on the market. A good squirt in the face with some hose water will send the deer running. The danger is that the system has to be on 24/7 and you and your friends have to remember that the system is on 24/7.

Special Fencing: Deer are incredible jumpers and will easily spring over a six-, seven-, maybe even eight-foot fence. But a double fence seems to deter them. The double fence can even be a cheap wire one placed about three or four feet out from the taller attractive fence. Another proven deer-repellent fence is a picket fence with irregularly placed uprights, some tall some short some medium but without a regular pattern. It will give your rose garden a sort of *Hansel und Gretel* cottage look, but the deer are confused by the high and low pickets and won't jump it.

Canine Solution: A friendly dog cavorting about the rose bushes, both day and night, is usually sufficient cause for the hungry deer to eat your neighbor's daisies and leave your garden in *Peace* (a hybrid tea from 1945).

EARWIGS

Forficula auricularia

The common earwig came from Europe with the arrival of merchant ships. Earwigs can be found all over the United States and southern Canada but are far more prevalent in the south and southwest. Curiously, they are one of the few non-social insects which care for their eggs and first phase nymphs. They are basically scavengers and omnivorous, but they will also hunt for food. They do help break down decaying matter in your garden, turning it into compost. They also eat aphids. However, they will delve into some particularly juicy rose petals and stamens, if and when they feel inclined.

If you have an exceptional amount marring your blossoms, try to reduce their numbers in the following way. Take old newspapers and loosely roll them up and secure the newspaper log with rubber bands. Place these logs in the garden at night choosing the most infested areas. Pick up the newspapers at first light and discard them quickly in a trash bag. Earwigs are nocturnal and regularly squeeze themselves into deep, narrow crevices to sleep the day through. They'll scurry out of the newspapers so work quickly.

I once offered an older friend who came to visit the garden a particularly beautiful, full spray of *China Doll* (1946). I cut it and said just before handing it to her to put in her car. "Here, let me shake it to make sure I'm not giving you any bugs." About forty earwigs dropped out of the flowers and landed on the sidewalk. "You know. Maybe I'll give you something else next time you visit."

GOPHERS

Thomomys bottae

Pocket gophers are the scourge of all rose gardeners who live in semi-developed neighborhoods or out in the country. It's impossible to grow roses *en masse* without protection from their ravenous hunger for rose roots. In nature, gophers aerate the soil and ensure good drainage during winter storms. They help to prevent soil erosion. In addition, their habit of bringing plant material into their burrows aides the creation of topsoil. They are called pocket gophers because they can stuff their cheeks with food and carry it off to a storage den to be consumed later.

Pocket gophers make two kinds of burrows: a main run and a side burrow for extracting soil. Those tell-tale mounds of loose soil indicate a side burrow. You can find the main run by digging about two or three feet in the direction opposite of the mound fan. In spite of the large population living in a vast area of unused land, pocket gophers are solitary creatures and live alone in their own burrows. They eat roots or they pull plants down from above. They construct storage chambers, sleeping quarters, and chambers for their own waste. The males will enter female burrows and mate, usually in the spring. The gestation period lasts about 18 days. Females have one or two litters a year giving birth to two to eleven offspring, with the average being six. Females stop growing once they reach maturity but males will continue to grow their entire lifetime. Pocket gophers don't hibernate in winter. They just move to burrows further down the tunnel. Their tunnels always slant toward the surface. If you see a vertical hole, it was made by a mole. Moles, by the way, subsist mostly by eating earthworms and grubs. So if you have moles, it's a good sign that your soil is healthy. Moles also aerate the soil and mix in the organic material. Just be aware of their presence as their tunnels are quite close to the surface and create "soft" spots in the rose garden which may cause you to lose your balance if you're not careful.

Gophers are opportunistic. They will fight when one invades another's territory. If you kill one, another will take over the recently departed's burrow. They receive all the water they need from the vegetation they consume. They will also burrow underneath highways, driveways, and parking lots constructing underground passageways as long as fifty or so feet. Gophers control water seeping into their burrows buy using soil plugs which they insert and pull out as needed. They prefer to build their burrows in sandy loam, the soil most suited to growing roses.

Unfortunately, the natural controls on gopher populations are snakes, owls, and falcons. Rattlesnakes aren't welcome near people and fear of them is transferred to the non-poisonous useful snakes resulting in both types being unwelcome. Raptors either won't live near humans, have no place to abide, or hunt at the wrong time of day.

Gardeners must take preventive measures to control gopher infestations. First, and foremost, all roses need to be planted inside a wire cage. Pre-made gopher cages can be purchased at several hardware stores and garden centers. You can make a gopher cage yourself by purchasing strong, one-inch mesh chicken wire fencing, cutting it, shaping it, wiring it together securely, fashioning a bottom, and joining it to the rest of the cage. Bury the constructed cage inside the planting hole with about an inch of the cage showing all the way around on top. Adjust the size of the cage to fit the fully-grown bush and not the specimen you're planting. **Remember.** Roses grow. If you're squeezing the roots into a gopher cage, it's way too small! For large climbing roses which are likely to be in the ground for decades, use a stronger gauge wire. These are stiff and hard to work with but they will last for years.

Several varieties of gopher traps are on the market. Follow their instructions carefully and take care not to spring the trap on an unprotected finger. Buried traps are only effective if they are completely covered with dirt and mulch to prevent light from entering the burrow. Take care not to block the main tunnel. Air must continue to flow through the passage if you want the gopher to be fooled.

My house and garden are in the middle of a long established residential neighborhood and therefore none of my roses are planted in gopher cages. When a mound of soil appeared two feet from my patio, I dismissed it. There are no gophers in my neighborhood. Later that day, the next door neighbor's old and usually silent dog was barking the most curious "woof." I looked over the fence and saw Boots staring at a flower bed, watching helplessly as a gladiolus leaf wiggled back and forth and then slowly disappeared underground. Still, my denial was unchanged. Then the following day, my *Handel* (1965) which was climbing on the backside of my potting shed looked odd. It had been growing just fine. Now it looked droopy all over. I rested my hand on its largest cane. It wiggled loosely. I tugged it quite gently and the entire plant came up out of the soil with not one root attached. It was as if it had been sheared off underground. A gopher! The house behind me had been vacant and on the market all summer long and a maverick gopher had moved in. My roses were all at risk! All my time, work, and money could be for naught.

Immediately, I flew off to the garden center and bought strychnine logs, gas bombs, poisoned corn, and a box trap with enough spring power to slice a piglet in two. I'd lost all concern about nature and caring for animals and being gentle to all living creatures. I wanted the gopher dead and I wanted to see the body.

I used everything. I was genuinely lucky to find the main tunnel. I dug into it, carefully inserted my box trap, made sure the air could flow through it, and then covered it over gently. I returned about every five minutes to check the trap. Sure enough, the third time I looked the ground wiggled. I let it die in peace. Returned that evening and lifted the trap and the now stiff gopher. I'd never been a hunter, but I walked about my backyard that day carrying this trophy with as great a pride as any Neanderthal had showing off his mastodon catch for the day.

More environmentally friendly potions are now on the market. Gophers don't like tilled soil. So if you can, a three foot wide, three foot deep parameter that gets roto-tilled regularly would be a deterrent. Battery powered thumpers will also keep the quiet loving vermin away. Plenty of rosarians, however, have said, "I just get up early in the morning and shoot them with a gun."

LADYBUG BEETLES

Coccinellidae

During The Middle Ages, farmers used colonies of ladybugs to rid their vineyards of insect pests. These critters were so effective at this that they were dedicated to Our Lady, the Blessed Mother, thus their name. They continue to be one of the most beneficial insects in a rose garden. Both the adults and their larvae have a voracious appetite for aphids. There are a couple of different species of them, some with two spots and some with more or none. Unfortunately, ladybugs can't determine whether or not the aphid it's eating has been sprayed with insecticide or has been drinking the sap of a bush fed with a systemic fertilizer/pesticide. That's why I don't advocate your using these products in your garden.

You may purchase a bag of ladybugs from several local garden centers. The adults have a migratory habit, however, and will often just fly away upon release. Here's a little trick to get them to "stick" around. Before you open the bag of ladybugs, place one twelve ounce can of 7Up in the sun until warm. Then, shake the can vigorous for 30 seconds. Point the opening of the can away from you and at the bag of ladybugs. Pop the top. The resulting spray should cover the bugs in a harmless sugary glue which seals their wings together allowing for a couple of days of good garden hunting lasting until the early morning dew or a rainfall eventually washes them clean.

LEAF CUTTER BEES

Megachile spp

Damage from leaf cutter bees is easily recognized. These California natives are relatives of the honey bee but are a bit smaller and darker. They are responsible for pollinating many wildflowers and plants in meadows and urban gardens. They chew on healthy green leaves in very neat circular patterns and carry the chewed leaves off to build a hive. They often place their nests inside an old log, directly in the ground, or a hollowed out rose cane. The rose will recover from the minor damage caused and the chewed up leaves usually don't die or even brown at the edge.

Leaf cutter bees are not aggressive, have a mild sting which is only used when they are handled. The beneficial impact of this critter far out weighs any damage to private gardens. Learn to feel privileged that these wonderful bees have selected a few of your leaves to help build their new homes. I have always kept a rotting log or tree trunk around as decoration and am pleased that it might be a home for this beneficial bee.

You may find the following facts interesting. Leaf damage from these bees is extraordinarily neat and orderly. Their hives contain the typical hexagon cells filled with pollen and nectar and one egg. Although the bees mature at the same time, they exit the hive as adults, one at a time, according to their proximity to the entrance hole! Here's another curious fact I learned this summer. More than 300 species of bees exist in the Pinnacles National Monument, down the road from Salinas. Go visit and look for the wild roses.

LEAF MINERS

Several varieties of moths, flies, sawflies and even some beetles and wasps produce miniscule thread-size larvae which feed on plant tissue. These larvae have developed a clever way of avoiding being eaten or crushed. They hide within a plant's mid-tissue layer and feed on the cells of the plant from wall to wall keeping the floor and ceiling, so to speak, intact. The result is a curving line of dead tissue visible on the leaf showing the path of the feeding tunnel.

More voracious larvae will skeletonize a leaf. If you manage a healthy garden and promote a balance, a sufficient number of predators will arrive and feed on the larvae's parents, thus keeping the population under control. Don't worry about the damaged leaves. My observation is that they are usually closer to the ground and therefore won't likely be close to any flowers you might cut.

Leaf cutter bee damage

Buddy's Snail-Proof Watering Hole

SNAILS

Helix aspersa

An import from the Old World, this Euro-trash is a notorious pest in California gardens, especially those on the Central Coast. It was originally introduced as a food source in the 1850s and escaped. With no real enemies, it overpopulates itself wherever found and causes millions of dollars of damage to farmers, overwhelms native species, and disgusts many gardeners. There's nothing quite like stepping on one in your stocking feet while fetching the morning newspaper or throwing a dinner party only to notice a snail has slimed itself across the picture window in the dining room and stuck itself in the middle for all to see.

Snails are especially nasty to new rose growth and fresh petals. They also love to hide in the drain holes of large black plastic pots. They push the soil out of the hole, giving your rose (unbeknownst to you) less soil to grow in and putting it at risk of drying out.

Because snails are truly hermaphroditic, every one you see has the ability to lay about 100 eggs in a batch. They can both hibernate in cold weather and aestivate in dry weather by sealing themselves shut, usually in a dark unreachable spot. They are nocturnal feeders and will come out and slide across the lawns and sidewalks whenever there's sufficient moisture.

I have tried every method of eradication I've ever learned of and I still have snails and their naked cousins, slugs. Best practice—if you see one, kill it. If you discover a mass of them sleeping in between two black pots, pick them off, one-by-one, and drop them into a can containing an inch of chlorine bleach. They die immediately. Bury the remains in an unused portion of your garden. They don't like crossing fireplace ashes. They get a small electric shock if they slide across copper tape. Unfortunately, the copper

in high humidity quickly develops a patina which gives them easy access. The pellet form of snail and slug control devices is better than the powder form and less likely to be used by your cat as litter. These compounds are especially useful in areas you can't control.

Snail poison is lethal to household pets so devise ways to apply it which prevent your dogs and cats from having any contact with it. For example, cut the top off of a large tinted plastic soda bottle, put it on its side in a dark place frequented by snails, make sure that it won't roll around, and spread some bait inside it. The snails will find it, eat it, and die.

To avoid snails, leave as few places for them to hide as possible. Snails love to congregate inside such ubiquitous garden flowers as agapanthus, clivia, and other smooth leafed plants where they don't eat their bedding, they just curl up inside it and hide. Bait the areas around these plants and keep them well away from your garden beds. If you can manage it, a couple of free-range chickens will do a great job consuming them. Snails are edible. You'll need to raise them for about ten days on wet corn meal to make sure anything harmful in them is purged.

Terrestrial snails can't swim. Buddy's favorite outside watering dish is an old ceramic telephone pole insulator. When inverted, it has a large top basin and several shallow rings descending to the ground which prove to be impenetrable snail barriers. So Bud gets a taste of bird in the top basin and doesn't have to worry about a drowned snail in his water bowl.

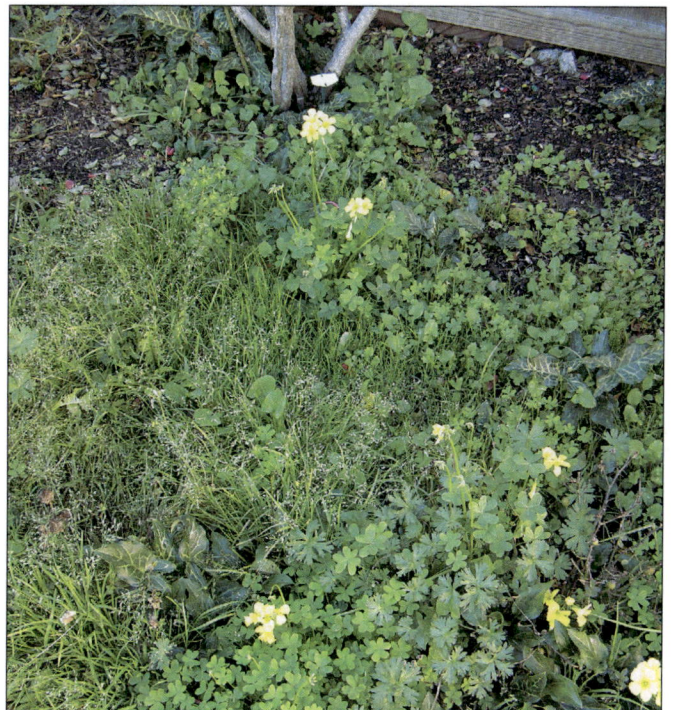

Group photo of fescue, geranium, dandelion, arum italicum, and bindweed which could be avoided with 4-5 inches of heavy mulch

SPIDER MITES

Tetranychidae

Usually a pest for drier, darker parts of a rose garden, spider mites feed on the sap from damaged cells of rose leaves. Their whip-like mouthparts play havoc on the soft leaf tissue. They can be identified by their telltale webs on the underside of the leaves but they themselves are barely visible. The worst infestations of spider mites occur in gardens were insecticides have been heavily used and all the predatory insects have been mass slaughtered. If you do notice a few areas infected by spider mites, simply give them several good showers with the garden hose. They prefer a dry environment and the dampness should be sufficient to control them.

SPITTLE BUGS

Cercopidae spp

Most apparent in the spring and early summer when the roses have lots of new tender growth, spittle bugs are among the easiest critters to identify. They are the nymphal stage of an acrobatic insect called a froghopper, truly able to leap the equivalent of a tall building in a single bound. These juveniles chew into the plant tissue and pass the draining liquid through their bodies at an exceptionally rapid rate. The swiftness of this action causes the juice to mix with the air and create bubbles. Nature has given these baby bugs the advantage of avoiding drying out in the hot sun and hiding from a hungry bird's eye. The foam has a disagreeable taste. They rarely cause much of a problem to the rose bush and can be flushed away with a garden hose and some dish soap. Spraying the ground around your roses after you prune with dormant oil will cause their eggs to be unviable.

THRIPS

Frankliniella occidentalis

I do not spray insecticides in my garden and therefore, I have never had much of a problem with thrips as there are sufficient beneficial insects living in my garden to control them. Thrips will appear in the spring and drill holes in pink and white roses. The most common type is the Western Flower Thrip which is a serious concern for greenhouse operations. The lifecycle of a thrip goes from egg, first larvae, second larvae, pupae, and adult in about 18 days. The adults live for about a month. The thrip has just one mandible which it uses to puncture soft plant tissue and extract the sweetness. A few days after they appear in a healthy garden, Minute Pirate Bugs show up and eat the thrips. Minute Pirate Bugs are tiny little "Jack Sparrow"-type marauders who can't rest until every thrip is eaten. It's on behalf of these

great natural helpers that I recommend you never use systemic chemicals on your roses. Keep your roses well watered and fed. Remove damaged or weakened growth and don't store refuse too close to your rose gardens.

A good test to see if you have thrips is to cut an affected flower, turn it upside down over a sheet of white paper, and shake it. If a few critters which resemble a hyphen fall out, they are probably thrips.

WHITEFLIES

Trialeurodes vaporariorum

These tropical invaders can destroy a greenhouse filled with valuable plants in no time flat. They are classified in the large insect order, *Homoptera*, which includes cicadas, froghoppers, and aphids and exhibit many of their cousins' attributes. They mostly appear in my rose garden at the end of the growing season and attack the aromatic leaves of my *Rosa eglanteria* and spread to other roses nearby. They multiply at an incredible rate. Brush up against a bush and whiteflies launch themselves into the air resulting in a cloud of them fluttering around in your face.

Whitefly traps are on the market and they do work. You have to replace them every month or so to keep their allure intense. Severe cases of whitefly can be treated with insecticidal soap. Stronger pesticides exist but are useless in neighborhood gardens as more whiteflies will just fly into your garden from across the street.

As I noted, they are seasonal in my yard and coincide with the garden shutting down anyway. So I just ignore them or squirt at them with the hose. A good application of fish emulsion in September and regular waterings will give your roses enough vigor to sustain the attack.

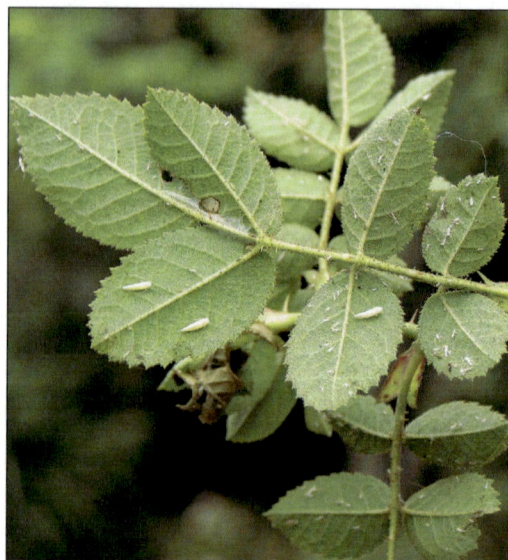

Whitefly infestation

Green Invaders

City gardens are often inflicted by plant invaders. Self seeding irritations like dandelions, scarlet pimpernel, chickweed, or alyssum can be controlled by having a thick layer of mulch in place. Oxalis and nutgrass must be dug out and removed. Pulling up oxalis simply spreads the bulbettes in the soil. Ripping out nutgrass takes away the grass blades and roots but leaves the bulbs intact. Bermuda grass can be pulled up, but believe me, you won't get it all. It's best to keep at it. Pulling up what you can and spraying the far parameters of your garden to stop it from invading. Spraying herbicides within the garden is likely to do more damage to the roses than to the weeds.

Most of the weeds we find in our rose gardens can be found in broken land in the wild. By broken land, I mean roadsides, river banks, and forest edges. This is exactly the same natural habitat of wild roses. Search the Internet using the Latin names of the plants listed below for additional information.

BABY'S TEARS

Helxine soleirolia

This member of the nettle family, *Urticaceae,* also has two other curious common names Mother-of-Thousands (propagational) and Mind-Your-Own-Business (attitudinal). I remember how in Arlington, Virginia I nursed along a pot of baby tears for years. I was quite proud of how I kept it looking so good and so green when the outside world was covered with snow. Little did I know that the darker portions of my yard in Salinas would become baby tears heaven and my pride come from ripping it out in gobs.

Baby's Tears plants just love shady spots. They love the nutrient rich run off from my roses. They grow in cracks and crevices. They appear on the north side of my raised rose beds and in a matter of days choke the bud unions. In fact, it seems to enjoy setting a mass of leaves and roots right into the mulch so that when you pull it up you also lose your mulch. A product called Moss Out claims to eradicate it. I bought some, but then never tried it.

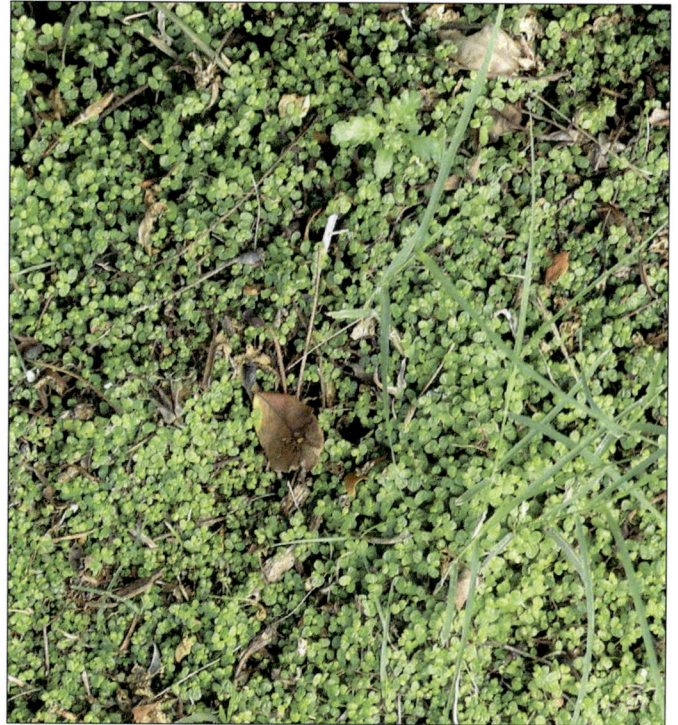

Baby's tears

BERMUDA GRASS

Cynodon dactylon

This weed to a rose garden is the equivalent of termites in living room walls. I have dug. I have sprayed. I have mulched, all to no avail. Once this baby tropical grass gets in, it's really hard to get it out. It has regular joints in its stems which develop their own set of roots.

The runners it sends out burrow deeply into the garden bed and then send a blade of grass vertically up to the sun. Those underground shoots spread quickly. RoundUp® is useless because of the grass's habit of setting out new roots at each little segment. Best advice is to continue to dig it out whenever it recurs. Let the bed rest for a week and see what new blades emerge. Then get those out. Persistence is the only way to remove this invasive weed. It is tender but not to the degree of winter chill we get in Salinas.

Bermuda grass

BINDWEED

Convulvulaceae

Many separate species are lumped into the common term, bindweed. All exhibit the fast growing, vining habit and the trumpet like flowers. Each species has developed its own niche, some flourishing along California's beaches and others populating hills and stream-sides. It is one of the temperate world's most difficult weeds to eradicate. The seed coats are quite hard and have kept the seeds viable for more than twenty years. Bindweed sets seed in August and September so once you see it, dig it out. Its roots will go deep into the soil. Some rosarians allow the bindweed to form a little mound and then paint the leaves with a brush dipped into RoundUp®. This herbicide sends its poison down to the roots.

Its seeds are mildly toxic. The plant itself was used medicinally as a natural laxative. Always wear gloves in the garden especially if you are pulling up infestations of bindweed. The sap is known to irritate the skin so don't put your gloved hand to your face.

Bindweed is usually spread by birds. The seeds pass through their digestive systems and often remain viable. In addition to their natural vigor, the seeds get deposited with a bit of avian fertilizer. It's not surprising therefore that my worst infestation occurred among the roses planted beneath a bird bath. Once established, bindweed is hard to get rid of. When you first see them dig them out and never let them go to seed.

The common Morning Glory is a member of the convulvulus family and manifests most of its weedy relatives' aggressive habits. A cousin of mine in his first year of gardening attempted to create a compost heap into which

he threw his end of the season garden and yard trash, including the long and leggy morning glory vines. He followed instructions carefully and the result was a rich heap of compost to apply to his second-year vegetable garden. First, he noticed one, then another, then realized that the entire garden was covered in sprouting morning glories.

Bindweed

Nutgrass

NUTGRASS (NUTSEDGE)

Cyperus rotundus

The most difficult weed to eliminate from the garden, nutgrass has been my terror since day one of rose gardening. Nutgrass has four different parts: the green blades of grass, the white roots directly beneath them, the umbrella like flower and seed capsules on the top, and the source of this evil, the tiny tubers (nuts, kernels, time bombs) which sleep comfortably 12 to 18 inches below the soil surface. This powerful sedge penetrates plastic weed barriers and all forms of mulch with ease. Most herbicides are not effective. RoundUp will kill only the green portion and the attached white roots, but will not penetrate the tuber. The tubers can remain in dry soil for two or three years only to sprout again when conditions are right. When moving plants from one location to another in your garden, you can spread nutgrass with ease. Tilling the soil will only slice the tuber and multiply them. If you let it go to seed, all those seeds will find their way during its dormant cycle into your soil.

Recent research on getting rid of it includes an organic method, the application of granulated sugar and minimal watering to heavily affected areas, on multiple occasions. The theory is that the super richness of the soil will eventually be too much for this poor soil loving scourge. A chemical product, SedgeHammer, is purported to eradicate the weed. Another product, Image, is also lauded as a cure when applied directly to the plant base and allowed to seep down into the soil. As I haven't used either method yet, I don't know the drawbacks.

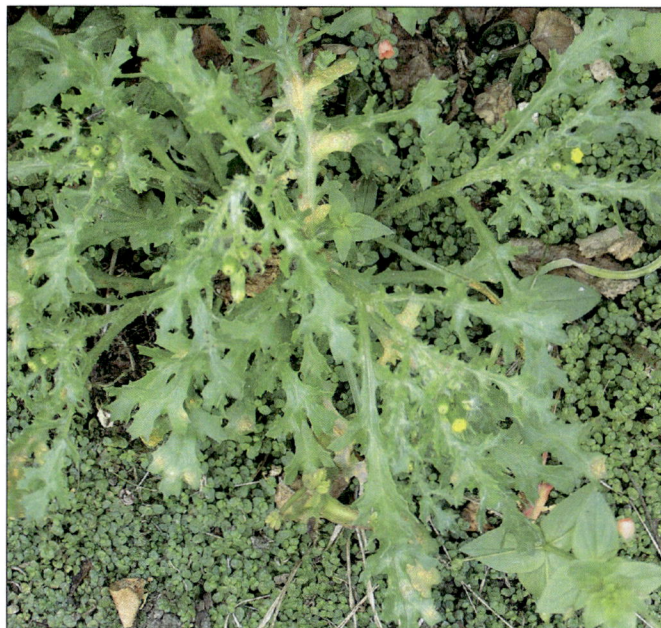

Common Groundsel

COMMON GROUNDSEL

"Old Man in the Spring," *Senecio vulgaris*

As my garden mulch dissolved and left bare earth exposed, this opportunistic weed showed up. It shares similar characteristics with dandelions, sports yellow many petaled flowers, cut leaves, and airborne seeds. It's easy to pull out but really can be prevented by a good layer of mulch. Be careful if it has gone to seed as jiggling the plant will cause it to spread its seeds everywhere.

Curiously, this weed also suffers from rust but this common affliction doesn't kill it or stop it from spreading.

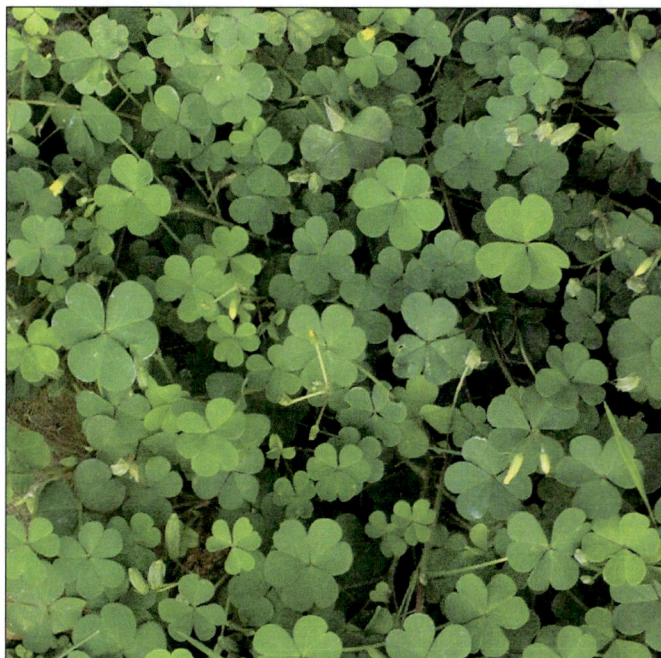

Creeping Wood Sorrel

CREEPING WOOD SORREL

Oxalis corniculata

This is that clover-leaved weed that gave my *Gizmo* (1998) such trouble. It creates a thick mat of vegetation with many roots, stems, flowers, and seeds which hide in the tiniest of crevices. Because of its creeping nature, it's hard to eradicate.

You think you got it all only to discover that a tiny bit of stem was left behind and re-established the plant. It is similar in leaf to its South African cousin but has a different growth habit. Its flowers are tiny. Its habit is spreading. This weed is also around throughout most of the season establishing itself in crevices, under stone paths, into brick walls as well as lawns and garden beds.

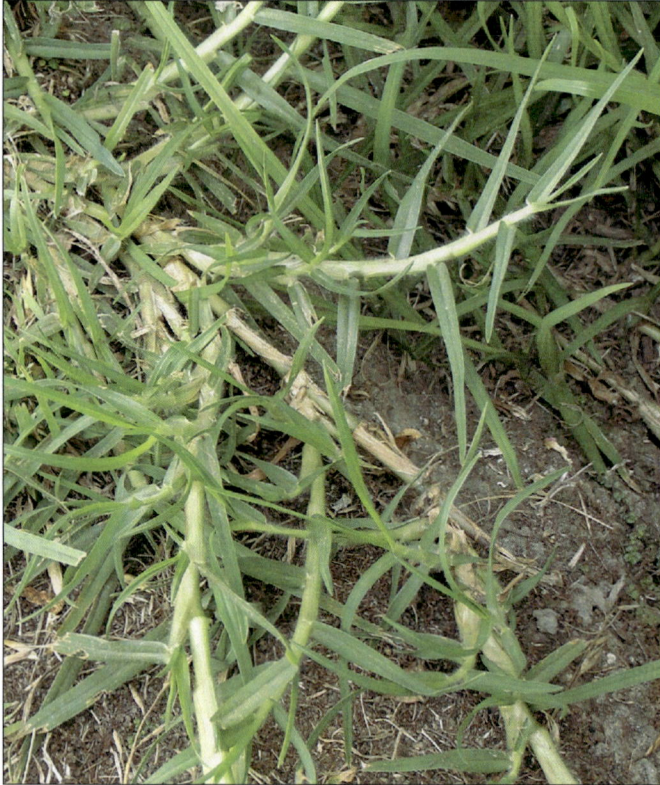

Kikuyu grass

Wood Sorrel is a nuisance to nurseries as I often see it growing on the soil beneath perennials and on the top of plants for sale. If you are buying potted plants from a nursery, give them a good inspection before you select them. Don't bring problems home. Don't import seeds. It might be useful to scrape the top half-inch of soil from the pots of recently purchased plants and leave it at the nursery.

CUTLEAF GERANIUM, CRANESBILL

Germanium dissectum

Also opportunistic, this true American version of the common garden plant known as cranesbill sprouts on bare soil and will form a mound of long stems and deeply lobed leaves. It has tiny purple flowers which unfortunately are too tiny and nondescript to give the plant commercial viability, but fertile enough to cause some problems on un-mulched soil. It's related to all true geraniums of which scores of varieties are available. The non-sprawling varieties make decent companion plants. **Remember.** What is commonly called geranium is actually a pelargonium, a related but different genus.

KIKUYU GRASS

Pennisetum clandestinum

This is a large, heavy and variegated grass. It's a little easier to get rid of as its underground runners are less likely to break apart than Bermuda grass. It's also killed by frost at least at the surface. Unfortunately, I've dug up roots growing nearly three feet down and counting.

OXALIS, BERMUDA BUTTERCUP

Oxalis pes-capre

This notorious South African weed has invaded our part of California. It can't survive where the ground freezes solid but it goes on a rampage where it doesn't. Oxalis springs forth from a pea-sized corm buried about six inches down. This horrible weed has the habit of producing bulbettes along its stem and around the corm. So if it's pulled up, the little bulbettes remain for the next opportunity to grow. Spraying with white vinegar will kill the leaves and give it a set back. Not letting it ever flower is the best eradication method. As soon as you see those characteristic clover-shaped leaves, get rid of it.

As you probably know, pulling the top part of the plant out only kills the top part. It doesn't do a thing to the corm which will regrow. Perhaps enough pulling will deny the corm the ability to store sufficient nutrients to grow again. Don't let it get established at all.

Common Spurge

If you have the time, you could dig up and run the soil through a fine sieve, thereby catching the corms. This method won't work if you have lots of organic matter in your soil. I find it best to spray oxalis hard with white vinegar when it first rears its ugly head. Whatever you do, don't let it flower! The seeds are carried about and will colonize other parts of the garden. Curiously, there are several horticultural varieties which are quite attractive and are available in several different colored flowers and leaves. These do not have the vigor of their cousin.

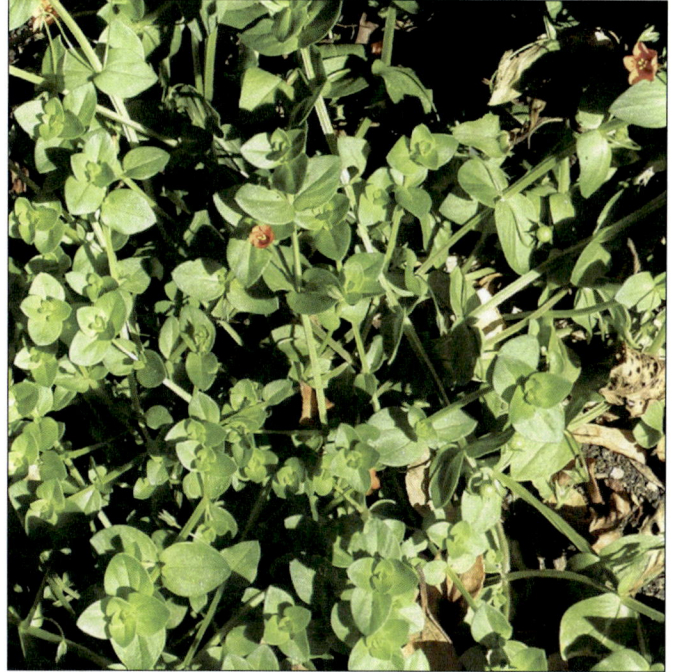

Scarlet pimpernel

SAN FRANCISCO BLUEGRASS, KENTUCKY BLUEGRASS

Poa unilateralis, Poa pratensis

There are numerous different varieties of this most common plant. It self seeds quite easily in our climate and quickly finds a secure place in the garden. Mulching will prevent its spread. It re-seeds rapidly and will create a lawn if you don't stop it.

SCARLET PIMPERNEL

Anagallis arvensis

This summer flowering weed has always been present in my garden. Its tiny russet orange flowers and prostrate growth are easily recognized. It has a central root from which its stems stretch out. Where scarlet came from, I'm not sure. It spreads easily by its microscopic seeds. It's easily yanked out, just do so before it gets a chance to bloom.

TALL ANNUAL WILLOWHERB

Epilobium brachycarpum

This particular weed is vividly green and plush. It gets rather tall but is easily pulled out. The older it gets the redder the stems get. I've noticed a lot of it in the garden some seasons and none in subsequent years. It has a fondness for sprouting beneath rose bushes and growing up through them. It also loves hard to mulch locations. Just like other weeds in this group, don't let it flower.

Other Concerns

VEGETATIVE CENTERS

Occasionally you might find a new cane growing directly out of the center of a flower. This anomaly tends to occur in specific varieties and is usually attributed to excess fertilization. You may also check out the tips of established leaves to see if there is any fertilizer burn on them which would make this diagnosis a slam dunk.

My other observation is that this variety wants to grow faster than it has viable outlets. Don't cut any long stem flowers from the bush this season. When you do remove spent flowers, cut the flower stem directly below the peduncle and allow all the remaining leaves to stay on the bush. Make a mental note of this rose bush and prune it less severely in January. You might as well prune the vegetative center off as it will never be substantial and is likely to fold over in a strong wind and carry much of its parent cane with it.

CHLOROSIS

Keep in mind that chlorosis, green veins on yellow leaves, is a symptom not a disease. It occurs when rose bushes are denied an adequate supply of nutrients, most probably nitrogen. This condition can be present because the soil lacks this nutrient. It can also happen if damage has been done to the root system. If it shows up on only a part of the

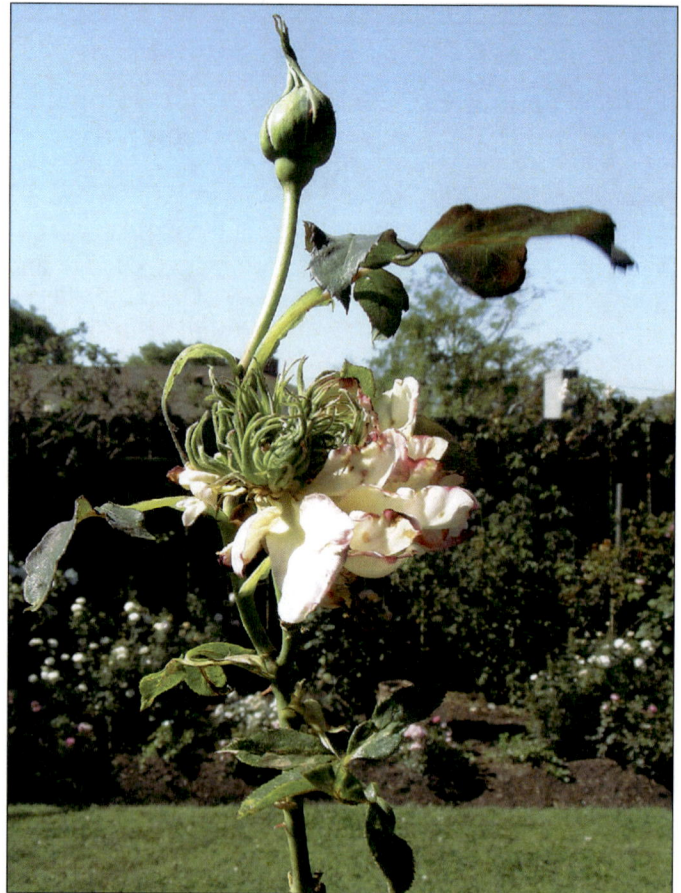

Vegetative center

plant, it most likely has a root problem. Poor drainage can be the culprit. Work more organic material and sand into your soil and dig a twelve-inch trench about two feet from the root line of the shrub. Most roses growing in raised beds aren't troubled by this condition. If the bush is producing chlorotic leaves and lacks overall vigor, you need to get a trowel and check the bud union and the soil at the base of the bush. Tree roots or galls might be strangling the roots and preventing good uptake of nutrients. Roots sitting in soggy ground will rot causing the entire bush to live off of only the surface roots. Fix the drainage and the rose is likely to bounce back.

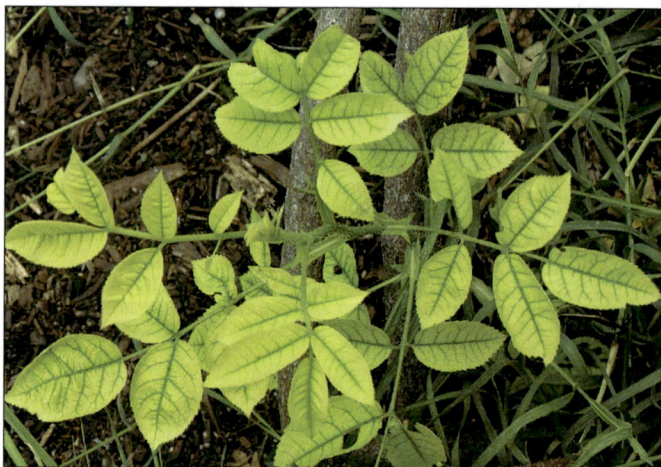

Chlorosis

References and Resources

The following websites will provide helpful information on a variety of topics mentioned in this book.

Monterey Bay Rose Society: www.montereybayrosesociety.org

Northern California Nevada Hawaii District or ARS: www.ncnhdistrict.org

American Rose Society: www.ars.org

HelpMeFind: http://www.helpmefind.com/rose/index.php

UC Davis Integrated Pest Management: http://www.ipm.ucdavis.edu/index.html

Baldo Vallegas' Page, Sacramento Rose Society: http://www.sactorose.org/rosebug/

Combined Rose List: http://www.combinedroselist.com/

Heritage Rose Foundation: http://www.heritagerosefoundation.org/index.htm

San Jose Heritage Rose Garden: http://www.heritageroses.us/

San Jose Municipal Rose Garden: http://www.sjparks.org/regional/rosegarden.asp

Sources of Hard To Find Roses:

Antique Rose Emporium: http://www.antiqueroseemporium.com/

Heirloom Roses: http://www.heirloomroses.com/

Hortico: http://www.hortico.com/

Regan's Nursery: http://www.regannursery.com/

Roses of Yesterday and Today: http://www.rosesofyesterday.com/

Vintage Gardens: http://www.vintagegardens.com/

Author's Biography

JOSEPH TRUSKOT

Winner of numerous awards from the American Rose Society for his articles on America's National Flower, Joseph Truskot has helped hundreds of individuals improve their ability to grow roses through his informative presentations and effective writing in *The Bay Rose*, the Monterey Bay Rose Society's monthly newsletter. A talented exhibitor, he has won numerous awards for a variety of different roses including Queen of Show on two occasions. He was awarded the Bronze Medal, the MBRS's highest honor in 2002. He has grown roses since 1986. However, it was his purchase of a house and yard in Salinas, California that set him on his quest to build the perfect rose garden, a goal he hasn't quite attained.

Joseph Truskot was born and raised in Lorain, Ohio and graduated with a degree in education from Miami University in Oxford, Ohio. He served as a Peace Corps Volunteer in Iran, a management intern for C.A.R.E., Inc in Belize, Central America and, while working on his Master's Degree at the School for International Training in Brattleboro, Vermont, drove a flower delivery truck and assisted the floral designers as needed.

His other great passion is for classical music. For nine years, he served as the director of training for the American Symphony Orchestra League (now the League of American Orchestras), then located in Washington, DC. During his time at the League, he served on the resident's landscaping committee for Fairlington, a large condominium complex located in Northern Virginia where he planted his first hybrid teas: Talisman (1929), Mirandy (1945), and Garden Party (1960).

In 1990, Joseph Truskot became the executive director of the Monterey Symphony, a position he held for twenty years. He is a director emeritus of the Association of California Symphony Orchestras and was its president and a long-time board member. He was also a board member of the National Steinbeck Center in Salinas. Currently, he is host of Central Coast Public Radio, KUSP Santa Cruz's On Site Program and a regular on air personality for its classical music presentations.

In addition to music and roses, he is an accomplished writer, potter, and quilt top maker. He lives in Salinas in the middle of his roses with two cats, Buddy and Frederick.

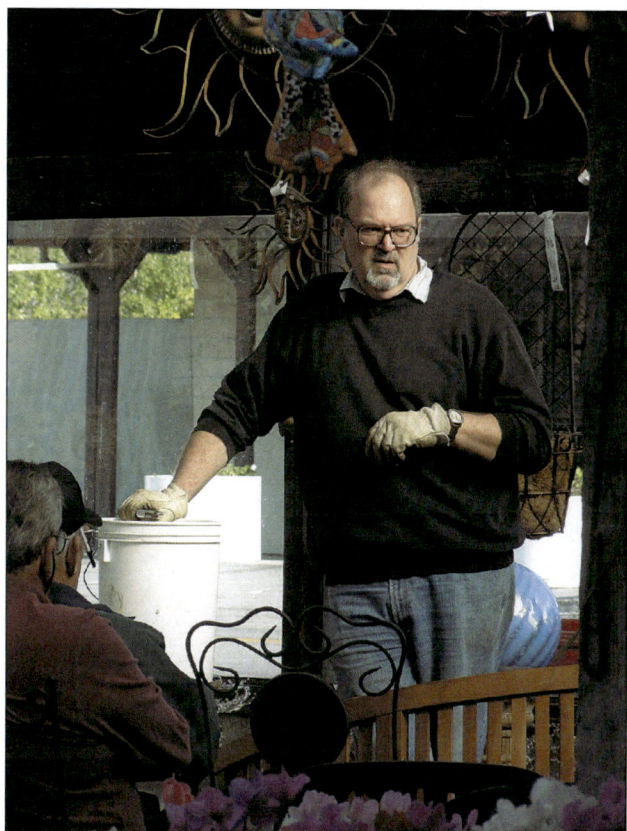

Author giving a pruning demonstration at Alladin's Nursery, Watsonville, California.

Photo by Adriana Leonardich

Index

Joseph Truskot